Endorsements for

Christ Rescued Me! ....from the "Church of Christ"

"Lee Anne Ferguson, a former life-long "Church of Christ" member, has done the true Body of Christ a great service through this excellent book. It exposes the multitude of heresies contained in the cult of Campbellism and its related sects, also known as the "Restoration Movement," founded in the 1820's by religious charlatans. I have been in Christian apologetics and counter-cult evangelism since 1981, and I can assure you that Lee Anne's book will not only help protect God's sheep from wolves and false prophets (Mt. 7:15), but it will also serve as an excellent theological resource and witnessing tool to be shared with "Church of Christ" members themselves. I heartily recommend her book to all!"

Larry Wessels, Director, *Christian Answers TV*, Christian Debater, Austin, TX

"I pray the Lord will give this book a wide hearing and large audience because it should be read. It should be read thoughtfully, prayerfully and with humility. This book is both sad and wonderful. It is sad because of the pain caused by an evil and false religious system, but wonderful because of its testimony of God's grace in leading the author out of darkness, into the light of the gospel of Christ, and then to use her painful experiences to make her a servant to Christ and others.

This book is true! It gives a true representation of false, man-centered, works religion. This is a textbook description of a system that goes under many names but at its core is always the same. It always elevates man and emphasizes his works and rejects the gospel of God's free grace. This book gives a true, thorough and repeated representation of the true gospel of the Bible. It faithfully communicates what God has done to save sinners.

This book is loving because it is written with a concern and compassion for those bound in a system that will cheat them in life and death. The heart of the book is the desire for others to be delivered from the darkness and brought into fellowship with Jesus. This would mean present and eternal joy for those whose hearts are opened by God.

This book is offensive. Many will take offense at its message but it's really the gospel they are offended at. It's the offence of the cross that causes men to stumble. They refuse to accept the truth that they can contribute nothing to their salvation. When confronted with this truth many are infuriated and their hearts are shut closed. Only God can open them.

I heartily commend this work knowing it will be sour to some but in God's hand may prove sweet to others. Some may malign and mock it but it may prove to be an arrow in God's hand to pierce the hearts of others and bring them to peace in Jesus Christ."

Grover Dean, Pastor, Grace Baptist Church, Glasgow, KY

Christ Rescued Me!

....*from the*

"Church of Christ"

Lee Anne Ferguson

True ♡ Gospel
Publications

Summer Shade, Kentucky USA

Christ Rescued Me! *....from the "Church of Christ"*

Copyright ©2019 by Lee Anne Ferguson. Printed in the United States of America. All rights reserved. Except for brief quotations for reviews, no part of this book may be reproduced in any form or by any electronic or mechanical means, including information storage and retrieval systems, without written permission from the publisher.

To order additional copies at special quantity discounts, contact:

True Gospel Publications
4369 Summer Shade Rd.
Summer Shade, KY 42166
Email: gospel4life@live.com

Front and Back Cover Design: Designer_pro247 at Fiverr.com
Front Cover Photo: A photo of the author and a photo of the view from "God's Meadow" (mentioned in book), combined with Shutterstock images for the hands, church and sky.

Unless otherwise noted, all Scripture texts in this work are taken from the *King James Version* of the Bible. Caps are the authors in instances where KJV translators didn't capitalize references to God.

Disclaimer: The author endorses the statements of those who are cited favorably herein, but not any errors they may have elsewhere.

ISBN: 978-1-7329259-0-8

Library of Congress Control Number: 2018914104

gospel4life@live.com

Acknowledgements

First and foremost, I want to express deepest gratitude to my Father in Heaven, for all He has accomplished in His Son to save a wretch like me. He has not only blessed me with His everlasting love, but also with the love of a husband who has stuck with me throughout all the trials and tribulations that we've been through, and has supported me through all the personal sacrifices, struggles and studies that have gone into the writing of this book. *"In all these things we are more than conquerors through Him that loved us"* (Rom. 8:37). I'm also thankful for all the children and grandchildren that God has blessed us with. My prayer is that this testimony will be their true spiritual heritage of what it really means to be rescued and saved by Christ.

I also thank God for the encouragement and endorsement of Larry Wessels, Director of *Christian Answers Television* (now CAnswersTV on YouTube), and for many of the excellent theologians and Christians who've been involved in his ministry over the decades (who are too numerous to name here), for without them this book would have never been complete.

I'm also thankful to God for the correction, clarification and confirmation of those who have helped to test my own spiritual insight. Although it's been deemed best that they remain anonymous until God grants them the boldness that their disclosure would require...*God knows who they are.*

And last, but not least, a special thanks goes to God for Pastor Grover Dean, for encouraging me to trust God's promises enough to "cast my book upon the waters" (Eccl. 11:1). Like a modern-day Charles Spurgeon, he too has had to count the cost of standing for the true gospel of Jesus Christ, against the rising tide of doctrinal compromise and spiritual barrenness, even at the risk of losing everything....*because Jesus is worth it.*

Dedication

This book is dedicated to my precious Lord and Savior Jesus Christ, for He is the One Who has granted these *"spoils won in battles" (1 Chron. 26:27)*, in order to edify His true Church and to illustrate His radical, rescuing love in calling His people out of darkness into His marvelous light (1 Pet. 2:9).

The constant longing that I have had for the deliverance of those still in darkness, has not been a burden lightly endured. But now that this labor of love has been completed, my heart's desire and prayer to God is that He will get this book into the right hands and use it as a means to orchestrate their rescue and to lead them into a deeper understanding of His love and the true gospel of Christ that sets the captives free. To God alone be the glory!

Table of Contents

Introduction..1

Part 1: *"If we would judge ourselves, we should not be judged"*

Chapter 1: Oh My Goodness!...17

Chapter 2: Justified by a "Believing Immersion"..............................23

Chapter 3: Proud to be "Humble"...27

Chapter 4: Replacing the Gospel with Disputable Things................33

Chapter 5: Moth-Eaten Patterns...39

Chapter 6: Pulpit Perversions...45

Chapter 7: Heart-Breaking Providences...51

Chapter 8: "From the Frying Pan into the Fire".............................61

Chapter 9: Pragmatism: Thread in the Cornbread!.......................67

Part 2: God's Awe-Inspiring Providences and Divine Appointments

Chapter 10: New Beginnings..75

Chapter 11: Blessed Assurance..81

Chapter 12: Painful Persecutions...89

Chapter 13: Standing Alone at a Crossroads.................................95

Chapter 14: "Politically Correct" Theology..................................103

Chapter 15: Ecumenical Anarchy...107

Chapter 16: The Falling Away..115

Part 3: Believing a False Gospel Leads to Eternal Damnation

Chapter 17: The Water Gospel 123

Chapter 18: Fatally False Interpretations 129

Chapter 19: Baptismal Regeneration is a False Gospel 133

Chapter 20: The Galatian Heresy 139

Part 4: How God *Really* Saves

Chapter 21: God Saves by Giving 147

Chapter 22: God's Perfect Redeeming Love 151

Chapter 23: God's Foreknowledge and Predestination 155

Chapter 24: The True Nature of the Atonement of Christ 159

Part 5: Compelling Conclusions

Chapter 25: Whosoever Will 167

Chapter 26: Subjective Morality: The Iniquity of Holy Things 173

Chapter 27: Deism Leads to Me-ism 181

Chapter 28: Open-Theism Opens the Door to Doubt 185

Chapter 29: The Sufficiency and Authority of Scripture 189

Chapter 30: Sad and Natural Outcomes of CoC Theology 193

Appendix 1: Acts 2:38 Exegesis/The Greek Rule 205

Appendix 2: Breaking Through the CoC's Heretical Language Barrier 209

"For I determined not to know anything among you except Jesus Christ and Him crucified." (1 Cor. 2:2, NKJV).

Introduction

Jesus asks, *"Who do you say that I am?"* (Mt. 16:15-17, NKJV), in order to set the stage for the divine revelation that one can only come to the *true* Christ by a special act of God's grace illuminating the *true* meaning of Scripture to one's heart and mind (Jn. 6:45), without which, one will fall for a *false* christ that can't save (Mk. 13:5-6). And this, being at the pinnacle of all divine truth, launches the primary purpose of this book: *to exalt the true Christ of Holy Scripture and to expose the false christ of man-made religion.*

To advance the cause of Christ, I truly hope that serious, biblical, honest and prayerful consideration will be given to this testimony, even though it comes from one of the least worthy and least significant of God's sheep. If not, it will have to be taken up with my heavenly Father, Who chooses the foolish and the weak to confound the high and mighty (1 Cor. 1:26-29).

Time is too short to keep holding out for someone more prominent to take on the vital task of uncovering important details that have been swept under the rug for way too long, while precious souls are at stake. These testimonial sketches have already taken years to document and piece together. So, although it is *definitely* not my natural inclination to be involved in controversy, the time has come when to remain silent would be an insult to God's grace which has enabled me to do this work, for His grace is sufficient and His power is made perfect in weakness (2 Cor. 12:9).

In light of the many written works that were done in the distant past to adequately expose spiritual deception in the so-called "Church of Christ" (CoC hereafter), this is not an exhaustive account, but is mainly a testimony to the fact that Christ rescues His people and enables them to know and love *Who He really is* (Jer. 9:23-24, 1 Jn. 5:20). It also testifies that His pre-eminence cannot be hindered by any amount of so-called "freewill," for He *actively rescues* His sheep and doesn't *passively* allow any to perish (Mt. 18:11-13). So, consequently, the heretical aspects of CoC doctrine also end up "coming out in the wash," in a way that has never been done before.

Nevertheless, my heart's desire is to win souls, not a popularity contest. After all, Jesus said His people will receive hatred from the world...*Not "likes"* (Mt. 10:22, Jn. 17:14). So this is not your typical, modern day, scratch-the-surface-kind-of-book that follows the script of hyper-socialized media, which exploits the fallen masses desire for absolute autonomy and reduces them down to the lowest, common denominator by literally "feeding" their weakest passions and shallowest thinking. The addictive platform of Facebook following *alone* has proved to be a perfect reflection of human freewill on steroids....*further confirming the fact, that when left to our own will, we are never truly free.* It's no coincidence, that those who fight the most against becoming what they perceive as being a "robot" for God, are ironically the most likely to become *robotically enslaved* to the things of this world, which is a sign of God's judgment (2 Thess. 2:10-12).

Christians are not called to conform to culture, but to conform to Christ, Who gives *true* freedom. Instead of following the crowd, we're called to follow Jesus, to follow the script of *His Book*, to *"reason with them from the Scriptures" (Acts 17:2)* and to faithfully answer for the hope that is within us (1 Pet. 3:15). Since the CoC is a religion of the head and not of the heart, it must be dealt with head-on, with tightly-knit expositions of Scripture, powerful proofs, compelling conclusions and heart-subduing evidences that engage the intellect and invites readers to *"let us reason together" (Isa. 1:18),* to conclude once and for all what the evidence demands....*that the so-called "Church of Christ" does not represent true, biblical Christianity.*

This is not to shame CoC members, but to warn them, for many are truly God's sheep who've been led astray, and are some of the most wonderful, sincere people in the world, who I love dearly (1 Cor. 4:14). But since *"open rebuke is better than secret love" (Prov. 27:5, 1 Tim. 1:13),* this labor of love has required the rebuke of an evil system that has taken them captive. By God's grace, some can genuinely be saved, despite CoC obscurity, but Jesus always rescues His sheep and leads them on their way out of such darkness.

This is in no way, shape or form any kind of personal attack, but is rather an urgent expose' of destructive heresies, for those who remain enslaved by such cannot inherit God's kingdom (Gal. 5:19-21). It is a heartfelt plea born out of a deep and abiding love for God and His people. But it's inevitable that many will be offended and will refuse to submit to Scripture and the true Christ, for the gospel itself is a Rock of offense (Rom. 9:33). Yet Jesus said, *"Blessed is he who is not offended because of Me" (Lk. 7:23,* NKJV*).*

Formerly being a fourth generation member of the CoC myself, I realize that I will also have to submit myself to the judgment of others, because of its effects on my own life and that of my family. I may even have to endure

Introduction

smear campaigns and more cruel reproaches for the sake of Christ. But I have counted the cost. The fires of suffering have only served to confirm the truth and to purify my life with a more complete renunciation of worldliness and a deeper dedication so necessary for this work, which has been the result of the love of Christ being poured into my heart by the gracious, sanctifying work of the Holy Spirit (Rom. 5:5).

What started out as a blog and *Theological Thoughts* column in a local paper years ago, became a huge turning point in my life when false accusations, malicious schemes and typical cries of "misrepresentation" were put forth to try to discredit, silence and weaken the resolve to honor my Lord and Savior by reaching out to His sheep with the true gospel. But His truth did not return void. And though I'm sure it was not the intention of those in opposition, the overflow of such hostility against the gospel has provided the occasion for this book to shine forth the beauty of God's truth, in stark contrast to the CoC's soul-eroding errors (1 Cor. 11:19).

Accordingly, God has granted the grace necessary to continue standing firm against this master-piece of Satan, which disguises itself under the banner of Christ in an attempt to gain Christian credibility (2 Cor. 11:12-14).

Tragically, it made its way to "our neck of the woods" (South Central KY) through John Mulkey in the early 1800's, who is still idolized today.[1] The church he split has become the only state-funded religious shrine in Kentucky. In fact, "Old Mulkey" became my family's favorite park, where commemorative plaques of our spiritual heritage puffed up our pride in thinking we were the ones "in the right."

Looking out over the beautifully wooded landscape, peppered with family-friendly picnic and play areas, one would never imagine that one of the most horrific pulpit crimes of all time had been committed there.

Mulkey was heavily influenced by Barton W. Stone[2] and Alexander Campbell, who were both leaders of the Restoration Movement, which claimed to restore "unity," based on what they termed "the ancient gospel."[3] But what they actually "restored" was the Roman Catholic, sacramental concept of salvation, primarily, Baptismal Regeneration.[4]

As a side effect, this virulent strain of *Mulkey malarkey* has infected our towns, churches and families, under the guise of "Church of Christ" (a misnomer) for over two centuries.[5] Though the CoC denies its history, or at least tries to revise it, (for it claims Christ as its founder), it still holds its *true* founders in high-esteem and continues to teach their peculiar doctrines, while elusively polishing them up in an attempt to sound more Christian.

For instance, the CoC denies teaching baptismal regeneration, by redefining it to only mean ascribing power to the water itself, which it claims not to do. *But baptismal regeneration also dictates that one can only be spiritually born again thru water baptism, which the CoC does indeed teach!* Yet it absolutely refuses to call it what it is, for it must try to hide its Romanistic doctrines and interpretations at all costs. So, when its shady history is questioned, it minimizes it as a "non-issue." This language barrier will become more evident throughout this work, *especially in Appendix 2.*

Formerly well-known as "Campbellism," this counter-reformation began to hide its true identity. Because, in the 1800's there were still those of the reformed camp who stood strongly against this Romanist system, seeing it for what it really was. So by claiming to have no formal creeds, it was better able to fly under the radar. And with the spiritual decay of society, along with a severe lack of discernment, the churches, that once stood strong in reformed confessions of faith, began to sacrifice truth on the altar of "unity," resulting in the rise of the "restoration" cults. The link between the decline of the former and the rise of the latter has been undeniable.

This same kind of superficial unity also sparked *The Downgrade Controversy* in the late 1800's, when sound doctrine was being downgraded into obscurity, so that false doctrine could gain the ascendency. Today it's known as the Ecumenical Movement, headed by none other than the Roman Catholic Church. However, it is now evolving into a "one world" hybrid that is neither Catholic nor Christian, but is rather a New Age, philosophical, technological, psychological, political and social gospel that's spreading like cancer and shipwrecking the faith of many... *calling for the urgent need to be exposed, abandoned and repented of.*

The CoC's very own *Duck Dynasty* reps have been on the forefront of this falling away for years. Its "duck, duck, goose" gurus continue to give spiritual advice on ecumenical and political platforms, while simultaneously preaching in CoC churches and universities across the nation, which has proved that there's no "decoy" too outlandish to further its "quack-ology!"

Therefore, this documentary also systematically provides an expanded view of how and why the "Church of Christ" has always been destined to be a temporary religion, a mere stepping stone back to Rome, as reflected in its

Introduction

title and peripheral issues already being compromised, in order to make way for a one world religion. But its baptismal regeneration formula is still remaining intact for ecumenical integration. This book also reveals how and why the CoC's that are refusing to go along with the inevitable transition are now "sitting ducks" that are experiencing a prophetic, mass die-off.

Consequently, it will be shown that rank Arminianism$_6$ is at the root of it all, and how it finds its most consistent and fullest expression in sacramental systems of salvation, which ultimately develop as a result of rebellion against God's absolute freedom and sovereignty in all things.$_7$

Sacramental salvation is the natural outcome of *minimizing* God's sovereignty in salvation and *maximizing* man's "freewill" ability to save himself by "cooperating" with God's grace. By unfolding what happens when it is consistently taken to its logical and sad conclusion, it's hoped that others will take heed and learn to *"try the spirits whether they are of God: because many false prophets are gone out into the world" (1 Jn. 4:1).*

By clarifying issues that have been obscured, and exposing their overall incompatibility with Scripture, this testimony is hoped to be used by God to call His people, who are still caught up in lies, to *"come out from among them,"* so that they too may bear witness to the true gospel of Jesus Christ.

The Spirit of God is still calling out the *true* Church, the *true* Body of Christ. And with the resurgence of reformed theology, more and more people are catching on to the fact that the CoC shares a similar soteriology (salvation theology) with the Roman Catholic Church, which the early reformed martyrs stood so strongly against, even under the penalty of death. This will be shown to be the chief reason why the evil spirit behind the CoC system fights tooth and nail against reformed creeds, and why it is now ineffectively developing even more sophisticated arguments to try to counteract these confessions of faith that reveal the true gospel...*which it must try to misconstrue in order to keep its false gospel from being exposed.*

The mystery of God's divine providence allowed me to be deeply entrenched in the CoC for decades, so that I could obtain an experimental knowledge of just how spiritually destructive a false gospel really is. But thankfully He never allowed me to rest quietly in that fatal delusion. He began a good work in me by slowly removing the veil from my eyes so that I could see Jesus as my only hope, Who then gave me the ability to break through the CoC's secretive, sacramental system, in order to launch a full-scale invasion of truth, to help lead others out of legalistic bondage into freedom in Christ and *true* obedient faith, which comes only by God's grace.

Due to my own past affiliation with the CoC, it is my qualified duty to anticipate and annihilate its fatally flawed arguments, and to responsibly represent what its theology actually entails. This insider approach avoids all speculation, and is biblically supported with a fair understanding and compassion toward all involved. Although this is not an exhaustive account, the incidents, conversations and practices are real and accurately depicted.

Legitimate, inside information, as well as supplemental CoC sources, are all used to reveal that *"we wrestle not against flesh and blood, but against principalities, against powers, against the rulers of the darkness of this world, against spiritual wickedness in high places" (Eph. 6:12).* By *"speaking the truth in love,"* a clarifying distinction has been carefully made between the evil spirit behind the CoC system, and those who are captives of it, by reflecting only upon the deluding effects it has on those believing its lies, the abuse that occurs as a result, and how the gospel and those who proclaim it are marginalized and persecuted because of its deceptive errors.

What Paul felt concerning his fellow Jews, is how I feel toward those who are still captives in the CoC; my heart's desire and prayer to God for them is that they may be saved. *"For I bear them record that they have a zeal of God, but not according to knowledge" (Rom. 10:1-2).*

Though many claim to know God, they are unable to biblically explain what He actually accomplished at the cross. Many claim to believe Jesus is *the* Savior, and yet, they are unable to use *possessive pronouns* when it comes to confessing a complete trust in Jesus Christ as *their* personal Savior. Many claim to believe the gospel, and yet, they betray their profession when they are unable to biblically define what the gospel even is! As a dire consequence, they end up simultaneously holding to beliefs that *deny* Jesus' power to save and the true gospel He came to proclaim, which is equivalent to *"having a form of godliness, but denying the power thereof" (2 Tim. 3:5).*

Upon this precipice, it will be shown how the *different* spirit behind the CoC system leads people to a *different* Jesus and a *different* gospel, which Scripture so strongly warns about (2 Cor. 11:4). Unwittingly, the CoC furnishes its own refutation by embracing a false gospel, which is a fundamental denial of the only way a sinner can be justified before a holy God. Therefore, the CoC condemns itself, and in effect, ceases from being a

Introduction

true church, though it ironically claims to be *the only true church...just as Romanism does.* So, with this being the case, the CoC system collapses and falls under the same condemnation as Romanism and the Israel of Apostle Paul's day, which embraced God but rejected His message (Rom. 10:1-3).

This is not a matter of splitting hairs, for there is *nothing* more important than knowing the way of salvation through Jesus Christ. And the issue is not whether doctrine or Christ saves, which is just a false dichotomy. The issue is *what* the gospel really is, *Who* Christ really is, and *how* He really saves. We are commanded to *believe the gospel (Mk. 1:15),* not a false version of it, which God places under a divine curse (Gal. 1:6-9).

When a system claims to be Christian but doesn't have the doctrine of Christ, (the *truth* about the work and Person of Jesus Christ), it doesn't have the true God and Savior, but falls under the condemnation of 2 John 7-11 as being a deceiver and an anti-Christ. *That's what makes this so serious.*

◊◊◊

Over fifteen years ago, I began to realize that the christ of the "Church of Christ" was not matching up with Scripture, for God was leading me to seek, to know and to trust in the *true* Christ. But, before then, I had been a self-righteous "Pharisee of Pharisees," a devout follower of the CoC my entire life, heavily involved in its advance, and knowing it's doctrines inside and out. I unfortunately raised my children in it for many years, and even taught its Sunday school for well over a decade. After all, I was trained very well.

My grandmother would have had it no other way. She had already set the precedent for all of us to become strict adherents of the CoC. But God, in His great mercy, kept me from becoming another carbon copy, and He kept me too spiritually inquisitive to continue to conform to CoC obscurity.

No wonder grandma was never too enthused when I'd come running into her kitchen as a child, with new discoveries about God's creation; like the beautiful designs I'd find on a butterfly or the design of His perfectly formed snail and periwinkle shells I'd collect from the nearby branch that inspired my artwork. She always made it clear that it was forbidden to talk about God on an intimately personal level, because it made her so uncomfortable.

Grandma would even shy away when I'd refer to the field next to the branch as "God's Meadow," a special place I'd go to pray as a child, for God always seemed to be revealing Himself there in the light of creation, as Creator of all things (Rom. 1:20). So it was very confusing to my quiet little spirit when grandma's air of condescension always relayed the message that it was a waste of my time to write about it, or to express it artistically.

Because, as my Sunday school teacher, she would religiously teach me gospel hymns and Bible stories. Even so, the emphasis was strictly on good, moral behavior, to the exclusion of genuine faith in Christ, along with the mundane challenge of surface-level questions at the end of class...*as if Jesus was just an impersonal, imaginary, storybook character with good morals.*

So it would always throw grandma for a loop when I would ask her much deeper questions, like whether she looked forward to being with Jesus (sadly she never could answer in the affirmative), or about all the Scriptures concerning the link between predestination and salvation, because our church always seemed to skip (or stumble) over those parts.

When pressed for clarification, obscure answers were always backed with the same escape clause, "Well, we just can't be sure what that means; we just have to try to do the best we can and hope for the best." Yet I knew deep down that God must have revealed them in His Word for a reason, for *"The secret things belong unto the Lord our God: but those things which are revealed belong unto us and to our children forever"* (Deut. 29:29).

Looking back, it has become increasingly clear that our minds were blinded by the CoC's theoretical theories, which would cast such doubt, obscurity and confusion upon Scripture. However, God is not the author of confusion (1 Cor. 14:33). That is what deception does. It dismantles the capacity to think God's Word through, according to the language in which it was written, its historical context, the identity and purpose of each author, and who it was originally being addressed to in each situation. True, biblical *exegesis* interprets what the original text actually conveys and means *in context*, whereas the CoC's unbiblical *eisegesis* inserts foreign meanings into the text, which creates a *pretext* to hide the true meaning.

Without the standard rules of interpretation, people are led to believe truth and error are just differences in opinion. This began in the Garden of Eden when the serpent tempted Eve to doubt what God had actually said (Gen. 3:1). Those who are unstable and unlearned are still taking portions of Scripture that are hard to understand, and are twisting them to their own destruction (2 Pet. 3:16). *"In whom the god of this world hath blinded the minds of them which believe not, lest the light of the glorious gospel of Christ, Who is the image of God, should shine unto them"* (2 Cor. 4:4).

So even if one acquired a Ph.D. in theology, it would still never be a cure for *spiritual* blindness. Because, when it comes to *spiritually* understanding God's Word, and loving Who He really is, we must first be *born from above* and enlightened by the Holy Spirit. For *"the natural man receiveth not the things of the Spirit of God; for they are foolishness unto him; neither can he know them, because they are spiritually discerned"* (1 Cor. 2:14).

Sometimes the truth hurts, because it's hard for our sinful flesh to accept God's absolute sovereignty. We all have our weak points and blind spots. And, while it's true that we can't understand *all* of God's ways, what He has revealed to us, we are to accept and shout from the housetops, and what He speaks to us in the dark, we are to speak in the light (Deut. 29:29, Mt. 10:27). For *"No man, when he hath lighted a candle, putteth it in a secret place, neither under a bushel, but on a candlestick, that they which come in may see the light"* (LK. 11:33).

By these truths many are strengthened in their faith, for *"he that doeth truth cometh to the light that his deeds may be made manifest, that they are wrought in God"* (Jn. 3:21). But, there will be some who reject and rebel against the truth, for *"every one that doeth evil hateth the light, neither cometh to the light, lest his deeds should be reproved"* (Jn. 3:20).

Today, the "hive mind" stronghold in our technologically advanced era is also dumbing down minds to the point of disabling the ability to *think theology through.* And when false notions are called into question or exposed, many have a theologically conditioned response, where they automatically assume a false persecution complex that triggers a hostile defense mechanism. Instead of a willingness to submit to the judgment of Scripture with a *teachable spirit,* many take personal affront.

Through the subtle art of redefinition, many are being tempted to compartmentalize between the character of Christ revealed in Scripture and the character of *another Christ* that's being promoted by society's false religious systems. Many are willingly brainwashed against deep theological studies that challenge faulty interpretations and preconceived notions. A false gospel that's hammered home repeatedly, programs minds to shut out anything that challenges it, and blinds them to its spiritual ramifications.

Still, we must not get discouraged, for Jesus said His people will be led by the Spirit into all truth (Jn. 16:13). They will be given the *"Spirit of truth; Whom the world cannot receive" (Jn. 14:17)*. They will know the truth and the truth will set them free from the dominion of sin and false religion (Jn. 8:31-32). They will *"be saved and come to the knowledge of the truth" (1 Tim. 2:4)*, for God teaches them by opening their understanding to Scripture (Lk. 24:45). Those who savingly believe in the true Christ will not abide in darkness (Jn. 12:46), for God has ordained the means to rescue them.

This is why I write and *"endure all things for the elect's sakes, that they may also obtain the salvation which is in Christ Jesus with eternal glory" (2 Tim. 2:10)*. It is my duty as a servant of the Lord, to use the means that He provides, in order to unpack the truth, where Scripture interprets Scripture. It speaks for itself. What seems obscure in one place will be made clearer in another, so that it can all be taken as a whole to get the full meaning.

Acts 17:11-12 tells us of Apostle Paul's encounter with noble-minded Bereans. These men and women were not only ready to receive God's Word, but they also searched the Scriptures daily for themselves, to see if all they were being told was true. Not only does this scenario show us that women are to be involved in theological matters too, but that we all need to apply ourselves to know the truth, even if it threatens our status quo.

Therefore, *Theological Thoughts* are prayerfully woven throughout the fabric of this work, to help readers to *think their theology through,* for we are commanded to commit ourselves to the Lord so that our *"thoughts shall be established" (Prov. 16:3)*. And comparison/contrast writings are often the means that God uses to bring our thoughts into sharper focus. Proclaiming the light of the gospel and exposing the lies hidden in darkness, helps God's people to discern the difference between the spirit of truth and the spirit of error (1 Jn. 4:5-6). By evaluating the evidence, they can make *informed* decisions on what to believe, *based on what God's Word actually conveys.*

"Group think," on the other hand, thrives on spiritual ignorance, and manipulates minds on the basis of gaining control and authority. This is why many, who embrace the CoC system of thought, don't even realize what they're being taught to believe, or the serious implications of those beliefs. And when false religion convinces people that absolute truth is not really knowable or obtainable, it blasphemously implies that God is not *able* to reveal Himself and His truth to His people. That's when the devil slips in.

Introduction

The more people can be convinced that God has failed to preserve and reveal His truth…. the easier *a replacement system* can be carried out.

Philippians 4:8 says our thoughts are to be upon things that are true, honest, just, pure, lovely and of good report, all of which are a perfect description of the gospel of Jesus Christ. Yet, mixing the gospel with worldly views, shows a low esteem for the authority and sufficiency of Scripture. Worse yet, truth mixed with error is no longer truth at all (1 Jn. 2:21), but becomes false, dishonest, unjust, impure, ugly and a bad report. Sowing seeds of the gospel mixed with worldly philosophies and opinions of man, leads to a false Jesus, and therefore, becomes a false gospel. No wonder Scripture warns us to *abstain from all appearance of evil* (1 Thess. 5:22). For what could be more manifestly evil than a false gospel that leads to Hell?

The idea that one can "chew up the meat and spit out the bones," also has its limits when it comes to bad theology, because it can lead to becoming an excuse for tolerating deceptive doctrine, or for allowing it to go unchecked. Scripture warns that *"a little leaven leaveneth the whole lump" (1 Cor. 5:6)*. It also warns that we cannot be partakers of the Lord's Table and of the devil's table (1 Cor. 10:21). Even common sense tells us that chewing meat that's mixed with bones can be a choking hazard.

When Paul identified *false brethren,* he was being wise, discerning and loving by warning others. Yet the world still continues to accuse faithful Christians of being unloving and judgmental when they warn of *God's judgment*. But we are to never cower or shrink back from exposing serious departures from the Christian faith behind an unbiblical concept of love.

While "the truth sounds like hate to those who hate the truth," Christians are still *commanded* to commit themselves to pulling down strongholds and *"casting down imaginations, and every high thing that exalteth itself against the knowledge of God, and bringing into captivity every thought to the obedience of Christ" (2 Cor. 10:4-5)*. This extends to stern warnings to *"have no fellowship with the unfruitful works of darkness, but rather reprove them" (Eph. 5:11)*, for true *"love rejoices in the truth" (1 Cor. 13:6)*.

Therefore, exposing error and proclaiming the gospel are two aspects of the same task, which may be one reason this documentary has proven the old adage true… that *"truth shines brightest against the backdrop of error."*

"For there must be also heresies among you, that they which are approved may be made manifest among you" (1 Cor. 11:19).

Christ Rescued Me! ....from the "Church of Christ"

Notes:

1 Loy R. Milam, *Old Mulkey: A Pioneer Plea for the Ancient Order,* (Tompkinsville, KY: Pioneer Paths Publishing, 2014), p. 6. Quoting from the actual minutes of the Mill Creek Baptist Church of Monroe County, KY (August of 1809), we read the following heretical charges brought against John Mulkey: "We then concluded that he denies the essential doctrine of the Gospel, such as denying in our esteem that Jesus Christ satisfied the demands of law and justice for his people, or died as our surety, or that any man is saved by the righteousness of Jesus Christ imputed to them."

Also see: Cecil E. Goode, *Heart of the Barrens,* (Glasgow, KY: South Central Kentucky Historical Society, 1986), p. 83, states as follows: "Of course, we know of the famous division in the Mill Creek Baptist Church then in southern Barren County but now in Monroe County. John Mulkey led off in 1809 a major portion of the church to join the Stoneites or Campbellites."

Also see: Warnell Cawthorn, *Pioneer Baptist Church Records of South Central Kentucky and the Upper Cumberland of Tennessee 1799-1899.* "The Baptists were afraid that Stone and Mulkey's doctrine tended to deism by reducing the death of Jesus to the level of the death of other men....a doctrine contrary to the Christian religion, and boldly charged Mulkey with being a heretic" (p. 436). "In 1809, John Mulkey led off a large faction of the Mill Creek congregation to the "New Lights." Many of these returned to the ranks of the Baptists within a short period of time" (p. 448). The irony is that Mulkey was famed as the "man with the majority," yet the *majority* caught on to him and his heresies once he threw off his disguise (p. 437). But this is secretly glossed over in the CoC.

See also: William Phillips, *Campbellism Exposed,* (Cincinnati, OH: J.F. Wright & L. Swormstedt, 1837), p. 198, states as follows: "They have been heard to boast that they had destroyed the Baptist church in Kentucky. We are gratified to discover that this boast concerning the Baptist church was founded in mistake. For that church, though in some places for a time, apparently trammeled and divided by the spread of Campbellism, has since risen with increased strength."

2 Barton W. Stone, *Biography of Elder Barton Warren Stone,* taken from Loy R. Milam, *Old Mulkey: A Pioneer Plea for the Ancient Order,* (Tompkinsville, KY: Pioneer Paths Publishing, 2014). Pages 42-46 shows that Stone revealed in his own words what caused him to blaspheme the God of the Bible. He had a stronger love for people and himself than for God. Instead of humbly submitting to God's inescapable sovereignty in salvation, he rebelled, called God a monster and built an altar to the god of "human freewill"... "*who changed the truth of God into a lie, and worshipped and served the creature more than the Creator*" (Rom. 1:25).

Introduction

Jesus made it clear that our allegiance to God and His cause must supersede all else, even our own parents whom we are commanded to honor. He warns that if it doesn't, we are not worthy to be His disciples (Mt. 10:37-38, Lk. 14:26). Jesus proved that what seemed to the world to be a sin of disrespect and cruelty toward His closest earthly relations, wasn't that at all, in light of His higher calling (Mt. 12:47-49, Lk. 2:49). A great way to honor parents is to share the gospel with them.

[3] Also see: Iain Murray, *"Revival and Revivalism: The Making and Marring of American Evangelicalism 1750-1858,"* (Carlisle, PA: The Banner of Truth Trust, 1994). "It is attended with many advantages to bring into view *ancient heresies*, for often what modern innovators consider a new discovery, and wish to pass off as a scheme suited to remove all difficulties, is found upon examination to be nothing else than some *ancient heresy* clothed in a new dress" (p. 270, emphasis mine).

[4] Bob L. Ross, *Campbellism: Its History and Heresies*, (Pasadena, TX: Pilgrim Publications, 1981). "Needless to say, this "plan" falls into the category of sacramental and sacerdotal salvation; **sacramental**, in that it necessitates a ceremonial ordinance; **sacerdotal**, in that it necessitates the "assistance" of another person ["priest"] for one to "obey" it. It is therefore, in a definite sense of the word a salvation by works---not only the work of the one "obeying," but also the work of the one "assisting" (p. 77, emphasis in original). "None of the men primarily responsible for the origin of the Campbellite church was ever baptized according to the present Campbellite doctrine of baptismal regeneration. We shall show from the historical records of the Campbellites themselves that Thomas Campbell, Alexander Campbell, Walter Scott, and Barton Stone, the "big four" of Campbellite history were never immersed to "wash away sins." Remember this fact as you read of the Campbellite church's history, for it renders Campbellism the most inconsistent religious movement on the face of the earth today" (p. 5).

"Notice that Stone and his followers did not go to a "Church of Christ" (like our modern ones) for baptism! This was for the very simply [sic] reason that **no such outfit existed!**" (p. 57, emphasis his). "There are a few other men that the Campbellites name as having a hand in the "restoration" movement, but with regard to these men, such as O'Kelly, "Raccoon" John Smith, Abner Jones, and others, the same fact applies to them as to the Campbells, Scott and Stone. That fact is: **not one of these individuals had been baptized to obtain the remission of sins**, for this doctrine was concocted within Campbellism during the early 1820's and was not put into practice until 1827 by Walter Scott" (p. 60, emphasis his).

[5] Warnell Cawthorn, *Pioneer Baptist Church Records of South Central Kentucky and the Upper Cumberland of Tennessee 1799-1899*. "*Mulkey malarkey*" also highlights the fact that John Mulkey (like all the other "restorers") never practiced what he preached. While he wreaked spiritual havoc and division, he himself was never re-

baptized according to the "ancient gospel" he forced upon others. For again we read, "John Mulkey never denied his baptism at the hands of the Baptists" (p. 438).

[6] See: Gary D. Long, *Definite Atonement*, (Phillipsburg, NJ: P&R Publishing Co. 1976), p. 79, states: "Historic or consistent Calvinism received the theological nickname "five point" Calvinism as a result of its reply at the Synod of Dort in 1618 to a five point manifesto formulated in Holland in 1610 by a group whose teaching later became known as Arminianism, named after its theological father, Jacob Arminius (d. 1609)." Those who still take a gospel stand against Arminian heresy today are also called Calvinists. There are also those who claim to be neither Arminian nor Calvinist, but there is no middle ground. Because whenever one takes away even one point of Calvinism, a total collapse into Arminianism is inevitable.

For example, one cannot *consistently* claim to believe in eternal security if they refuse to acknowledge the *definite* atonement of Christ. It is absolutely impossible without committing theological suicide. But sadly, as a systematic attempt to overthrow and undermine the biblical truth that true Calvinists stand for, Arminians often misrepresent them and falsely accuse them of being fatalistic (submitting to random fate), which is actually a trait of both *Hyper*-Calvinism and Arminianism.

Fatalism (or random chance) is completely at odds with historic Calvinism and true Christianity which affirms God's divinely ordained means for bringing about His purposes, and affirms His sovereignty over our choices and even "chance." *"The lot is cast into the lap; but the whole disposing thereof is of the Lord"* (Prov. 16:33).

Both Arminianism and *Hyper*-Calvinism are evangelistically unfruitful, like the wicked and unfaithful servant in Jesus' parable of the talents (Mt. 25:14-30). Amazingly, Jesus "killed two birds with one stone" in that parable. For it could be a perfect depiction of *Hyper*-Calvinism's fatalistic absence of evangelism and refusal to use God's divinely ordained means for reaching the lost.

It could also depict Arminianism's confusion of categories regarding God's sovereignty and our responsibility, but these issues will be examined further in later chapters. However, their spiritual depths are not for the faint at heart, or for those who are not ready for what the Bible calls "strong meat" (Heb. 5:12, 14).

[7] (*Catholic Almanac*, (Huntington, IN: Our Sunday Visitor Publishing, 1994), p. 223, when referring to the sacraments, Romanists say they "perpetuate the redemptive activity of Christ, making it present and effective."

This is how both Romanism and the CoC views baptism, due to their common misinterpretation of certain Bible verses, such as Acts 2:38. Both claim that baptism actually *causes*, *conveys* and *confirms* the benefits it signifies, which makes baptismal regeneration a powerfully deceptive *replacement* for the true gospel.

Part 1

"If we would judge ourselves, we should not be judged"

(1 Cor. 11:31).

Chapter 1

Oh My Goodness!

"There is none righteous, no, not one... there is none that doeth good, no, not one"
(Rom. 3:10-12).

One of the earliest, funniest and yet most telling memories I have of my childhood, is when I'd come home from church and turn moms clothes basket upside down so that I could pretend it was a pulpit. Then, I would drape her black slip over my shoulders like a judge's cloak (because that's how I perceived the preacher). I'd then line up all of my dolls and stuffed animals, pretending to preach to them, while holding my little Bible in one hand and pounding my fist on my imaginary pulpit with the other! And I remember *distinctly* what my main message always was, which was the same basic message of all the "Churches of Christ;"..."*If you don't be good, you're going to Hell!*" Even then, I had CoC doctrine *down pat!*

Jesus, on the other hand, never said "be good." Yet, He did say, *"be perfect" (Mt. 5:48).* But since "being good" seemed more within our reach, that then became our main focus. Despite the fact that no one is able to be good either....*at least not in a saving sense (Ps. 14: 1-3; 53:1-3, Eccl. 7:20).* We had absolutely no idea that we needed the righteousness of Christ credited to our account by virtue of God's mercy. For the *"wrath of man does not produce the righteousness of God" (Jas. 1:20).* No amount of pounding on the pulpit with guilt trips and threats of Hell could produce it.

Although I was convicted of sin at a very early age, due to all of the Hell, fire and brimstone sermons, I was never given a satisfactory solution. And though our church gave a sense of purpose and belonging, I remember growing up and *straining* to try to hear exactly what the gospel even was (it was absent). Because the main purpose to be found in the CoC was the installation of spiritual growth initiated through baptism, and the achievement of full, human potential by obedience to the "second laws of pardon" (explained further in the third chapter).

So instead of being directed to the Savior, and the need to have saving faith in His righteousness as our only hope, we were directed to look within for the power to overcome sin. Although ours was a "Christianized" form of moralistic humanism, it still had Eastern philosophy undertones. Instead of being told that sin had so infected us that we could never have any hope of being spiritually good enough for such a holy God, His holiness was played down by implying that we had the natural potential to do such a thing.

Apostle Paul, on the other hand, stressed that *"they that are in the flesh cannot please God,"* for he knew and confessed that although he had a *creaturely will* to "be good," it wasn't a degree of good that could attain salvation, due to weakness of the flesh (Rom. 7; 8:8). Paul knew that he could be *morally* good, but not *spiritually* good enough to live up to God's perfect standard of righteousness, for his "willpower" to do good could not produce righteousness unto salvation. So he realized that his only hope was for God to accept Jesus' perfect righteousness on his behalf (Phil. 3:8-9).

But these biblical truths were unheard of in the CoC, for our doctrines caused us to be more self-conscious than God-conscious. *"For they being ignorant of God's righteousness, going about to establish their own righteousness, have not submitted themselves unto the righteousness of God. For Christ is the end of the Law for righteousness to everyone that believeth"* (Rom. 10:3-4).

Although lip service would be given to such verses, our system of works was safeguarded by theological term-twisting. Instead of being taught that Jesus satisfied God's law perfectly on behalf of His people, we were taught that Jesus merely lowered the bar so that anyone could just slip in, as long as we just tried to live up to our full potential and do the best we could.

And certainly, that is commendable in the natural realm. But it's impossible for someone *spiritually* dead in sin to do anything that is *spiritually* acceptable to God. Throughout Scripture we're reminded that we are morally responsible to our Holy Creator. Yet it never indicates a natural, spiritual ability to please God. Those who've not been quickened (made spiritually alive) by the Spirit are *"dead in trespasses and sins"* (Eph. 2:1).

On the contrary, CoC doctrines implied that the word *dead* in this verse only meant half dead. Though the CoC claimed to "speak only where the Bible speaks" it failed to teach that *dead meant dead* (spiritually speaking), and not just a polluted or tainted kind of dead. Even though the *effect* of being dead in sin is indeed a polluted, tainted will that cannot rightly respond to God. This inability is a result of spiritual death (Jn. 8:24, 43).

Scripture doesn't lie, but the CoC system did, by confusing the difference between dead and half dead, which kept us from ever completely giving ourselves up for dead in order to freely receive God's grace in Christ alone. So Scriptures, such as Romans 2:14-15, were construed to create an obedience-based system of salvation, based on the common assumption that all are *born* with the law of God written on their hearts. Here the CoC utilized Rome's "Natural Law" interpretation to promote the idea of man having the *natural ability* to get saved apart from divine intervention.

But the Gentiles being referred to *didn't* have the law of God *naturally*. Yet they could be accepted by God and have His law written on their hearts by virtue of being *supernaturally* regenerated by the Holy Spirit (Jer. 31:33, Ezek. 36:27). For by *natural* generation we are all *"children of wrath" (Eph. 2:3)* unless the *"law of Christ"* is written on the tablet of our heart by God's gracious intervention, whereby we then become obedient partakers of His divine nature (Study Ps. 37:31, Isa. 51:7, 1 Cor. 9:21, 2 Cor. 3:3, Gal. 6:2).

This entirely differs from external religiosity, *"common"* grace" and the *common* light of nature or conscience possessed by all humans, which distinguishes us from lower life forms that are not created in God's image. Our *heart* is the seat of our conscience, and it's at enmity with God and desperately wicked until made anew by God (Jer. 17:9, Rom. 8:7, Heb. 8:10).

Although the CoC denies that its version of salvation hinges on law, its "works of obedience" assumes a legal standard of performance, for there must be a principle of law that's being obeyed or performed. The very *word* "obedience" indicates a standard (a law) whereby behavior is determined. So by basing salvation on works instead of *true* obedient faith in Christ alone, the CoC commits a fatal error, and is in complete opposition to Apostle Paul's declaration in Romans of what true salvation is all about.

The CoC is notorious for smuggling in false interpretations, which confuses things that differ and creates a false dichotomy between "works of obedience" and "works of the law." This CoC play on words will be further examined in later chapters. But the root of this problem is the CoC's distorted anthropology of man being born with a "spark of goodness," which has man falling upward, instead of downward into sin. This Gnostic view of the Fall nourished the belief that if we had just enough *head knowledge*... God would "grade on a curve" if we didn't make the grade.

Growing up, I remember encountering some Christians outside the church who I perceived to be over-zealous fanatics. Because they would seem so full of joy and enthusiasm when they would talk about Jesus and what He did on the cross. And, for the life of me, I could not figure out why in the world anyone would be so joyful about Jesus merely making a way for us to save ourselves through works of obedience. Because, for me, it had always been *horrible* news (and rightly so), because I just *knew* I was going to fail on "my part" and end up in Hell. *Any honest person would!*

So I always sensed something was terribly wrong when I was in the CoC, for I didn't have a single ounce of joy in what Jesus did on the cross. Yet I loved my religion and all of the religious things that we did. However, after I was baptized *literally* "for the remission of sins"... I *quickly* realized there had never been a true eradication of condemnation or the love of sin. In other words, there was no change. And the sins that baptism "supposedly" remitted were immediately replaced by myriads more. My conscience was not purged from dead works so that I could serve the living God (Heb. 9:14). Instead, I was consumed with legalistic fear and the constant burden of trying to maintain my own salvation, rather than being concerned for the souls of others from a regenerated heart full of love and peace.

This was why heartfelt testimonies of salvation were non-existent in CoC gatherings. Even in our personal lives there were only contrived confessions of faith that were so vague that "faith" came off as merely being an abstract concept devoid of any absolutes. In fact, the only acceptable "testimony" for those of us in the CoC, was a recounting of one's baptism, and a prideful boasting of how one was "walking in the light" of one's own works.

No wonder those of us who were caught up in the CoC could not grasp the depths of Christ's death on the cross. We were in bondage to a never ending treadmill of work-righteousness. And this was also why we could never tolerate testimonies of Christ's saving power from anyone outside the church. For CoC theology suggests that Jesus' work comes short of actually saving anyone, unless one makes His work effectual by adding one's own meritorious works into the equation. Strictly speaking, Jesus' merits would only kick in once we had done all that we could, which created such a low view of Christ and a high view of man, making one wonder why the "Church of Christ" wasn't named the "Church of Man"... but that'd be too obvious.

No wonder many of us ended up on psych meds to try to overcome the pressure of a condemned conscience. Ultimately, it was a failure to grasp the seriousness of sin, and how we could never do enough works to make up for a single sin we had ever committed. Instead of facing reality, we delved deeper into denial, prescription drugs and worldly distractions. This is the inevitable result when there has been no true, Holy Spirit conviction of how bad sin really is, and therefore, no true, Holy Spirit regeneration.

There is no true possession of the gospel in the CoC. There is just possession of a system that Jesus supposedly left us with. But the true gospel is that Jesus actually *accomplished* redemption on the cross for His people, rather than just making a system available, where one can redeem themselves. Jesus *never* made a way for God to lower His perfect standard of righteousness! On the contrary, Jesus *fulfilled* God's perfect standard of righteousness *on behalf* of His people. He died for *their* sins so that they can have His perfect righteousness credited to their account, and so they can serve God out of a loving and reverent fear, rather than a legalistic fear.

Yet we were theologically conditioned to believe a *different* gospel and "hope for the best," thinking our good would somehow outweigh the bad. Although, reality constantly testified to the fact that it was impossible! Since we were not *internally* ruled by Christ, we were *externally* ruled by an oppressive religious system. So, like Judas who followed Christ with his feet, but not with his heart, the practical implications of following CoC doctrine played out in our lives in varying degrees and it was anything but "good."

For my great-grandmother CoC theology manifested in a lifetime of severe depression, due to living in legalistic fear that she could never be good enough to get to Heaven, despite her obsessive and futile efforts to try to do and say everything perfectly. For my great-grandfather it manifested as severe, demonic oppression, that became even more profound once he took Arminian theology to the next level and got involved in the Pentecostal movement of his time, which also sprouted from the rise of Restorationism, as evidenced in history and its similar use of Baptismal Regeneration (but with a different twist). Yet what *it* claimed to "restore" was the apostolic sign gifts: speaking in tongues, prophesying new revelation, etc.

No wonder he ended up vandalizing their "Church of Christ" by painting it in large, black letters..."*and they shall prophesy*" (Acts 2:18). Because, like many others who become disenchanted with the CoC, he thought that it was the charismatic gifts that were missing in the church, when sadly...*it was actually the gospel that was missing*.

For my grandma, it also played out in obsessive perfectionism, but with the addition of psych meds in hopes that she wouldn't end up like her parents. But without the true gospel, she too continued on a steady decline. As for grandpa, he made a profession of faith at an early age and was baptized by a Baptist preacher. Yet, after he married grandma, CoC leaders told him he'd be a detriment to the church if he didn't get re-baptized by them *literally* "for the remission of sins." So, rather than renounce his former profession and violate his conscience, he stopped going to church.

Yet grandma continued to go, having us all indoctrinated into the CoC system and its unbiblical baptismal formula for salvation. Consequently, she would worry when one of our body parts (even a finger) didn't go all the way under the water, because in order for a sacrament's mystical qualities to work, it must be performed perfectly (an impossibility). So, like Pharisees who carried Christ in their Bibles, but not in their hearts, we all struggled spiritually due to growing up in utter isolation from the true gospel.

Since the CoC misinterpreted verses, such as Hebrews 6:4-6, to mean that one could lose their salvation, we naturally concluded that one could never get it back (v. 6), which was why we would often fall deep into despair and self-condemnation. Grandma even wrote in her diary about how she wished we could realize that God is merciful. But she could not see that our churches contradictory doctrine of "God is merciful....*'if'* we do our best".... *could never be reconciled with its misinterpretation of such verses.* So all we could do was "hope for the best," despite a chronic sense of doom.

As a consequence, we were all driven into a pressured life of over-achievement, worldly competition, materialism and self-absorption. But the CoC's *"just do the best you can and maybe God will have mercy"* motto, re-baptism, psych-meds, perfectionism and financial gain could never replace the true gospel of Jesus Christ, and He warns those who attempt to do so.

"Ye are they which justify yourselves before men; but God knoweth your hearts: for that which is highly esteemed among men is abomination in the sight of God" (Lk. 16:15). Rather than justifying ourselves based on our performance, we needed to judge ourselves according to God's perfect standard, Jesus Christ. Only then could we have realized the futility of our sinful condition and truly turned to Him in order to be *justified by faith*.

Chapter 2

Justified by a "Believing Immersion"

The CoC teaches that faith + works = justification
The Bible teaches that true faith = justification + works

True, blood-bought Christians are *"kept by the power of God through faith unto salvation" (1 Pet. 1:5)*. For *"it is God that justifieth" (Rom. 8:33)*, based on Jesus' perfect obedience, not their own (Titus 3:5). Yet the CoC system was completely at odds with this great Christian truth, and would evade the force of biblical passages that make it so clear. It did this by departing from what the apostles actually say, and supplying what it supposed them to mean. For instance, the CoC taught that being justified by faith meant, *"by an **act** of faith*, or a **believing immersion** in the Lord Jesus Christ."

But even works that flow from faith cannot satisfy divine justice. Yet the CoC still insisted that "justification by faith" meant that one is justified on account of saving grace *imparted* through baptism, when *performed* in faith. Its deliberate omission of Jesus' *imputed* righteousness as the only ground of justification, was equivalent to affirming a false gospel, for it *replaced* His imputed righteousness with an *imparted* righteousness thru the sacrament of baptism. Subsequently, "believing" became synonymous with being baptized, which made all the Bible passages on faith seem non-sensical.[1]

"But let us examine this Campbellite gloss a little further. It tells us, that the apostles, by faith, intend a *"believing immersion,"* an act springing from faith. If so, it will do no violence to the Scriptures to omit the word "faith," and to supply its place by that which it is said to mean. Then let us try a few texts. Our Lord says, *"O woman, great is thy faith"* (great is thy *believing immersion*.) St. Paul says, "With the heart man believeth unto righteousness" (with the heart man is *immersed* unto righteousness.) (Emphasis his)[2]

Rather than allowing Scripture to define its own terms, the "Church of Christ" imports its own definition onto biblical terms. For another example, the term *faith,* in Ephesians 2:8, was deceptively interpreted by the CoC to mean, "by grace ye are saved through ***a believing immersion,*** instead of faith, which *"is the gift of God; not of works, lest any man should boast."*

The CoC's absurd evasions actually contradict everything the Bible has to say about true, saving faith. The irony is that although many unbelievers try to discredit the Bible based on its supposed "contradictions," the CoC ends up creating its own, while still claiming to be a Christian religion! Yet God purposely allows such things to confound those who are wise in their own eyes (1 Cor. 1:27, Lk. 10:21). As a matter of fact, He gives the proud just enough material in His Word for them to build a case with. In other words, they have "just enough rope to hang themselves," so to speak.

A great illustration for this point is the false contradiction that the CoC creates between Paul and James. In Romans 3:27-28, Paul says, *"a man is justified by faith without the deeds of the law."* But James 2:24 says, *"By works a man is justified, and not by faith only."* Yet both mention Abraham to prove their points and both even use the same Greek word for "justified." However, they don't use it in the same sense, for they are both addressing two different matters. Paul tackled work-righteousness and the false belief that one could earn salvation, whereas James dealt with false professions of faith and those who try to abuse God's grace as an excuse to live in sin.

For example, in Romans 4:3, Paul appeals to Genesis 15:6, where Abraham is "justified" (counted righteous) *through faith* in the perfect righteousness of the coming Messiah (Jn. 8:56)....*before* Abraham had performed any works of obedience. However, James 2:21 appeals to Genesis 22, where Abraham's God-given faith is "justified" (proved) by a willingness to offer Isaac on the altar; a willingness that he was enabled to exhibit....only *after* he had already been justified freely by God's grace.

Did you catch that? Both Paul and James are actually presenting two sides of the same coin. Like all the other supposed "contradictions" in the Bible, they are actually in perfect harmony. Both make it clear that works are not the means of salvation, but the outgrowth of salvation. Likewise, true, God-given faith always manifests itself in works of obedience and in the ability to trust Jesus alone for salvation. But a faith that doesn't, proves to be the "faith" of devils, for it contains no God-given power to prove its claim. And that kind of "faith" is what produces a misguided trust in work-righteousness, rather than a saving trust in Jesus' righteousness alone.

The CoC also creates a false contradiction between God's promises and warnings. Although Scripture exhorts God's people to hold fast to their faith, and warns them against falling away (Heb. 10:23, 26-29), it simultaneously promises that He is the only One Who can keep them from stumbling (Jer. 32:40). There is *No* contradiction! Because God's promises and warnings are actually means that He uses to secure the perseverance of the saints. The fact that God often puts His warnings and promises within close proximity, proves that His sovereignty in salvation is compatible with our duty to obey (e.g. Jude 21, 24). God works in mysterious ways.

Perhaps this is why James 2 (and other such passages) becomes such a noose for those who confuse things that differ, in an attempt to establish their own righteousness. But since they lack the ability to harmonize their case with the rest of Scripture, they often end up trying to prove that Paul was only addressing the Mosaic Law rather than good works in general.

Then, by still subtly trying to establish the principle of law for their justification, they only dig themselves deeper by promoting a "do more, try harder" moralism that makes God's grace seem like something that just "helps those who help themselves."

That is not a saving grace, but *a fall from grace* that makes it look like we have to meet God halfway by somehow contributing to the finished work of Calvary by "cooperating" with His grace, where Jesus just merely "fills the gap." This version of "grace" is a faulty foundation that's built upon the sinking sand of humanistic philosophy, rather than the solid Rock of Jesus Christ, Who actually *"fills all things" (Eph. 4:10)*.

True grace is not merely an aid for us to try to save ourselves, it is God's divine power that *actually accomplishes* His purposes, which means that those who fall away from faith in Christ as their only hope, prove that they were never true, born-again believers to begin with (1 Jn. 2:19).

Saving grace is not merely "prevenient," as far as the Methodist usage of the term is concerned.[3] To put it simply, it is not *generally* in operation, waiting for just anyone to come along and "make it effectual." Unlike *"common* grace," *saving* grace is not just something God generally dishes out to all. God resists the proud but gives grace to the humble (1 Pet. 5:5).

Saving grace is reserved only for those who humbly repent of their sin and turn away from their own futile attempts of trying to justify themselves. It's reserved only for those who trust in Jesus alone to save them. For only Jesus' merits have perfectly satisfied God's holy law, so that guilty sinners, who come to God for mercy, can be made righteous through Him.

Notes:

[1] For classic examples of this kind of CoC double-speak, see: Benjamin J. Williams, General Editor, *Why We Stayed*, (Los Angeles/London: Keledei Publications, 2018), pp. 68, 70. Also see pp. 74 and 82 for more up-to-date examples of the CoC's "*imparted* righteousness" through sacraments.

[2] William Phillips, *Campbellism Exposed*, (Cincinnati, OH: J.F. Wright & L. Swormstedt, 1837), pp. 54, 55.

[3] For more information on Methodism and its founder, see: Stephen Tomkins, *John Wesley: A Biography,* (Wm. B. Eerdmans Publishing Co., 2003), pp. 168-169. He reveals how *consistent* Arminianism inevitably leads to atheism, sacramentalism and complete apostasy. It turns out that John Wesley was an adulterer and Roman Catholic sympathizer who professed to be an atheist to his family, even while he still hypocritically pushed perfectionism on those in his "holiness" movement.

According to John Wesley's treatise on Baptism, published in 1756, he was also a baptismal regenerationist. This is also revealed in his *Doctrinal Tracts* (p. 252).

Also see: Robert G. Tuttle, *John Wesley: His Life and Theology*, (Zondervan, 1978), p. 341. He reveals how *consistent* Arminianism leads to what some call "Catholicostal" mysticism. This seems to be a natural outcome when one believes that Jesus came to bring a *method* of salvation, rather than a *message* of salvation.

Chapter 3

Proud to be "Humble"

"Pride goes before destruction, and a haughty spirit before a fall" (Prov. 16:18).
"Beware ye of the leaven of the Pharisees, which is hypocrisy" (Lk. 12:1).

In order to live with such glaring contradictions we had to learn to dissociate our religious convictions from reality, or else go mentally insane from having to face what we were not spiritually equipped to handle. The biblical word "predestinate" could *especially* trigger a psychotic episode.

So, when we would read the Bible, we had to learn to compartmentalize what we read from what we were taught in church. For any ray of light threatened our CoC conditioning, and had the potential of forcing us to face the truth that would have set us free, the truth that we were unknowingly trying so hard to run from....*God's sovereignty in salvation.*

Instead, we were driven like addicts to the obsessive compulsion of perfectionism, where some very abnormal behavior patterns inevitably emerged, adrift with moral lapses, inconsistencies and mental breakdowns. But due to a preconditioned and artificially induced standard of evaluation of our symptoms, we were plunged into a socially sanctioned, pseudo-science perspective, rather than a purely biblical perspective.

So, consequently, we became perfect candidates for being duped into *Big Pharma's* diagnosis of "chemical imbalance"....a medical myth that has been successfully debunked for decades.[1] Far from promoting spiritual growth in the midst of life's problems, the CoC's system of theology served to promote neurotic and psychotic tendencies. Yet there was such a deep denial of these kinds of dissociative disorders and delusions, especially within the family context where our theological views were actually lived out. Instead of being led to Jesus Christ as our only hope, the need to be saved by Him was minimized, and the true meaning of mercy was distorted.

Although ours was a more socially accepted form of dissociative dysfunction, we still unknowingly utilized the concealment devices of the CoC's psychotic system, which allowed us to live out our delusions under the pretense of religion and what was *falsely called science* (1 Tim. 6:20).

Sadly, what we really needed was spiritual regeneration, rather than dead religion. Church attendance was compulsory and sermons were cold and dry. However, we learned some basic facts about Jesus, for in order to appear Christian, we had to *at least* be programmed to intellectually acknowledge and confess His existence as the Son of God Who died for our sins, but *Not* as someone Who fully satisfied divine justice so that we could fully entrust our souls to Him. Instead, "our part" had to supplement His.

This warped view was due to Christ's death merely being portrayed as an abstract suffering and dying for our sins, instead of a substitutionary atonement, where He actually *satisfied* God's just wrath and *achieved* redemption on behalf of those He died for (Heb. 9:12). In other words, we were not taught the true meaning of the term *"propitiation" (Rom. 3:25)*.

If there had ever been true testimonies of salvation in the CoC, one would have been thought to be prideful and arrogant in the least, or mentally imbalanced and disorderly at the most. This was due to the CoC teaching the lie that humility meant not being sure about ones salvation.

Certain verses were pulled out of context (e.g. 1 Cor. 4:5-6; 7:17, 14:36), to try to prove that God doesn't specially call any particular person to salvation, which contradicted the context as well as other verses that make it so clear that there is a *general* call for all sinners to repent and turn to Christ, but that God *effectually* calls His people with **"a holy calling....not according to works, but according to His own purpose and grace, which was given us in Christ Jesus before the world began"** *(2 Tim. 1:9, emphasis mine)*.

There was such a deep resentment in the church toward any who seemed to live holier than we did, *especially* if they gave credit for their godly living to the power of God's grace, rather than the oppressive CoC doctrines that we had to follow. Because we took pride in the fact that we *believed* one must live right. Yet we were hypocritical in how we *actually* lived, due to our false humility and self-imposed religion that had no true power against sinful indulgences. *"These things indeed have an appearance of wisdom in self-imposed religion, false humility, and neglect of the body, but are of no value against the indulgence of the flesh" (Col. 2:23, NKJV)*.

No wonder there was such a vicious animosity and jealousy toward any who claimed to actually be saved. I remember verses (e.g. Rom. 12:3) that were pulled out of context and used against them, to try to make them look like they were evil for daring to have blessed assurance in Jesus' power to save and change them through simple faith in Him alone. ₂

It was falsely assumed that *all* who claimed such assurance were abusers of grace who thought they had a license to sin. The CoC system contained no knowledge of how a *truly* saved person would battle sin and serve Christ out of love, rather than legalistic fear. Therefore, it had to resort to obedience-based control in order to keep its unconverted members in line.

So, consequently, we were theologically trained to believe that if anyone had a right to God's favor... it *had* to be us....*because we worked for it*. Since our doctrines nourished the belief that we were better than others, we were inevitably led to believe that God was indebted to us. So, sadly, we were not only set up for boasting, but for inevitable failure, for we were paradoxically *proud* to be "humble."

"Now to him that worketh is the reward not reckoned of grace, but of debt. But to him that worketh not, but believeth on Him that justifieth the ungodly, his faith is counted for righteousness" (Rom. 4:5).

Although our doctrines indicated that we had to be absolutely perfect or end up in Hell, deep down we all knew that we couldn't *really* pull off perfection. So we excused our sins (especially the sin of self-righteousness) by constantly and legalistically performing *what we thought* was repentance for our sins, according to our "second laws of pardon" doctrine.₃

This man-made idea is strikingly similar to the Roman Catholic sacrament of "penance" (the so-called *"second plank"* of justification), where one must try to regain the salvation one *initially* had in baptism, but lost again and again due to sins committed *after* baptism. In summary, subsequent works were necessary *after* baptism, as a *secondary* means of justification.

So, although I was constantly performing what I thought was repentance, there was never a true removal of guilt, for the sin supposedly pardoned through repentance one minute was replaced by another sin the next! And it had the potential to land me in Hell just as surely as the one previously pardoned! So, without the true gospel, I had to try to stay sane by either adopting an *antinomian* view of sin (an abuse of God's grace as an excuse to live in sin), or else become an obsessive-compulsive perfectionist.

Although our "second laws of pardon" were conditioned upon our own works, the CoC claimed that these works were exempt from Paul's condemnation of works salvation, because they were supposedly *works of a* *different category....*those that baptism had made acceptable for salvation. The CoC would also elusively dodge Paul's condemnation of works salvation by giving lip service to the fact that one couldn't earn salvation. But what was *really* meant was that one could not *initially* earn salvation, for one could not lay the sacramental groundwork for salvation, which Jesus supposedly did when He instituted baptism. But *after* baptism, "works" of repentance, faith, etc....*could* be meritorious, for they were now "baptized works," acceptable for meriting or earning salvation. So, the gist was that one couldn't earn salvation by works...*until after baptism,* which was still a salvation by works... *just misleadingly worded different.*

But despite the CoC's deceptive language, I still remember being torn to pieces when I would read in the Bible about how Esau sought repentance with tears but couldn't find it (Heb. 12:17). That alone planted a seed in my heart that God watered over the years, to help me realize that I needed to pray for Him to *grant* me repentance (2 Tim. 2:25).

Just because one is sorry for sin, doesn't mean one has a godly sorrow that leads to true repentance, which is realizing one's repentance even needs to be repented of! True repentance is realizing we can never repent enough to cover the sins we've committed and that Jesus' righteousness is our only hope of Heaven, for we have no *saving* righteousness of our own.

Our only hope was that God would accept the righteousness of Christ in our stead. Just like the song *"Rock of Ages"* says, *"Could my tears forever flow, could my zeal no languor know, these for sin could not atone, Thou must save and Thou alone."* Although we passionately sung these words with great, religious zeal in the CoC....*we just didn't get it!*

It's not that we didn't carefully contemplate our beliefs, but we were just not spiritually equipped to "test the spirits" in order to recognize and reject false doctrine. There was no true freedom in a religion that lacked the means to detect lies. If we had been given discernment by the Holy Spirit, we would not have remained indifferent to the consequences of deception.

Intimate involvement in the CoC was a strong, contributing factor in the way my family and I viewed God and religion. It also affected how we related to each other, for our approval of one another was always based on performance instead of unconditional love. The false standard of comparing ourselves with others, rather than God's holiness, led to pride, superiority and cookie-cutter conformity (2 Cor. 10:12). No wonder grandma and all five of her daughters strangely became duplicate valedictorians! And my mother *still* struggles with depression and the external pressure to perform.

In Luke 10:41-42, Mary had an exalted view of Christ, for she knew that everything she needed was in Him alone. She was content to sit at Jesus' feet, even at the expense of losing others approval and praise, for He meant more to her than anything else in the world, and He promised that His blessing would never be taken away from her, because it was eternal.

Martha, on the other hand, had to be reminded of what was most important, for she was caught up in the temporary cares of the world, working in her own strength, distracted from *"the one thing needful."* Likewise, we were all like "Martha's on a mission" in the CoC, basically dictating to Jesus how He needed to reprimand those who weren't as "good" as us, and how He needed to back us up and reward us for all of our earthly efforts to perfect our lives and impress others.... *"for Him" of course.*

Since our obedience-based system started with man and reasoned outward from man to God, we ended up with a god that was a lot like man. So we became the center of our own universe, where a superficial joy, freedom and peace had to be forged through our own performance.

Because when human reasoning is the starting point of religion, it always ends up self-centered with a sub-biblical view of God. This is why it cannot be stated strongly enough just how far these dangerous errors led us away from the truth. Although we sincerely thought we were "doing right," we were actually being led further and further away from the true God and Savior of Scripture. Sincerity is no guarantee of Heaven. As it has often been said, *"The road to Hell is paved with good intentions."*

But God looks past the whitewash of "doing right," for He sees the heart. Though the CoC passionately practices what appears to be "obedient faith," repentance, worship, baptism, communion, etc.,....*without true salvation it's all vain, empty and void of life, power and true godliness.*

The CoC denies the power of the true gospel, by replacing it with a false gospel that claims man has the power to *spiritually* please God apart from divine intervention. Good works, done by a fallen will that's never been set free from the love of sin and truly regenerated by the power of the Holy Spirit, are actually an abomination to God, and have no saving merit. They are done out of legalistic fear and attempts to bribe God, by obligating Him to save based on works. But dead religion can never produce spiritual life.

Christ Rescued Me! ....*from the "Church of Christ"*

Notes:

₁ Ruffalo, M. (2017, September 28). *The Myth of the Chemical Imbalance.* Retrieved February 1, 2018 from: https://www.psychologytoday.com/blog/mental-illness-metaphor/201709/the-myth-the-chemical-imbalance.

Here Mark L. Ruffalo critiques the chemical imbalance theory of mental disorder and examines why the chemical imbalance myth persists today despite being widely refuted by a number of prominent psychiatrists. You will find that the answer lies behind *"Big Pharma."*

See also: Pies, R. W. (2011, July 11). *Psychiatry's New Brain-Mind and the Legend of the "Chemical Imbalance."* Retrieved May 16, 2018 from: http://www.psychiatrictimes.com –

Here he states as follows: *"I don't believe I have ever heard a knowledgeable, well-trained psychiatrist make such a preposterous claim [that patients have a chemical imbalance], except perhaps to mock it....In truth, the 'chemical imbalance' notion was always a kind of urban legend—never a theory seriously propounded by well-informed psychiatrists."* –Ronald W. Pies, M.D., Prof. of Psychiatry, the State Univ. of New York and Tufts Univ. School of Medicine.

₂ For some classic examples of how God often uses His people to provoke the self-righteous to jealousy, see: Genesis 4 about Cain and Abel, Genesis 37:4-11 about Joseph and his brothers, and Rom. 10:19; 11:11, 14, where God makes it even more clear that He does this for His own divinely intended purposes.

₃ See: Bob L. Ross, *Campbellism: Its History and Heresies,* (Pasadena, TX: Pilgrim Publications, 1981), pp. 138-146. "Now where do Campbellites get this idea of a "second plan of pardon" which differs from their first one? It is primarily built upon a warped interpretation of the case of Simon, the sorcerer (Acts 8:9-24). Campbellites teach that Simon was saved, then fell out of grace. Since he was told to *"repent and pray God, if perhaps the thought of thine heart may be forgiven thee,"* Campbellites conclude that this must be the second law of pardon" (p. 145).

For more up-to-date proof that the CoC still teaches this heresy, see: Jerry Sparks, *The Gospel in Five Seconds, Volume 20,* Issue #3, p. 8. Retrieved March 3, 2018 from: http://www.housetohouse.com/the-gospel-in-five-seconds

Note: *"House to House Heart to Heart"* is the largest publication among all "Churches of Christ" since 1995. It is also their most prominent YouTube channel. Therefore, it will be used throughout this book as one of the main CoC sources that perfectly illustrates its most up-to-date heresies.

Chapter 4

Replacing the Gospel with Disputable Things

"Ye blind guides, which strain at a gnat, and swallow a camel" (Mt. 23:24).

Although the cross and Christ were always mentioned in the CoC, their glory and truth were emptied of worth and value by a heavy emphasis upon works and disputable things that caused us to be in constant dispute. But, sadly, that was preferred over the offense of the cross, which is *how God saves.* Instead, we unknowingly became *"enemies of the cross"* by constantly looking for a loophole. *"For the preaching of the cross is to them that perish foolishness; but unto us which are saved it is the power of God" (1 Cor. 1:17- 18, Phil. 3:18-19).*

The offense of the cross is that it doesn't make appeals for us to "do" anything to be saved. The cross proclaims that there's nothing anyone *can* do to be saved. It reveals our desperate need to have our sins *imputed* to Jesus and His righteousness *imputed* to us through the gracious gifts of repentance and faith in Him, in His perfect, obedient life, and in His finished work on the cross, because *faith itself is obedience to the gospel (Rom. 1:5).*

But this was unheard of in the CoC, which taught the opposite...*that obedience itself is faith.* It taught that faith is a meritorious work that we do, rather than a work that God does in virtue of Jesus' merits (2 Thess. 1:11). Thus, it incorporated more into faith than just faith in Christ. And those who opposed its unbiblical view were falsely accused of isolating faith from "other biblically-sanctioned means of salvation"....*such as baptism.*

Rather than being honored with the privilege of suffering for the offense of the cross (Gal. 5:11), our church attracted worldlings by soft-peddling *another gospel* that avoided the topic of *imputed* righteousness like the plague, despite the fact that Scripture is saturated with it (Romans 4 *alone* mentions it many times). Our plan or "loophole" was far less offensive to religious pride, and far more in line with our sacramental system, which was central to how we were to *save ourselves....with "a little help from Jesus."*

So Bible passages, such as Acts 2:40, were taken out of context and misinterpreted to mean that trusting the Lord merely meant trusting Him to help us to do what it took to *save ourselves*. When in actuality, Jesus made it abundantly clear, that even if we've *done all* that's commanded of us, it is still *unprofitable for salvation*, for it is only our reasonable duty (Lk. 17:10). When the Apostles were asked, *"What must I do to be saved?"*... they simply said, *"believe on the Lord Jesus Christ"* (Acts 16:30-31).

However, the CoC would stress the *doing* of God's will in verses such as John 7:17, but would leave out the fact that *doing His will meant believing solely upon Jesus Christ for eternal life* (Jn. 6:40) and how everything else would fall into place after that. So, instead of being humbled at the foot of the cross, we were taught to "walk in the light" of our own prideful works, due to a fundamental denial of the sufficiency of Jesus' work on the cross.

So disputable, peripheral things were turned into essential for salvation things. For the CoC severely confused categories by systematically basing part of our salvation on marginal issues, and by *picking and choosing* which commands to keep and which ones to reject. Consequently, by majoring in the minors, its convoluted logic caused our "dogmatic" doctrines to vary, and caused the cross of Christ to be made ineffective in our lives, for no one could ever agree on what were the *most important* "salvation works."

So one CoC would be dogmatic about how a kitchen in the church would damn to Hell, yet would hypocritically be okay with snacks for children or a water fountain. Another would be dogmatic about how it was essential to be baptized only in a creek, while another would have a built-in baptistery. One would be dogmatic about how the Lord's Supper had to be taken while standing, whereas another would teach that it was okay to sit. One would be dogmatic about women only wearing dresses, while another would not.

And on and on the crazy inconsistencies and variations went. To be biblically blunt, our "dogmatic" doctrines were like shifting sand...*always changing*. Because one can in no way, shape or form be consistently dogmatic about peripheral things that are disputable and questionable!

However, these silly scenarios are seen in many Arminian sects. For instance, some CoC's have the same head covering theology as Mennonites and Amish.[1] And, just like them, some will have women to *partially* cover their head, while other sects will have them to cover their *whole* head. The irony is that the face is a major part of the head, yet none of them wear face veils, and even their forehead is exposed, which is the most prominent part of the head, and the part that is first noticed! But when any of these legalistic sects are questioned as to why such inconsistencies exist, the answer is always along the lines of... "Well... *we* just don't do it that way."

Muslims also have variations within their different sects, with some being more consistent with head covering doctrine than others. So one must wonder how most legalists would feel if they had to encounter *consistent* Muslim women everyday that might make them think they are going to Hell for not covering their *entire faces and foreheads!* Perhaps they would then get a taste of their own medicine and repent for dogmatizing things that are so unnecessary.... *things that have nothing to do with salvation!*

True modesty is simply dressing *decently* so that one doesn't draw inappropriate attention to oneself. Yet legalists draw an *incredible* amount of attention to themselves by an outer show of vain glory, which causes them to stand out like a sore thumb as the spiritual elite (such as the Pope).

The trivial differences between the Amish and the Mennonites, which are both of the Anabaptist Movement, are similar to the trivial differences between the "Churches of Christ," the "Disciples of Christ" and the so-called "Christian Church" of the Restoration Movement.

For example, the Amish heavily emphasize a works-salvation, based on having "no phones, no lights, no motor cars, not a single luxury," whereas Mennonites place more emphasis on a *different* set of works for obtaining salvation. Likewise, the CoC system heavily emphasizes attaining salvation and avoiding Hell, based on having no musical instruments in the church, whereas the "Disciples of Christ" and the "Christian Church" allows musical instruments, yet they place more emphasis on a *different* set of works for obtaining salvation.

The "International Churches of Christ" (or the Boston Movement) have a more aggressive methodology for recruiting members, which has caused them more exposure as a cult than the typical "fly under the radar" CoC's. Yet they still hold the same basic theology. *All* of these groups still have the same soteriology (salvation theology), no matter which way they slice it or dice it! And this is why they often set up a false dichotomy between Paul's writings and Jesus' Sermon on the Mount, in order to try to set the stage for their own earthly kingdoms of human reformation, based upon works. No wonder we were never encouraged to pray *"Thy Kingdom come,"* for the CoC teaches that Christ's kingdom has *already* been consummated...and that the CoC is it... both now and forever![2]

All Arminian sects mix Bible terminology with work-oriented phraseology, in order to try to sound more biblical, and to make self-righteousness seem more palatable. These deceptively contrived phrases are jam-packed with theological connotations that have nothing to do with the true gospel. For example, the Anabaptist sect calls its system of works "an obedient love-faith relationship with Jesus Christ."[3] Roman Catholicism calls its system of works "faith working through love."[4] And the CoC eloquently calls its system of works "appropriating God's promises through "obedient faith."[5]

◊◊◊

The first "Church of Christ" I grew up in had formerly been a "one cup" church. A particular preacher began teaching that everyone had to drink the fruit of the vine from the same cup, or else they wouldn't have "obedient faith" on an *"essential for salvation work."* This stance was based upon a single Bible verse concerning the Lord's Supper, which was grossly exaggerated and taken to a ludicrous extreme (Mt. 26:27).

After that fad died out, another preacher came in among the gullible and had them focusing more on the second half of that verse, to promote a *different* "essential for salvation" twist on the Lord's Supper. Since it says *"drink ye all of it,"* it was taken to mean that anytime they took the Lord's Supper they *had* to make sure they sipped down every last drop of juice in their individual cups, or else be in danger of Hell fire!

A major cause for such confusion was that the CoC leaned heavily upon a discreetly elusive system for interpreting Scripture and for coming up with modern innovations of ancient heresies. This unspoken system enabled CoC's to become the "harbingers"[6] of *unique* doctrines and commandments of men that would set them apart as the *only ones* "in the right."

For example, Jesus first instituted the Lord's Supper on a Thursday (Mt. 26:17-19; 28:1, Mk. 14:12-16, Lk. 22:7-15; 23:54). Yet the CoC dogmatically chose every Sunday (assuming the meals in Acts 20 were the Lord's Supper, although *the cup* isn't even mentioned there). Ironically, another cult could have just as easily been formed by trying to base salvation on dogmatically taking the divine ordinance every Thursday... or every single day (Acts 2:46).

Like many Arminian sects, the CoC put human logic on par with God's divine decrees, which created a prison of performance, where our religious identity became heavily shackled to a man-made system. As a deadly consequence, disobeying the CoC system became equal to disobeying God; the same pit Romanism leads to, and what Paul warned about (Col. 2:22).

No wonder Jesus described this kind of nonsense as *"straining at a nat and swallowing a camel" (Mt. 23:24),* for it leads to eating and drinking damnation to one's own soul *(1 Cor. 11:29-30).* One can only imagine just how guilty the CoC may be of the body and blood of Christ, by implementing a system that displaces and distorts the truth concerning Jesus' body and blood, insults the Spirit of grace, and *replaces* His gospel with non-essential assumptions and commandments of men that are hostile to the gospel.

The irony was that the most crucial aspect of salvation, which is saving faith (in the true Christ of Scripture) being a gift from God apart from any human effort, was *replaced* with disputable things that dishonored the name of Christ, and eclipsed the biblical view of the gospel. No wonder Romans 14 strongly warns against making disputable things essential to salvation! In Jesus Christ there are no "doubtful disputations."

There is *"simplicity in Christ" (2 Cor. 11:3).* But the CoC complicated the gospel by reducing Christianity to a mere system of moral codes that even the heathen will adhere to in order to feel better about themselves. Because the spirit behind the CoC system wickedly attempts to put God within human reach by reducing Christianity to mere formalities that can be accomplished by natural, human abilities. However, Jesus said, *"Verily I say unto you, Except ye be converted, and become as little children, ye shall not enter into the kingdom of heaven" (Mt. 18:3).* So, until CoC members become like totally dependent children upon the righteousness of Christ alone, they will not be able to enter into God's heavenly kingdom. *"For many, I say unto you, will seek to enter in, and shall not be able" (Lk. 13:24).*

When a religious philosophy centers on the false notion that "God won't just reach down to us, we must reach up to Him with our works"... then its revelations on salvation will vary. But since God must reach down to us, His revelation remains consistent. Jesus warned of thieves and robbers who climb up another way to try to gain entrance into God's kingdom, for they would rather do *anything* than come to the true Christ of Scripture and submit to God's supreme sovereignty in salvation (Jn. 10:1), even if it means *replacing* the true gospel with a false one that leads to eternal damnation.

Christ Rescued Me! ....*from the "Church of Christ"*

Notes:

₁ For a sampling of some of the CoC's legalistic views concerning head coverings, see: La Vista Church of Christ, *Command or Custom?* Retrieved April 28, 2019 from: http://lavistachurchofchrist.org/LVanswers/2003/2003-10-01.htm

₂ For a perfect example, see: Robert Meyers, General Editor, *Voices of Concern*, (Saint Louis, MS: Mission Messenger, 1966), p. 59.

₃ David Bercot, *Will the Theologians Please Sit Down*, (Amberson, PA: Scroll Publishing Company, 2009), p. 9. Although his book was to be a diatribe against theology, it turned out to be just another Arminian attack on *reformed* theology.

It is no coincidence that Bercot "dialogued" with both Mennonites *and* those of the Restoration movement! Every sect has its own unique catalysts for ecumenical integration. For the CoC, it's been the likes of Phil Robertson, Max Lucado, Leroy Garrett, etc. And for the Mennonites, it's been David Bercot! He even wrote favorably toward Romanism on page 173, further confirming the fact that the Anabaptist religion is also gradually being reabsorbed back into Rome where its doctrines originated. Like the CoC, it too has always been destined to be a temporary bridge back to Rome. As a fulfillment of biblical prophecy, all apostate churches (*harlots*, as the Bible calls them) are coming full circle (Rev. 17:5).

₄ *Catholic Catechism*, Chapter Three, Article 1, #162

₅ Alvin Jennings, General Editor, *Introducing the Church of Christ*, (Fort Worth, TX: Star Bible Publications, Inc., 1981), p. 230.

₆ Alexander Campbell established the "Millennial Harbinger" magazine in 1830, as a major tool for developing *unique* doctrines, which are still molding CoC practices today. It was also used to promote his strange eschatological (end times) views and his claims of "restoring" God's kingdom on earth. He ignored the biblical tension of the "already" and the "not yet." This is why the CoC still claims to be that "restored kingdom on earth." But the *true* gospel of the kingdom that Jesus preached, is the gospel of God's sovereign rule and reign over sin, death and all things... *including salvation* (e.g. Mk. 1:14-15), which will only be fully consummated in the end.

No wonder CoC's have never been able to biblically prevail in any kind of open debate against true Christians. For this reason, they have elusively retreated into the shadows, for the most part, while preferring to just stick with disputing among themselves....like a dog chasing its tail.

Also see: Robert Meyers, General Editor, *Voices of Concern*, (Saint Louis, MS: Mission Messenger, 1966), p. 230 -- CoC's would often boast about "skinning the sects," until their constant defeat led them to start turning in on themselves with the threat of being *skinned if they left,* which will be demonstrated in the next chapter, especially p. 40.

Chapter 5

Moth-Eaten Patterns

"But woe unto you, scribes and Pharisees, hypocrites! for ye shut up the kingdom of heaven against men: for ye neither go in yourselves, neither suffer ye them that are entering to go in" (Mt. 23:13).

Our desire to be on the cutting edge of "restoration" revelation, and the fleshly desire to feel that we had a corner on spiritual superiority, caused our church to lose all Scriptural integrity. The "divinely revealed pattern" theology that became so integral to our religion, was diametrically opposed to Jesus' doctrine of unity based upon truth. Instead of unity in His Person, emphasis was placed on unity in a "pattern."

The results were nothing less than catastrophic. Jesus was reduced to being a mere pattern for us to follow toward our own godhood, rather than an actual Person of the Godhead. This is why Christ profits the "Church of Christ" system nothing, even though it assumes His title (Gal. 5:2).

I can remember distinctly in Sunday school, how there was always a tremendous amount of emphasis placed on Noah's Ark and all of the "patterns" that he had to go by, in order to get it *just right*. The Ark was used as a perpetual illustration of how we too had to get the "pattern" *just right*, in order to be saved. We were *never* taught that the Ark represented Christ in all of His perfection, or how His perfect righteousness is all that can keep one afloat through the destructive waters of sin and death.

That was unheard of in the CoC, for it sinks like the Titanic for having the wrong Christ! The heretical implications of pattern theology are staggering. Because, if Jesus was just a pattern or example for us to follow, that would mean that He fulfilled God's commands for *Himself*, which is blasphemous!

Jesus was completely sinless, which is why He was able to fulfill God's perfect standard of righteousness... *in order to justify His people from their sins*. He was the perfect Lamb sacrifice *to cover their sins*. It was *Not* just so they could have a pattern to go by in order to fulfill God's commands for themselves... *as if anyone could ever even come close to doing such a thing!*

No wonder severe division has always existed among CoC's. Although they were initially established on the basis of forming unity on the "New

Testament Pattern," each group's idea of unity had to be centered on *that certain group's interpretation* of what it thought that pattern was. Because, when doctrines are built upon speculation and private interpretation, rather than absolute truth, then each group just ends up picking and choosing what it thinks will best suite the interests of that particular group.

The CoC is a classic example of how "group think" operates, and how local, man-centered authority is established in order to control converts. This self-styled hierarchy of power promised us liberty, but brought us into bondage, so that we feared to ever even question authority (2 Pet. 2:19).

Words cannot describe the overwhelming influence that was exerted over our mind. It was even far more acceptable to question Scripture than to ever question our religion. To question church authority was equivalent to questioning God. It was even implied in *every* CoC, that all *other* CoC's were headed for Hell if they didn't follow that particular churches pattern.

The old saying is "the proof is in the pudding," and in the CoC's case it seems to be banana pudding! For I just recently obtained a photo of one its church signs perfectly illustrating its threats of "divine retribution" toward any who would even think of leaving. It states: "Remember the banana, when it left the bunch it got skinned." This was our fear.

The CoC's controlled opposition, Leroy Garrett, straightforwardly admitted in his book, *What Must the Church of Christ Do to Be Saved*?--

"We must face the fact that this tragic habit of splitting into sects and sub-sects is due largely to a faulty "Restorationist" hermeneutics, which says there is an identifiable pattern for the work and worship of the church which spells out details, which when adhered to "restores" the true church" (p. 40). "We have erred in our claim that there is a uniform pattern of organization and worship in the New Testament churches and that we have duly "restored" that pattern. This is evident in the fact that we can't even agree among ourselves as to what that pattern requires. We have not only differed but divided over almost every aspect of the life of the church…. are we to conclude that God has given us a prescribed norm or pattern that is so obscure that we ourselves cannot make head or tail of it?" (pp. 131, 132) -- (SCMe-Prints@stone-campbell.org., ©2010). (Emphasis his)

By peeling away the essential doctrines of the faith and replacing them with disputable things, the solid foundation upon which a consistent view of the gospel should stand, gave way to a slippery slope of sin-filled sludge. By trying to patch up a faulty framework with patterns that have nothing to do with the gospel, our man-made system ended up usurping the authority of Christ. This is what happens when the microwave mentality of man comes up with his own methods, rather than trusting in God's divinely intended purpose to convert His people by way of the Holy Spirit convincing them of the *absolute truth* of the gospel of Jesus Christ. Consequently, the CoC system fell off the ledge of legalism into the deep abyss of apostasy.

By constantly chipping away at the gospel, sanding off its rough edges and *replacing* it with the fig leaves of work righteousness, the spirit behind the CoC hides Jesus under legalistic layers that redefine the gospel into obscurity. By *"suppressing the truth in unrighteousness,"* Jesus is hidden from the people, suggesting that He must first be found in the waters of baptism. This way the CoC's sacramental system could gain the monopoly on salvation by appearing to be the only means of obtaining it, thereby making its "church" all the more authoritative. For baptismal regeneration is the "golden calf" *replacement system* of the Restoration Movement.[1]

Scripture reveals who is *really* behind all false religions that hide the gospel from people. It also makes it clear that it is only the true gospel that can set them free from the curse of a false one. For *"if our gospel be hid, it is hid to them that are lost: In whom the god of this world hath blinded the minds of them which believe not, lest the light of the glorious gospel of Christ, Who is the image of God, should shine unto them"* (2 Cor. 4:3-4).

"The doctrines of grace separate the Christian faith from the works-based religions of men. They direct us away from ourselves and solely to God's grace and mercy. They destroy pride, instill humility, and exalt God. And that's why so many invest so much time in the vain attempt to undermine their truth. The religions of men maintain authority over their followers by 1) limiting God's power, 2) exalting man's abilities, and 3) "channeling" God's power through their own structures. A perfect salvation that is freely bestowed by God for His own glory is not a "system" that can be controlled by a religious body or group" (Emphasis his). [2]

Although we religiously tacked the name of Jesus on to the end of all our prayers, we were not taught what it really meant to pray in His name, that He was our only hope, our only access to God, that we can have *direct access* to God through Christ, by faith in His finished work on the cross, and in His righteousness alone as our only hope of salvation. Through Him, *"we* have **access by faith** into this grace in which we stand" (Rom. 5:2). "For through Him we both have **access by one Spirit** unto the Father" (Eph. 2:18, emphasis mine). Even the absence of physical water cannot keep us from the love of Christ and **access to God through faith in Him** (Rom. 8:35-39, Eph. 3:12). No external circumstance can prevent *"whosoever will"* from partaking of the Water of Life *freely*....by God's grace alone, in Jesus alone.

The CoC denomination (though it deceptively claims not to be one), teaches that *it* alone is "a place of sacramental encounter with God."[3] But true salvation is *Not* in its so-called "church membership package deal," which comes with a load of legalistic luggage.[4]

There are no fig leaves to gather in order to try to hide our sins, and no baptismal waters to swim through to get to Christ. There are no tedious tenets of legalistic patternism, no mechanical sacramentalism, no self-proclaimed hierarchy of power with the monopoly on salvation, no complicated steps, no baptismal mediators to go through, and no patterns to unpeel or perform to get to Christ. There are not many ways to salvation, only one way. Jesus said *He is the way.* He never said that He merely *paved a way* through a pattern of performance or a lockstep, 5 step, check-off list. *"There is a way that seemeth right unto a man, but the end thereof are the ways of death"* (Prov. 14:12).

Not surprisingly, the CoC authority pattern of organization is completely void of any real evangelistic outreach, for its idea of reaching out, is to get the lost to come to its "church" and perform all of its unbiblical mandates of moral reform without the power of the true gospel to genuinely transform them. I can remember wracking my brain to try to figure out how in the world I could ever get others to come to my church and go through with all of this. Naturally, I would become so very discouraged and confused.

Our legalistic system created stumbling blocks and obstacles that kept us from true, living faith in Christ, and from true evangelistic outreach, for it dishonestly hid Jesus behind a scripted blueprint that is nothing like biblical Christianity. But only the Lord can give the discernment needed to renounce the *"hidden things of dishonesty"* in the CoC, where God's Word is not being rightly divided, but is being handled deceitfully, which causes division (2 Cor. 4:1-2). And Jesus said, *"a house divided cannot stand"* (Mt. 12:25).

Not only is the CoC's version of repentance a mere outward reform, its version of faith and confession is also mere mental assent to a minimal set of facts concerning Jesus. For the CoC does not represent true, biblical Christianity at all, which is also why its loosely-knit, moth-eaten pattern theology unravels at the seams. So in order to be a *true* Church of Christ, its false gospel and pattern theology would have to be completely moth-balled and replaced with the true gospel of Jesus Christ, which glorifies God's grace and mercy, not man's high opinion of himself and his man-made doctrines.

Although Jesus preached the gospel, which is Himself, the CoC claims that the gospel wasn't preached until after Pentecost, hence its obsession with Acts 2:38. However, the Bible shows that John the Baptist preached the same "remission of sins" doctrine *before Pentecost* that Peter preached *on Pentecost,* and both pointed to the righteousness of Christ for the remission of sins. But CoC leaders claim that their church didn't come into effect until Pentecost, although the Bible reveals that *God's* church was in full function *way before* Pentecost (e.g. Mt. 18:17, Lk. 12:32, Acts 2:47).

So considering the fact that the CoC teaches that one must be baptized into its church, and that salvation is only in its "Church membership package," it must first answer the question…..exactly what church did John's baptism put people into, if there was supposedly no church until Pentecost?

So far, no CoC leaders have ever been able to give a biblical explanation for such heretical inconsistencies, for then they would have to admit that *their religion did not originate at Pentecost*, but in the early 1800's by their false prophet, Alexander Campbell. But, sad to say, even after learning the truth, many would still rather follow in the footsteps of Esau, and forfeit an eternal inheritance for a bowl of Campbell's soup (Gen. 25:29-34). [5]

Apostle Paul asked, *"Is Christ Divided?"* (1 Cor. 1:13), for when spiritual leaders are elevated to the point of usurping the role of Christ in people's lives, the inevitable result is always confusion and division. But the Bible says that *"God is not the author of confusion, but of peace, as in all churches of the saints" (1 Cor. 14:33)*….and Christ is not divided.

The *true* body of Christ is His sheep, indwelled by the Holy Spirit Who never leaves them, despite the fact that they are often scattered by wolves in sheep's clothing, as a fulfillment of biblical prophecy. Those who belong to Jesus are drawn to Him by the Father, Who teaches them the truth and builds their faith and trust in Him so that they are led to true repentance and an obedient, like-minded unity in the Spirit (Jn. 6: 37, 44, and 65).

Notes:

[1] Bob L. Ross, *Campbellism: Its History and Heresies*, (Pasadena, TX: Pilgrim Publications, 1981), p. 38 states: "Actually, the Campbellite movement practically was dormant until the debating began and baptismal salvation was "discovered." It was upon the back of this two-headed monster that Campbellism began to advance." He also states: "Today, baptismal regeneration is the foremost doctrine of the Campbellite Church, just as it is in Romanism and Episcopalianism" (p. 44).

[2] James R. White, *The Potters Freedom*, New Revised Edition, (Calvary Press Publishing, 2009), p. 39. Available at: https://www.calvarypress.com

[3] See: Benjamin J. Williams, General Editor, *Why We Stayed*, (Los Angeles/London: Keledei Publications, 2018), p. 129.

[4] Allen Webster, *What Does the Church Have to Offer Me?* Volume 18, Issue #2, pp. 1-2. Retrieved May 16, 2018 from: https://housetohouse.com/wp-content/uploads/2016/02/v18n2.pdf -- Here, it is repeatedly stated as follows: "access to the eternal God is ….*in the {CoC} church membership package*" (Emphasis and brackets mine).

[5] For illustrative purposes only. Besides, I can find no evidence that the founders of actual *Campbell's Soup*® had any connection to the Campbell's of Campbellism.

Chapter 6

Pulpit Perversions

"There be some that trouble you, and would pervert the gospel of Christ" (Gal. 1:7).

Like most modern churches, there was an invitation system set up at the end of each church service, where emotional appeals, combined with songs, such as *Just as I Am*, were used to signal to the congregation what emotions or duties were to be called forth, in order to settle the issue of salvation...*by taking some kind of physical action.* The assumption was that a *physical* coming to the front of the church, to soothe a guilty conscience, was automatically equivalent to a *spiritual* coming to Christ. This was due to an extreme emphasis placed on the will of man, and the idea that man's choice has the final say as to whether one is saved or not.[1]

Due to growing up under CoC indoctrination, I was always under extreme pressure to unpeel many legalistic layers to try to get all the way to Christ. The first layer was going up to the CoC preacher and "accepting" Jesus by publically giving mental assent to the fact that He was the Son of God. The next layer was being baptized by a CoC preacher. So by the time I was fifteen, I made a so-called "decision for Christ" and went up to be baptized.

From there, the "process of salvation" had supposedly begun. I was told that I was now a Christian and would have to "grow in Christ" for the rest of my life to finally be saved in the end. I was taught nothing about being *eternally* indwelled and *sealed* by the Holy Spirit Who permanently *insures* that one will grow in Christ. Rather than being given the proper antidote for a sin-sick soul, CoC baptism was administered as an inoculation against such truths, which built up a resistance to true Christian conviction and faith.

As a sad consequence, I became very discouraged and letdown, for I had previously been under such deep conviction over sin that I had hoped for a miraculous change to occur once I was baptized. But when that didn't happen I became even more disillusioned and rebellious than ever.

I had truly wanted to obey the Lord but was heavily influenced by false doctrines that led me to believe that He had done all that He could for me, and that the rest was now up to me. So I developed a very low view of

Christ and His love. Although I believed in God with all of my heart, I had a hard time believing in a Savior that supposedly died for everyone but allowed many that He supposedly died for to perish in Hell. Our doctrines made me think that whatever He did for sinners, it must not have been enough to save us from ourselves, let alone save us from Hell. So although I thought that I had come to Jesus to be saved, I still lived in constant fear that He would allow me to perish in Hell if I didn't do everything "just right."

But I didn't realize then that I had come to *another Jesus,* one not represented in Holy Scriptures. It was a *different* Jesus and a *different* spirit that I had received; a Jesus who was unloving and untrustworthy unless I "did my part;" a Savior who couldn't really save, unless I saved myself; a taskmaster who would meet me in the waters of baptism, but leave me as soon as I rose out of the water and sinned again. So I began to feel as if I would have had more hope if I had drowned in the waters of baptism.

Yet, while going through the physical process, there was this grand illusion of resurrection to new life, because that's what we were led to believe baptism *literally* did. While under such suggestive, baptismal regeneration conditioning, one couldn't help but to imagine that one's sins *were literally being washed away in the water*, due to the trick terminology used. But in practical reality... it never played out that way.

Inwardly, I had become even worse, for to my former guilt I had added the sin of self-righteousness. But even though I was told that I was now a Christian, my conscience was still far from being purged from guilt, no matter how hard I tried to believe that I had actually come to Christ in baptism. I was told that I had peace where there was no peace (Jer. 6:14).

Instead of carrying God's pardon sealed in my heart by the Holy Spirit, through faith in Jesus, I then had to carry the added burden of trying to earn God's pardon by throwing myself into the CoC's "second laws of pardon." For although we were taught that baptism was supposed to *initially* put one into Christ, and *initially* put one into right standing with God, we were also taught that one could fall from grace *out of Christ* as soon as one sins.

This was a classic example of tap water theology, where one turns the grace of God on or off at will. One minute I would be repenting for a certain sin that would immediately be replaced by another....*and then another.* And yet, this was the vicious cycle that I had to learn to live with, as one who was still dead in sins and trespasses, for I had not been truly changed and born again by the sanctifying power and indwelling of the Holy Spirit.

Instead, I was deceived by a false support system that could only support me as long as I supported myself, by fulfilling the "second laws of pardon" that allowed me to "grow in Christ," which meant gaining more salvation brownie-points. So, like many, I became extremely "religious," but still lived just as worldly as any other lost sinner. Because, in the CoC anything went, as long as it was socially sanctioned and/or popularized on television.

Since we didn't have formal, doctrinal positions to safeguard any kind of true, biblical structure in our lives, we could believe or do anything outside the church that we wanted, as long as we just kept a misguided trust in the CoC's outward codes of behavior and its *unique* interpretations of Scripture.

This conditioning process produced a type of religious schizophrenia, for we had to disassociate our legalistic and perfectionist theology from our worldly lifestyles and our lust for worldly entertainment. This was the only way we could still claim to be Christian, and yet still fit in with the world. So, predictably, we ended up blending in perfectly with the world.

Instead of being separate from the world as "salt and light," our selective perceptions allowed us to choose those things which were of the devil, disassociate them from our theology, and still maintain our social status as a "Christian." After all, it was still fashionable to be considered a Christian. But in instances where it wasn't, we kept silent and made sure to never "rock the boat." Compulsive conformity was the name of the game.

We were chameleons when convenient, and conformed to the world instead of Christ. If the public school system promoted a dance, it was suddenly okay to go against the CoC's policy against dancing. So, although I was a strict CoC member by day, I became a "dancing queen" by night.

Martial Arts and yoga were also acceptable for church members, even if transcendental meditation and guided imagery were involved, as long as they were still socially sanctioned, promoted in a positive light on TV or "Christianized." No wonder I became a third degree brown-belt in Karate while in high school. So I was heavily initiated into Eastern thought and trained to access my "inner power," which seemed to parallel perfectly with the CoC's inner power concepts of *absolute,* human autonomy and freewill.

Although sound doctrine (orthodoxy) is supposed to lead to sound practice (orthopraxy), that couldn't happen as long as I was under the influence of the CoC and a superficial adherence to its doctrines, which led to being even more desensitized to evil. So I was a prime candidate for New Age deception, which eventually led to even deeper levels of the occult.

Sadly, by the time I was eighteen, my parents severely shunned me for marrying a guy they disapproved of, but not because of any true Christian convictions. Jesus was never mentioned at home, and not even a single word of prayer was ever heard in our house, for anything biblical was reserved *only* for church. So I had heard more about how I needed to be good for "goodness sake," so "Santa" would come, or so the "bad man" wouldn't get me. Yet my family had still hoped that I'd marry someone more up to "status quo," according to their external expectations.

But he and I actually had a lot in common. We were both heavily influenced by the world and disillusioned by religion. He was raised in a Catholic family, where he too was duped into believing that he was initially saved by a rite of baptism, and that *"God helps those who help themselves."* We only differed on exactly how we were to go about "helping ourselves."

For me, it meant that I had to do all that the CoC told me I had to do. This included the CoC's unique version of "growing in Christ," which included *religiously* taking the Lord's Supper *every* Sunday, *religiously* attending church *every* time the doors were open and *never* worshipping God accompanied by music...*or else!*

So instead of *truly* growing in the grace and knowledge of the Lord, I was growing more and more distant from Him and the truth that He came to proclaim. I *never once* remember hearing that Jesus would never leave or cast out those who truly come to Him (Jn. 6: 37, Heb. 13:5).

But, of course, I *hadn't* truly come to Him. I had come to *another Jesus* that could only be found in the waters of baptism and lost again when I would sin. I *never once* heard anything about Jesus' propitiatory sacrifice to *obtain* and *secure* the salvation of all who would fully entrust their souls to Him....*except through the gospel songs we would sing* (Isa. 53, 1 Jn. 4:10). But hymns, such as *Nothing but the Blood*, contradicted what was preached.

"You contact the blood in the water," is what they say around this section of eastern Kentucky. "You meet the blood in the water" is what others have stated. In this regard, Campbellism parallels Romanism. Romanism says the blood of Christ is in the wine; Campbellism says it is in the water. The only difference between the

Romanist and the Campbellite is the kind of liquid used and the actions relating to the liquid. The Romanist will drink the liquid of wine in order to reach the blood, while the Campbellite will be immersed in the liquid of water in order to reach the blood."[2]

In the CoC we had to learn to filter gospel hymns through the philosophy that Jesus' blood could only make us "savable," depending on our response to it. For instance, *Nothing but the Blood* was filtered through the philosophy that nothing but the blood made it "possible" for us *to save ourselves by our own freewill response*. And *Amazing Grace* became an unbiblical version of grace that only made it possible for a wretch like me to conjure up enough self-generated faith to make it effectual.

As a sad conclusion, our CoC lens filtered gospel songs through the Roman Catholic idea that God's grace is *necessary* to *do* everything it takes to be saved but not *sufficient* to save, without our help or cooperation. Despite the fact that... *Jesus said His grace is sufficient (2 Cor. 12:9).*

But, naturally, when doctrines of devils deceive people into believing their salvation is dependent upon them, they will end up having no *Blessed Assurance* (another song legalists can't sing in sincerity). So the prevailing mindset was that we had to *do* something to be saved, which logically led to thinking we had to *do* something to keep it, rather than believing we could be kept by the power of God, through an irrevocable gift of faith that could only come from Him (e.g. Rom. 11:29, Eph. 2:8-10, Phil. 1:29, 1 Pet. 1:5).

The irony was that John Newton, writer of *Amazing Grace*, also wrote:

"This is faith: a renouncing of everything we are apt to call our own and relying wholly upon the blood, righteousness and intercession of Jesus."[3]

And *Rock of Ages* was written by Augustus Toplady, who also wrote:

"Freewill is an Arminian idol. A man's 'freewill' cannot even cure him of a toothache, or of a sore finger, yet he madly thinks it is in its power to cure his soul. The greatest judgment which God himself can, in the present life, inflict upon a man is to leave him in the hands of his own boasted freewill."[4]

No wonder gospel songs sung in Arminian churches always contradict the false, watered-down gospel that's preached behind their pulpits. The end result is always a kind of compartmentalized thinking that distorts the truth, which was why the dutiful singing of gospel songs in the CoC took on a monotonous quality that could not be scripturally accounted for, because sincere praise was replaced with mechanical ritualism.

Gospel songs, such as *Down At the Cross,* clearly proclaim where Jesus' blood was *literally* applied to His people, and they have it *personally* applied at God's appointed time, by a *direct* operation of the Holy Spirit (whereby His Word becomes indispensible to guide them in faith and repentance), not by an *indirect* operation through an outward ceremony (e.g. Eph. 2:13-16). In fact, none of the gospel songs ever insinuate that it is, because it's not. It is only applied by the gracious work of the Holy Spirit through faith in Christ.

Although we could sing about the cross under the CoC's influence, we were unable to grasp the *message* of the cross…*that there is nothing anyone can do to save themselves….not even after baptism!*

However, when Jesus is the author and finisher of our faith, we can sing gospel songs with a sincere heart; a new heart that's enabled to obey Him out of love and gratitude, rather than legalistic bondage where sin has dominion. For only God can *"make you perfect in every good work to do His will, working in you that which is well-pleasing in His sight, through Jesus Christ; to Whom be glory forever and ever. Amen"* (Heb. 13:21).

Notes:

[1] For a more in-depth study on the false "invite Jesus into your heart" system popularized by Arminian operatives, see: Iain Murray, *The Invitation System*, (Carlisle, PN: Banner of Truth, 2002). Also see: Iain Murray, *Revival and Revivalism: The Making and Marring of American Evangelicalism 1750-1858,* (Carlisle, PN: Banner of Truth, 1994). History proves Arminianisms destructive infiltration.

[2] Bob L. Ross, *Campbellism: Its History and Heresies*, (Pasadena, TX: Pilgrim Publications, 1981), p. 98. Also see: Benjamin J. Williams, General Editor, *Why We Stayed*, (Los Angeles/London: Keledei Publications, 2018), p. 68. Here one is given the CoC's updated phraseology for what it is now describing as "God meeting us with the cleansing blood of Jesus in the waters of baptism."

[3] John Newton. (n.d.). AZQuotes.com. Retrieved December 20, 2017 from: http://www.azquotes.com/quote/350619.

[4] Augustus Toplady. (n.d.). AZQuotes.com. Retrieved December 20, 2017 from: http://www.azquotes.com/quote/542564

Chapter 7

Heart-Breaking Providences

"I have gone astray like a lost sheep; seek thy servant; for I do not forget Thy commandments" (Ps. 119:176). "The Lord is nigh unto them that are of a broken heart; and saveth such as be of a contrite spirit" (Ps. 34:18).

Outside the church I continued to live like any other lost sinner or so-called "carnal Christian." Although I was still considered religious by the world, my life was void of any true power to live godly. And since no one from church ever wanted to talk about the Bible outside of the church, I became perfect prey for the Jehovah Witnesses who did. Consequently, I studied with them once or twice a week for four years. After all, they too had sprouted from the Stone/Campbell Restoration Movement.[1]

So I found out that our religions had *ALOT* of things in common, such as: freewill Arminianism, moralistic humanism, works-salvation, extreme legalism, an aversion to the Holy Spirit, ignorance concerning the Trinity, etc. But, of course, I still found no solid, spiritual foundation to cling to.

Subsequently, the sense of darkness in my life kept growing at alarming proportions, especially after nine years of marriage and four sons later when I found out their dad was having an affair with another man's wife. I truly didn't understand how God could allow me to be so hurt, betrayed and rejected. Although I knew I was *far from perfect*, I thought I was "close enough" by "doing right," staying in church, praying, reading the Bible and loving my family. And I thought I had repented for every sin I could think of.

Yet I was further away from God than ever. So I wondered what in the world God wanted from me. Even after doing all that I could to save my marriage, it still failed, which puzzled me, considering how I thought God was supposed to reward my "good, moral behavior." I was so confused, heart-broken and lost that I became even more rebellious against God. That's when carnal, human logic, mixed with self-righteous indignation, became activating forces that plunged me even deeper into darkness.

My transformation began with changing my wardrobe and replacing all of my modest clothes with more worldly, seductive clothes. One underlying cause may have been to get revenge, but the main reason was to try to be someone I wasn't, for the "old me" had gotten hurt. I felt another blow like that would kill me, so I was determined to never be hurt again, by becoming a heartbreaker myself, only to end up even more broken-hearted.

Although I still kept up the appearance of being "religious" by day, I once again became a "dancing queen" by night, gathering crowds around me. So when the boys would go to their dad's house on the weekend, I started going to night clubs, and even tried to numb my emotional pain by experimenting with alcohol for the first time in my life, only to be disappointed, for it did not help at all and was just "not my cup of tea."

But since "keeping up appearances" was what really mattered in the CoC, it helped me to justify my actions and my anger. CoC sermons encouraged me to think that I was better than my ex-husband and his new mistress, all because I was "religious" and they weren't. I also became so driven by selfish ambition that I appeared successful from a worldly point of view, for I really seemed to have my act together on the outside. Although it was a messed up kind of survival mode, it seemed to work for me....*for a while.*

I was still heavily involved in the CoC, teaching Sunday school, and raising the boys on my own, while working as a medical housekeeper, until I found a way to get the boys out of daycare, which kept them sick all the time.

By painting my first mural at the medical center, I started a small, commissioned, mural art business and portfolio. Soon after, I was able to enroll in college full-time so that I could have the flexible schedule I needed to be with the boys. The problem was that I had to maintain a very high grade-point-average in order to keep my grants and scholarships, which put me under extreme stress and took time away from motherhood.

But the church pumped up my pride and self-esteem by singing me praises for such an undertaking. Never mind that I was losing focus on my original intent to spend more time with my children. Worldly success was what really mattered. I had to look good on the outside and appear to be superwoman. So I carved out a whole new image for myself; new hair style, new look, new figure and a new attitude of worldly self-confidence.

I appeared to be at my peak in talent, beauty and brains from a worldly perspective. But I remember being cut to the core by Jesus' words, *"What is a man profited, if he shall gain the whole world, and lose his own soul?"* (Mt.16:26). I began looking in the mirror and wondering who I had become. It was as if I was living a double life. No matter how together I seemed to be on the outside, I was dying inside, and the boys were starting to sense it. I too, sensed an impending doom, but instead of turning to God, I started to run from Him in rebellion....for I did *Not* trust Him.

With the influence of worldly friends, I delved even deeper into darkness. Then one weekend I even ended up in New York City, which was totally out of character for a little country bumpkin like me. Yet I tried to take my fill of worldly company, fancy restaurants, art galleries and sightseeing to escape the emptiness I felt inside. But I kept sensing that God was going to catch up with me, like He did Jonah. The sense of doom was so severe that I started having thoughts of throwing myself off the tour boat into the Hudson River. Yet, by God's mercy, I made it back to land.

Then suddenly, I heard a loud voice penetrating the darkness of my mind, screaming "Repent!" I turned around and there was a street preacher with Bible in hand, looking straight at me! As a small-town girl, I had never had such an encounter. Time seemed to stand still as my conscience was blasted with one blow after another. At first I thought, "surely not...surely God isn't just singling me out." So I looked around to see how many others were stopped in their tracks, and incredibly enough, I noticed ... *it was just me!*

I felt so offended that everyone else seemed to be able to get away with everything, yet I couldn't even get away with what I perceived to be *"just one little rebellious streak"* against God. Hundreds of people all around me seemed so caught up in the hustle and bustle of the world that they didn't even seem bothered. Yet I was cut to the heart by the thought that no matter how far I ran... *I could never completely escape God.* And though I was finally able to move on, little did I know then that I would treasure that moment forever... *because God was catching up with me.*

After years of trying to carry the weight of the world on my shoulders from a devastating divorce, deep darkness and rebellion against God, I was running out of diversions. All of the housework, yard work, homework, artwork, church work and every other work to distract myself were all having an accumulative effect. It was all taking an unbearable toll upon me, and I knew that I could not keep it all up for very much longer.

But instead of whole-heartedly turning to God, I was determined to fulfill every worldly desire before I died. Yet my plans got frustrated when I became so shaken by that street preacher. So I got down on my knees in a motel room and began crying uncontrollably. I begged God to forgive me for trying to run from Him, and I begged Him to get me back home safe with my boys, despite all the pressure to try to make up for their dad's absence.

After a turbulent air flight that almost scared the life out of me, God answered that prayer. So when I got back home I slowly began to distance myself from worldly friends, and I took a long, hard look at my life and the direction I had been going. I began to realize that it was a miracle of God that I wasn't kidnapped or sold into human trafficking or something. After all, I was stalked in NY by a guy in a black suit with a black brief case!

It occurred to me that I could have ended up like an ancestor of mine who had also been an artist. She had sunk into a deep depression, and instead of turning to God, she left her family and went to New York to pursue her artistic fantasy of opening up another art studio, only to be found floating in the Hudson River. So I was *very* thankful to make it back home. Yet little did I know that I'd be plunged into even deeper waters.

◊◊◊

CoC leaders made it a point to tell me that if my ex-husband didn't divorce his mistress and reconcile with me, he'd go to Hell. They made it painfully clear that if I didn't live a life of complete loneliness and leave the door open for him to come back, I would cause him to go to Hell and myself too.

So I pleaded 1 Corinthians 7:15—*"if the unbelieving depart, let him depart. A brother or sister is not under bondage in such cases."* But I was told that didn't apply to me because I had complicated things by dating before the divorce was final, even though I was previously encouraged to! [2]

As a painful consequence, my mind plummeted to the depths of despair. Spiritual anguish overcame me and manifested in paralyzing panic attacks, severe clinical depression, a complete nervous breakdown, chronic adrenal fatigue and what my doctor thought to be the beginning symptoms of MS.

I was at the end of my rope physically, mentally and spiritually. Although I had begun to desperately look outside of myself for relief, God kept me from finding any help or relief in friends, doctors, psych-meds or psychotherapy, which all seemed to only make me worse off than ever.

After a lifetime of *never* having blessed assurance, *never* being able to trust in the weak Jesus our church falsely depicted, *never* knowing the true Jesus, *never* being able to live up to all that was expected of me, *never* being

Heart-Breaking Providences

able to handle a life of perfectionism and condemnation....the thoughts of impending doom kept coming to my mind with even more force. I was no longer able to eat, sleep or do anything but vomit uncontrollably. I would quietly do it in the bathroom sink to keep the boys from worrying about me, because they would get so insecure and clingy when they knew I was sick.

But it finally got so severe that I had to keep a "puke pan" (for lack of a better term) with me at all times, even when I drove... even using it during doctor visits and counseling sessions. I even had to keep it in my college backpack so I could use it for stomach acid while taking finals in the hallway!

It was like having the worst case of the flu imaginable, but with no end in sight. So I landed in the hospital several times that year, while an elderly couple from church would take the boys in. But after the last hospital stay, I was so unable to function that the couple recruited another lady in the church to take me in for a few days, because my family was still shunning me while supporting my brother who was threatening and harassing me, (due to his experimentation with drugs and Satanism). And my ex was flaunting his mistress. So I was also suffering due to the sins of others!

I was so thankful for help, but the CoC's performance-based approval produced legalistic fear if we didn't "behave" well enough. So the boys and I were under constant pressure to act perfect, even in the midst of such crisis. No one in our church or family wanted to talk about God outside the church, or about the impact of divorce on the boys or the spiritual struggles I was going through. Though I was already carrying the weight of the world on my shoulders, with constant waves of nausea, even heavier burdens were being put upon me as I was told to *try harder, be stronger* or *do better*.

But it was as if a switch had been turned off in my body and in my mind, to keep me from ever attempting such feats again. I became so weak that I was barely even able to walk. I got down to skin and bones, and looked like death. Yet I couldn't bear the thoughts of leaving my boys without a mom. So with nowhere else to turn, I began to desperately seek God for help.

And suitably, I was led to Bible passages that seemed to speak directly to my brokenness, such as: *"When my father and my mother forsake me, then the Lord will take me up"* (Ps. 27:10). *"For thy Maker is thine husband....For the Lord hath called thee as a woman forsaken and grieved in spirit, and a wife of youth, when thou wast refused, saith thy God. For a small moment have I forsaken thee; but with great mercies will I gather thee. In a little wrath I hid My face from thee for a moment; but with everlasting kindness will I have mercy on thee, saith the Lord thy Redeemer"* (Isa. 54:5-8).

While I tried to cling to those words for dear life, the holiness of God and the worth of Heaven began to come upon me like a fiery force that could not be shaken, for I felt that I had lost all hope of obtaining it. As a heart-rending result, I was losing the will to live... *but was too afraid to die.*

After weeks of not being able to eat, sleep or barely even keep water down, the paralyzing fear of Hell constantly flooded my mind with horror. I got weaker and weaker as my conscience became so wounded at the realization of how bad sin really was; an eternal offense against the eternal God, with eternal consequences. I was so heavy-hearted and weary of my life, all I could do was cry out to God for mercy from a heart truly broken over sin, for I knew I deserved Hell.

At that point I began to give up on ever being able to repent enough or be good enough. I realized that I had nothing of eternal worth to commend myself to God, not even my good works. Because I finally realized that I could never do enough good to make up for a single sin or failure in my life.

Then, all of a sudden, a fiery dart penetrated the depths of my soul with the thought that I may have been predestined for Hell. Instantly, I was so struck with horror and broken in spirit that I began to feel as though my sanity would break. With faintness of heart, I dreadfully gave myself up to God to do whatever He willed to do with me, as I hung in doubtful suspense.

Then it was as if all the strength of my body and mind began to melt away, ready to sink into Hell forever. In such distress of soul, I seemed past recovery and bound for eternal torment. It was as if I was being crushed into the ground by the weight of sin as I fell into the depths of despair.

I painfully accepted the fact that I lacked the perfect righteousness I so desperately needed to enter God's holy presence. And, by remembering Scripture, I realized that the curse that had been pronounced upon me by the moral law of God could never be reversed by anything that I did. *So all I could do was pray the most intense prayer of my life...* and I distinctly remember it like it was just yesterday--

"Dear God in Heaven, I've tried everything I know to do to try to be good enough and I just keep failing. I can't do it. I can never be good enough to get to Heaven. I know that You are God, and I know that You are holy and good, so if You see fit to send me to Hell, I know that You are just and that I have no choice but to submit to Your righteous judgment. I know I deserve to be in the fiery depths of Hell for eternity. Yet, even though I know I have no hope of Heaven, I will still serve you anyway, because You are God. I will serve You for nothing in return. Even if I am predestined for Hell, I will still serve You as long as I live...... *for there is nothing else.*

Immediately, it was brought to my mind...remembrance of the Savior. I remembered the *name* of Jesus. Though I'd heard it my whole life from behind the pulpit, I had never been able to trust in Him due to all the lies that were preached about Him. Almost simultaneously, memory of the words *"believe with the heart"* (Rom. 10:10) was brought to my mind. And, at that moment, my life seemed to hang by a thread at the very mouth of Hell, for I knew I didn't have that kind of heart faith. I was completely undone. I had no rest, no peace and no hope...*unless Christ rescued me.*

It began to dawn on me that no one from the church ever even *once* mentioned the name of Jesus to me during their routine, brownie-point visits. When I'd try to explain my spiritual struggles and lack of faith, I was met with complete complacency, for they were totally unfamiliar with such dealings from God. So as *miserable comforters* they could only say, *"where there's a will there's a way"*... and they were *NOT* talking about God's will!

Our beliefs gave them no reason to direct me to Jesus as my only hope. All they could do was encourage me to believe in myself and my own fallen will to "do right." As a result, I realized that I was actually losing all faith and hope in our churches "do more, try harder" moralism that placed such a low value on Christ, by implying that we could overcome sin with self-effort.

For the first time in my life, I began to highly esteem Christ, for I realized that my self-effort was a futile means of overcoming sin, and that I could never be good enough to deserve Heaven. Despite being on the verge of Hell with inexpressible anguish in my soul, the *name* of Jesus gave me a ray of hope. I was beginning to get a glorious glimpse of the *worth* of Jesus and the *worth* of faith in Him. Little did I realize, I was being drawn to Christ by God's grace through the means of prayer, as I pleaded with all my heart--

"Dear God in Heaven, if Jesus is real and if He is truly *the* Savior, please give me faith in Him, because Your Word says that He's the only way to Heaven, and that *believing in Him from the heart* is the only way to be saved. I realize from reading

Your Word that He's my only hope, but I know that I am *not able* to believe from the heart like I'm supposed to. I realize I need faith in Jesus to be saved, so would You *please* give me this faith if it be Your will? And if You allow me to keep living, please heal me for the boy's sake. I realize they need me now more than ever. Please help us Lord. *Please rescue me....* I ask in Jesus' name, Amen."

Unlike many of the outlandish "altar call" stories that are told in some circles, I didn't have an uncontrollable laughing spell, end up in a trance under a church pew, or get pressured into a false profession of faith. My emotions were not hi-jacked by mood-altering music playing in the background or by emotionally charged prayers being vocalized over me. Instead, after that night alone with God in intense prayer, I just left my soul in His hands as He kept gently drawing my mind to His Word.

Everything I read led me to realize how much I needed to *believe with all my heart in Jesus' ability to save.* So I continued to *constantly* plead for God to give me that kind of heart faith, because I realized that I was *completely* at His mercy. I prayed that He would help my unbelief, for I knew that I only had head knowledge of Jesus (and it wasn't even the true Jesus of the Bible). I didn't fully realize it then but....*I needed to know the true Jesus,* Who is able to save all who truly come to Him to be made holy (Heb. 7:25).

Amidst all of my struggles, it also began to dawn on me that no one in the church seemed to manifest a living faith in Jesus, for they never talked about Him or anything He had done in their lives. What became even more striking to me was that it didn't even seem to bother them, whereas I was tormented with the realization that I didn't have that kind of faith.

I was so stricken with grief and mental anguish over sin. But instead of being directed to Jesus, I was looked upon as just having an overly sensitive conscience that could easily be fixed by a stricter focus on "doing better." And when I struggled to make it clear that I couldn't, I was severely reprimanded. Yet I knew there was nothing I could do but seek God, so I kept using the means He provided (prayer, His Word), hoping His promise was true....*that those who truly seek Him will finally find Him (Deut. 4:29).*

So, along with my "puke pan," I started taking my Bible with me everywhere I went, even holding it to my heart all night while trying to sleep. Every thought of my mind, every desire of my heart, and every ounce of strength that I had left was directed to God for mercy as I began to flee to

Christ for refuge, so that I could lay hold of the hope that was set before me in God's Word (Heb. 6:18).

The ability for me to even plead for mercy was a mercy in itself. It was proof that God was not leaving me to myself in a false religion. Though I could not fully comprehend it at the time, God's goodness in my brokenness was that He was breaking my former, religious pride so that I could begin to see how fallen I was from His glory, and how I needed Jesus to rescue me.

For the first time in my life I knew that I was *not able* to pull off "my part" of salvation. I began to realize that the only part I had ever pulled off was all of the sinning. Even all of my good works were dead without Christ. I knew that only He could do all of the saving...*or else I would be lost forever.*

After a lifetime of apprehensions toward Christ and the gospel, I could no longer believe the CoC's lies that had set forth a way of salvation and sanctification that only led to a miserable end. It had shipwrecked any possibility of true faith, with a *different* Jesus and a *different* gospel; a Savior who couldn't really save unless I "cooperated" enough.

I could no longer try to believe in a blood atonement that only covered some sins, not all sins, such as my treacherous sin of unbelief; an atonement that couldn't actually atone, and a Redeemer that couldn't really redeem, unless I redeemed and reformed myself first.

Thankfully, God was not giving me over to such profane lies, for I could no longer even *attempt* to believe such absurdity. Instead, He kept directing me to the truth by *driving me to the light and testimony of Scripture, where Jesus is presented as a complete Savior.* He began opening the Scriptures to my mind in small increments here and there, just when I needed them.

As my spiritual struggle with demonic assaults and God's chastening continued to rage on in a battle for my soul, all of the gospel songs that we would sing in church also began coming to my mind in small increments...*as they were actually written...*Not as they had been filtered and watered-down behind the pulpit. I even began waking up through all hours of the night with gospel songs in my heart. Although I could barely even speak, I was being taught to make melody in my heart to the Lord.

And when I realized from the Scriptures that it was *God* Who was giving me songs in the night (Ps. 42:8; 77:6; 149:5; Acts 16:25), I was encouraged to keep waiting upon Him as He kept bringing me to the end of myself, where all I could do was pray *constantly* that He would grant me the faith I so desperately needed, in order to truly believe in the Jesus represented in the Bible and our old gospel songs; the Jesus Who wasn't just a potential Savior, but the *real* Savior (Mt. 1:21); the Savior Who didn't allow any that He died for to perish in Hell; the Savior Who *actually saves actual people*, rather than just making everyone hypothetically or potentially "savable;" *...the Savior Who actually rescues His people.*

"I will seek that which was lost, and bring again that which was driven away, and will bind up that which was broken, and will strengthen that which was sick" (Ezek. 34: 16).

Notes:

[1] For a more comprehensive history of how the major American cults sprouted from the "Restoration" movement, see: CAnswersTV YouTube Channel video titled, *"Rise of the Cults: Where did all These Strange American Religious Sects Come From?"* at: https://www.youtube.com/watch?v=HfVTXbFrvh8&list=PLCF0ADB29C0EB8C40

For even more evidence that American cults sprouted from the Stone/Campbell movement, also see: Dr. Robert A. Morey's article on *"Campbellism and the Church of Christ."* Retrieved May 10, 2018 from the FaithDefenders.com website at: http://njiat.com/JunePDFs/Campbellism%20and%20the%20Church%20of%20Christ%2004_30_09.pdf

[2] See: Robert Meyers, General Editor, *Voices of Concern*, (Saint Louis, MS: Mission Messenger, 1966), p. 61 states as follows: "There are good people in the Church of Christ who deplore the wrongs done in the name of dogma and the Lord. But the attitude more frequently among them is that the more one silently endures these absurdities, the more pleased God is with the forbearance. Because primary obedience is to the church--righteous indignation—that most purifying of emotions, is stifled in the Church of Christ. Blind loyalty is to the church, not to justice; to the church, not to morality."

Chapter 8

"From the Frying Pan into the Fire"

"While they promise them liberty, they themselves are the servants of corruption"
(2 Pet. 2:19).

After days and days of suffering that seemed to stretch on for eternity, God strengthened me enough to get back home to take care of myself and the boys again, which was nothing short of a miracle. To help the muscle twitches, weakness and pain in my legs, I had to constantly monitor my stress levels and avoid all processed foods. But a stress free life with four rambunctious little boys was next to impossible! I could not let them down, for they required a *tremendous* amount of energy and attention.

So I began to experiment with different kinds of smoothies to try to keep my strength up. Because, dystonic tremors used up so much of my energy, I developed hypoglycemia from chronic, low blood sugar, which was actually making the tremors worse and contributing to my nausea and loss of appetite. It was a vicious cycle that I could not break out of until God gave me the wisdom to force myself to drink a health smoothie every two hours.

However, until then, I continued to discreetly throw up in the bathroom sink with the water running, to keep the boys from worrying and feeling insecure. I had to be strong for them. But the silent suffering was so painful that I'd often wonder if God would ever come through for me, heal me and give me the faith I needed in Jesus. I would also constantly grapple with the dark thoughts of why God would allow such intense suffering.

It was as if God had put me on a "forced fast," to keep my mind stayed upon seeking Him. Although it was difficult to have to drink all of my meals in order to survive and take care of the boys, God gave me the will to live. Yet no amount of veggies, vitamins, herbs, or sardine and fruit smoothies could ever completely heal me. Yes…I said *sardine*, if that gives *any* idea of how desperate I was!

Unrelenting sickness, heart-ache, spiritual struggles and the conflicts of going through a major theological transition on top of everything else, were turning my life upside down. The devil, my own flesh and worldly influences were constant companions that would toss me to and fro as to which way to go in my sad condition. Some very insensitive remarks would also come my way, such as the suggestion that my struggles stemmed from missing church on some Sunday nights…. even though I was deathly sick and exhausted!

So around that time I really began to ask a lot of questions in the church, especially after becoming convicted over some of the lyrics in my rock and roll music that I wanted to start replacing with Christian music.

I asked some CoC leaders if it would be okay for me to listen to Christian music as long as it was just in the privacy of my own home. The answer was an unequivocal…*No!* I was told that worship can ne*ver* be accompanied by music no matter where it takes place, or it would be a sin.

So I asked if I was better off just sticking with the music that had bad lyrics at home, and the answer was yes! This was so shocking and confusing to me. It seemed so contradictory that the church would discourage and even condemn gospel music, yet encourage something with bad lyrics instead! I couldn't believe my ears!

Such incidents were just the starting point of many to follow, which I would file away for further analysis once I got out from under such spiritual bondage. *Things were just not adding up.*

But, looking back, I realize that if I had been told that it was okay to listen to gospel music at home, it would have compromised the CoC's legalistic rule of keeping worship music out of the church. Since they must have obviously realized that God can be worshipped anywhere, they had to protect their church tradition by saying music can't accompany worship no matter where it takes place.[1]

At this point, I need to clarify that I personally love singing gospel hymns without music, especially in a group setting, for music can be distracting when it's used to manipulate emotions, or when it drowns out voices, which are both common abuses today. But it's a peripheral issue that salvation should *never* be based upon, which was what the CoC system did. It even led to the extreme of protecting man-made traditions at the cost of directing someone against their conscience, back into worldliness.

Thankfully, God kept faithfully leading me out of such horrendous darkness by gradually continuing to break down all of my CoC conditioning. I began to go through horrific spells of being fully aware that I was so deep in darkness that it would take a miracle of God to bring me out of it. And yet, I knew that my only hope of being reconciled to Him was through Jesus.

So during such intense, spiritual torment, I began to often say out loud, "I choose Christ." Sometimes I'd even be driving down the road when a song like "Highway to Hell" would play on the radio, and I'd be compelled to turn it off and say out loud, "No! I choose Jesus!" Little did I know then, that *it was actually Him choosing me and enabling me to choose Him.* Little by little, He was rescuing me and pulling me out of all the darkness in this world and all the delusions that I had previously leaned so heavily upon.

Yet spiritual blindness, ignorance and error were still the devils playground in my life for months to come as I was still being drawn out of the kingdom of darkness that had kept me bound for so long. The devil hates losing his captives, but God began to give me a strange type of discernment that allowed me to get a taste and feel of how sick evil was.

In fact, it was allowed to make me so sick mentally, physically and *especially* spiritually, that my whole body would shake and writhe under the weight of it. And strangely, my attention would often be drawn to a certain pagan object in my house that would make me feel so sick that I would have to throw it away before I could get any relief.

For instance, one item that began to make me sick was a picture I had taken with Deepok Chopra (one of Oprah Winfrey's gurus) at one of his seminars on "quantum healing." I had treasured that souvenir but could no longer stomach the sight of it, so I ended up throwing it in the garbage. And immediately I began to sense relief in my spirit. After that, I began to throw away many New Age books that I had collected over the years, even though they blended *so well* with the self-help philosophies of CoC theology.

Simultaneously, I kept sensing that something was terribly wrong with our religion. So after asking many unsettling questions, the open contradictions and obscure answers left me with no choice but to write a letter to my church leaders, letting them know that I was going to visit other "Churches of Christ" to see if I could find the answers I was looking for.

To say the least, that did not go over very well! My resignation was met with complete resistance and hostility instead of compassion and concern. My children and I were heavily harassed by condemning letters and condescending visits from the church. My twelve year old was even sent a letter stating that he had better get his mom to come back to church or be in danger of Hell! We were told that we had to be joined to them as members or be lost. Acts 9:26 was even used to try to support that theory!

The church also only recommended one other CoC out of all the dozens of others in our area (we are infested). But when I chose a different CoC that was not hand-picked by them (one that happened to have a kitchen), I was officially ex-communicated with a nasty letter that had all of the Elders signatures on it (except for one brave soul that stood against such abuses of authority), which served to convince me even more that something was terribly wrong with our theology that would lead to such prideful actions.

So that was "the straw that broke the camel's back," so to speak. Although I continued to visit other CoC's, I never again joined any of them, for I found that they all had the same basic theology. But then, I unknowingly ended up in yet another branch of Arminian theology.

◊◊◊

Out of such a deep, spiritual hunger for God and His truth, I started watching televangelists. As a consequence, I began to seek the kind of church that I *thought* they portrayed; one that at least *seemed* alive and not dead as a doornail. Little did I know that I was being led into the same trap that so many find themselves in after leaving the CoC. "From the frying pan into the fire," I went into the Neo-Pentecostal/Word of Faith movement,[2] which initially seemed to be the answer to what was missing in my life.

God's great mercy and patience with me during my spiritual pilgrimage from the CoC was incredible. For, like most who make an exodus from the CoC, I embarked on a journey where I ignorantly entered upbeat, mainstream, mega churches, where the true gospel was replaced with the healthy, wealthy and wise, prosperity gospel; biblical counseling was replaced with self-help, humanistic psychology; true worship was replaced with repetitive "Jesus is my boyfriend" music; true prayer was replaced with "positive confessions" and New Age "Contemplation," and true conversion was replaced with wild, subjective experiences and freewill decisionism.

What I really found to be interesting was that their only major problem against the CoC was that it was not into their false tithing doctrine, music in the church, *hyper*-grace, the charismatic gifts of prophesy, speaking in tongues, etc. Because, like all other popular, modern sensations that move the masses, the main focus was always on shallow issues, the *exact* same Arminian roots as the CoC. They just added on a *different* set of "how to" studies, conferences and seminars on "doing better" or "trying harder" *at this, that and everything.* For extremism is the name of the game in any false religion, where one legalistic hang up is just exchanged for another.

Though most exit the CoC because of its spiritual void and extreme legalism, many are often surprised to find that there are pitfalls in the opposite extreme as well. There's never balance in Arminian circles because their theology is contradictory and inconsistent. This is why they often have a subtle mixture of both legalism and license to sin. So it's no wonder that I met up with many other ex-CoC members on my pilgrimage, who were also free-floating from cult to cult just as I was…. searching for answers.

◊◊◊

It was in those circles that I also got hooked up with Arminian "witchdoctors." But, of course, they don't confess that about themselves! Some were Amish, some CoC and some Word of Faith, etc. Despite their differences, they all still had the same basic theology at the root of their practice, with the added feature of Pantheism; the false belief that God is an impersonal "life force" that flows through *all things*….rocks, trees, plants, people…and would have to include the devil, *whether they realized it or not!*

It's the main philosophy behind every healing therapy that claims to utilize "universal energy," which they blasphemously refer to as the Holy Spirit, when it's actually *"the prince of the power of the air" (Eph. 2:2)*. By redefining God as an energy that can be hindered by "negativity," healing charlatans claim to have the *positive* power to detect and remove "negative interferences," through the use of dowsing tools.[3] These channeling tools range from their own hands, to pendulums, rocks, sticks (as in water witching), radionic devices that "diagnose" mineral deficiencies, or whatever can be used like a Ouija board to seek out hidden knowledge.

In a similar way, the CoC performs a type of "water witching" when it comes to baptism, by implying that one can channel Christ through water and *cause* Him to save by going through the baptismal formula. By believing one has to "contact the blood" in the water, one can easily be led into viewing baptism as a ritual similar to Catholic Mass, where a priest claims to "transubstantiate" or transform the physical elements of bread and wine into the actual body and blood of Jesus. Although the CoC denies an actual physical contact with Jesus' blood, and confesses that Catholic Mass is satanic, its doctrine of baptismal regeneration still dangerously implies the same kind of errors, which is one reason it's headed back to Rome.[4]

It was no wonder that I was so vulnerable to deeper levels of the occult. But thankfully God gradually began showing me through His Word that He cannot be channeled or called down from Heaven to enter anything, including baptismal water. His Word reveals that He is *Not* in everything and doesn't approve of everything. He is omnipresent, yet transcendent and not part of His creation (1 Kgs. 8:27, Ps. 139:7-16, Acts 17:24-28).

God is a personal Spirit Being, not an impersonal "energy force" that's subject to manipulation and change. He offers a personal relationship with us through His Son Jesus Christ, Who suffered, died and rose again so that sinners can receive God's mercy and have eternal life.

Notes:

[1] For a classic example, see: Benjamin J. Williams, General Editor, *Why We Stayed*, (Los Angeles/London: Keledei Publications, 2018), p. 94 -- "The grand finale of this argument is the conclusion that the inclusion of instruments in worship is an unauthorized innovation on the divine pattern of the New Testament. Those who worship without instruments are said to be standing squarely on divine authority. Those who worship with instruments are guilty of the sin of going beyond the boundaries of Christ's will and are thus outside of the fellowship of God's people."

[2] For a beginners guide on the origins and heresies of the Word of Faith movement, see: D.R. McConnell, *A Different Gospel*, Updated Edition, (Peabody, MA: Hendrickson Publishers, 1995).

[3] See: Ben G. Hester, *Dowsing: An Expose of Hidden Occult Forces,* Revised Edition, (Arlington, CA: self-published, 1984). Also see: Dr. John Ankerberg and Dr. John Weldon, *The Facts about Dowsing and Water Dowsing*, (ATRI Publishing, 2012).

[4] For more evidence, see: Alvin Jennings, General Editor, *Introducing the Church of Christ*, (Fort Worth, TX: Star Bible Publications, Inc., 1981), p. 108.

Note: The CoC *always* uses Romans 6:3-4 to try to justify its "contacting the blood in baptism" doctrine... *even though these verses don't even mention His blood*, which is so ironic, for the CoC claims to be "silent where Scripture is silent!"

Chapter 9

Pragmatism: Thread in the Cornbread!

"Many of them also which used curious arts brought their books together, and burned them before all men: and they counted the price of them, and found it fifty thousand pieces of silver" (Acts 19:19).

Other common phrases for modern pragmatism are..."whatever works for you" or "to each his own." And its rising influence on society is causing many to buy into it, literally. Its sick motto is that *"the end justifies the means"* or *"whatever produces positive results must be truth,"* which portrays God as a tool that humans can use to secure their own ends. So, if obeying the true gospel of Christ isn't what "works," then an alternative is chosen. And since the CoC system didn't have the true Jesus and the true gospel in the first place, it made us even more vulnerable to "alternatives."

And that's exactly what the New Age offers. After all, many alternative doctrines and therapies appear to be good, just as the forbidden fruit in the Garden of Eden appeared good....at first (Gen. 3:6). Because, according to Scripture, the devil loves to pose as an angel of light by getting people to believe "the energy" working behind certain doctrines and so-called "therapies" is God (2 Cor. 11:13-15). But such counterfeit light is nothing more than divination/witchcraft (e.g. Deut. 18:10-12, Jer. 14:14, Hos. 4:12).

So by desperately seeking a cure for my sickness through such avenues, God chastened me even more. After many unfortunate events, horrific experiences and a near-death episode, He had mercy on me and allowed my senses to be exercised so that I could finally learn to discern between good and evil (Heb. 5:14). For God's Word is a sufficient guide to help us distinguish the works of the Holy Spirit from works of the devil.

For that reason, I was eventually able to part ways with Arminian "faith healers." But since those of us who were from the CoC never learned the truth about the Holy Spirit in the first place, we were the most prone to that kind of deception. I can remember only one sermon that focused solely on the Holy Spirit and how He is a Divine Person of the Godhead. It was when our CoC was trying out new preachers, to replace the one that retired. Needless to say, that particular preacher did not get the position.

He was seen as being too controversial, for the CoC system limits the Holy Spirit to just being the mere *influence of the Word*, made effective by baptism. When in actuality, He's the divine agent Who effectively wields the Word like a sword that cuts to the heart (Heb. 4:12).

CoC sermons belittled the biblical concept of being eternally indwelled and sealed by the Holy Spirit. It was even mockingly asked how He could ever *actually* enter a person... *through the hand or foot?* Yet it was never denied that the devil entered Judas Iscariot. Therefore, it was implied that the devil had the power to enter a person, but that the Holy Spirit didn't. [1]

Naturally, the evil spirit behind the CoC system never wanted us to know about demonic possession, even though many of our members showed signs of it. So by having the wool pulled over our eyes, we became even more vulnerable to every wind of doctrine promoted by wolves in sheep's clothing, because we were not rooted and grounded in the truth.

So it's crucial to note that our church, like most other modern churches, didn't have a problem with Acupuncture, Iridology, Reflexology, Reiki, Bio-energetic assessments and many other healing therapies that claim to tap into what they call *universal* "energy" meridians.

This forbidden knowledge was meant to get us "in tune" with our own divinity and help us "tap into" our *inherent,* universal "spark of goodness," which demonically displaced God's Spirit and the fact that He only indwells and sanctifies His own. Though there has never been any real scientific evidence to prove significant, medical benefit from such, there is a lot of anecdotal evidence, which are merely placebo testimonials of those who've fallen prey for such a perversion of the gospel (Gal. 1:6-9, 1 Tim. 4:1).

I have a few testimonies of my own about the demonic power working behind such therapies, which is why I can now warn others to never underestimate the power of suggestion. It has been the devils main tool since the Garden of Eden. All he has to do to start the process is to get us to doubt God's truth and exchange it for a lie. By getting Adam and Eve to focus on temporary results instead of the long-term spiritual consequences of rebelling against God, they fell for the suggestion to eat forbidden fruit.

And this is exactly how pragmatism works today. It's just the same old lie that's been re-packaged, which reminds me of the time I went into business with one of those very persuasive "life coaches," to sell a product that they claimed to be a cure all. But once I started doing my own research I found out that it was full of cheap fillers, with barely any of the main ingredient that was supposed to help people. So I found another product that just had the main ingredient, minus all the fillers, at the same price.

Excited about what I'd found, I went back to them thinking they'd surely rather sell this instead, for they acted like they really wanted to help people. Little did I know then that I had gotten into what's called a Pyramid Scheme. So, to my surprise, they told me that they would be crazy to stop selling the flawed product because they were making a fortune off of people. And when they saw how shocked I was, they tried to convince me that it wasn't really dishonest, for if people really believed it helped, then it would!!

All that a peddler of pragmatism has to do is convince gullible people that something works and they will experience a major placebo effect. The question is, would they still buy into it if they knew they were just being tricked into thinking it was working? Sadly, many would, for they would rather exchange the truth for a lie as long as they get some temporary results. This is described perfectly in Isaiah 30: 9-10, where it says, *"this is a rebellious people, lying children, children that will not hear the law of the Lord: which say to the seers, See not; and to the prophets, Prophesy not unto us right things; speak unto us smooth things, prophesy deceits."*

This is why the ionic, detox, footbath scam is also highly promoted by Arminian charlatans. Similar to the foot pad scam exposed in 2008, it has fooled many. One can only imagine how cheated many feel after finding out they've spent tons of money to soak their feet in *electrode corrosion!* And it could happen to anyone, especially the sick and vulnerable ones who've been through the wringer by the medical establishment. But, having been there myself, I can honestly say that the biggest concern isn't the money people are being *duped out of,* but what they're being *duped into* spiritually.

Thankfully God's Word is loaded with biblical insight into what we need to look out for. For instance, 1 Timothy 6:20-21 helped to break the spell in my own life, by warning me that I should be *"avoiding profane and vain babblings and oppositions of science falsely so called; which some professing have erred concerning the faith."*

Like evolution, I realized that many healing therapies have no scientific evidence to back up their claims, and prove to be fraudulent once they are investigated. And these kinds of therapies perfectly fit into the category of "curious arts," mentioned in Acts 19:19. So when we subject ourselves to such, we are actually buying into a false religious system that severely distorts and perverts the biblical concept of God! The one common thread behind their philosophies is that most draw upon Arminian humanism and Eastern religion, which both have a freewill concept of self-salvation.

Therefore, there's no excuse for rebelling against God by getting involved in such dangerous practices. Because Scripture has clearly warned us to avoid anything that could put us into direct contact with demons that work behind the scenes to try to make the philosophies behind certain practices seem true (Eph. 5:11, 1 Pet. 5:8). They not only put one at risk financially, mentally and physically, but most importantly, spiritually.

"Beware lest any man spoil you through philosophy and vain deceit" (Col. 2:8). Even though *"many shall follow their pernicious ways"* we must remember that *"through covetousness shall they with feigned words make merchandise of you" (2 Pet. 2:2-3).* And I had to learn the hard way.

◊◊◊

In those circles, I also became involved in "prayer groups" that took Arminianism to its logical *extreme*, which *drastically* diminished hope in the finished work of Christ. The "energies of prayer" (as their preferred *Message Bible* puts it), was to be exerted by us, in order to take dominion back from the devil. For they blasphemously taught that God "lost control" over the world when Adam and Eve supposedly handed it over to the devil when they sinned. So our own works had to purge the earth of all evil before Christ would return. They ignored the fact that although Jesus has given His people power over *all* evil, only Jesus has *all* power (Mt. 28:18).

God still has complete dominion over all things, including the forces of darkness (Mt. 6:13, Eph. 1:21, 1 Pet. 5:11). No one, not even the devil, can do anything unless God allows it. And when Jesus comes again, He Himself will purge the world of all evil (Rev. 19). Until then, God gives His people keys to the door of Heaven (Jesus), for *the gospel* is life to those loosed for Heaven, and death to those bound for Hell (Mt. 16:19, 2 Cor. 2:14-17).

In contrast, Arminianism led to Dominionism, where man takes charge. No wonder absurd "spiritual warfare" tactics were carried out by self-proclaimed seers, prayer warriors, curse breakers, prophetic intercessors, inner healers and psycho-spiritual counselors who would give exhausting, legalistic orders to pray in tongues so many minutes a day; to make so many "declarations" per day (e.g. "pleading the blood"); to put a sign of the cross with "anointed" oil (or salt) everywhere...*to ward off evil,* or to utilize "specially formulated prayers" that allegedly gave us power to "speak things into existence" *like God*, to break "generational curses," or to "reverse the curse" of witches (who we were always in competition with, for we used the same conjured up devices they did). One "exorcist" even suggested cutting up pieces of "prayer cloths" in people's food to deliver them from demons! But one can only imagine trying to explain... *thread in the cornbread!* [2]

But, sad to say, it's all par for the course when Arminianism goes to seed. Do-it-yourself religion is fertile breeding ground that paves the way for being *"carried about with every wind of doctrine" (Eph. 4:14).* By redefining God as something that can be hindered or controlled by human freewill, almost any false doctrine can be implemented, no matter how ridiculous.

No wonder my grandma used a homemade pendulum (a string tied to a wedding ring) to try to determine the gender of my brother before he was born! And no wonder we were all willingly ignorant of such dangerous dabbling, and thought it was just fun and interesting to experiment with.

Although false religion can stir religious affections to a fever pitch, it can never save, for it robs people of the power of the true gospel and leaves them spiritually bankrupt. The CoC, and others like it, are rip-off religions with a sham salvation that is theologically thread-bare; for Arminianism is a fertile seedbed for every form of deception that offers spiritual diversions from the Sovereign Lordship of Christ, in attempts to fill the empty void.

But God calls us to repent and trust in Jesus' righteousness alone. I'm living proof that He still continues to rescue His sheep from all the messes they get themselves into. There is still so much to learn and we need Him to grant us the discernment to *"abstain from all appearance of evil" (1 Thess. 5:22),* whether it concerns our health, finances, relationships or eternity.

From experience, I know how hard it is to resist religious rackets and false claims when one so desperately needs healing, but we have to learn to *"trust in the Lord with all thine heart; and lean not unto thine own understanding. In all thy ways acknowledge Him and He shall direct thy paths. Be not wise in thine own eyes; fear the Lord, and depart from evil. It shall be health to thy navel and marrow to thy bones" (Prov. 3:5-8).*

Notes:

[1] William Phillips, *Campbellism Exposed,* (Cincinnati, OH: J.F. Wright & L. Swormstedt, 1837). See Chapter 3-- *Divine Agency of the Spirit: Irreverent and Blasphemous Language of Campbellites Respecting the Spirit.*

For more in-depth information on the CoC's *general* indwelling of the Holy Spirit doctrine, see: Alvin Jennings, General Editor, *Introducing the Church of Christ*, (Fort Worth, TX: Star Bible Publications, Inc., 1981), p. 164.

Also see: Allen Webster, *How is Your Hearing?* Retrieved May 3, 2018 from: https://housetohouse.com/wp-content/uploads/2016/02/v17n1.pdf

[2] See: Justin Peters, *Clouds Without Water: A Biblical Critique of the Word of Faith Movement,* available at: https://justinpeters.org/a-call-for-discernment/

Part 2

God's Awe-Inspiring Providences and Divine Appointments

Chapter 10

New Beginnings

…"forgetting those things which are behind, and reaching forth unto those things which are before, I press toward the mark for the prize of the high calling of God in Christ Jesus" (Phil. 3:13-14).

After coming to terms with the past, and seeing things more from a biblical perspective, God began slowly pulling me out of the fiery furnace of affliction, at least enough for me to finally remarry after seven long years of being a single mom. And though my husband also had to transcend the pain of his past, over time we helped each other draw closer to the Lord.

When we were very young, we would both send love letters to each other through my best friend, who happened to be his cousin. Sometimes I would also visit their Baptist church, where Tony and I would lock eyes, knowing there was something special between us. I would even tell my parents that I was going to marry him some day, which they seemed fine with. But when I was finally old enough to date him, things fell apart, due to our differing religious views.

After that, I became even more disillusioned and gave up on finding Mr. Right, for I had thought Tony was the perfect guy; a Sunday school teacher, always packing his Bible around, only to find that he wasn't so "perfect" after all! I remember him teasing me and saying, "You're one of those 'strict girls' ain't cha?" And I'd snap back, "Don't you fear God at all?!"

But a lot of water had passed under the bridge since those days, and for some reason we never could forget about each other. Then at my best friend's wedding, we met up again. I found out that he too had gone through a similar divorce, so we had a lot in common, but that also included trust issues after us both being so betrayed. Yet we began talking on the phone, and after a while we started dating and eventually got engaged.

Most didn't know it, but I called off our wedding the morning we were to be married. I was so afraid of being hurt again that I used the excuse that it was too overcast. For the old wives tale was, "if you marry on a rainy day, that's how many tears you will shed." But it finally came down to me having to take a leap of faith, trusting that God would work everything for good.

So I crossed over the branch, where I had prayed so many prayers as a child, and we were married in "God's Meadow." Both sets of our twins had been born only weeks apart, so it was very unique and special to see his twin daughters as the flower girls and my twin sons as the ring bearers!

Right before our vows Tony prayed for God's blessing upon our marriage, and...*at that very moment*...God seemed to literally part the clouds and beam the sun directly down upon us, and all of our loved ones got to witness it! We were all so filled with amazement at the perfect timing of it! And such unexpected mercy and relief came to my soul by the consideration of it, because I had struggled for years, wondering if God would ever bless me with marriage again... *especially* to my first love.

◊◊◊

Although Tony hated that I had become involved in so many cultic, Arminian circles, he wasn't the one to convince me they were wrong, for at that time he still wasn't completely right with God yet either. So our marriage was indeed overcast in the beginning, even to the point of him becoming violently angry and us separating for two months. But another act of God's providence occurred about that time when my mother made a surprise visit, with a bag of old school papers that I thought I had thrown away years ago!

Inside, was the old, heart-shaped candy box Tony had given me when we were teenagers. When I opened it, I found that it still contained the piece of bark that I had kept from the tree in "God's Meadow" where I had carved our initials! With astonishment, I broke into tears, for it was as if the Lord was reminding me to be patient and to not give up on our marriage, because for some reason Tony and I were obviously meant to be together.

God was also working on him, for not long after that, a homeless man with a long, white beard was walking down the road in front of our home. So Tony went to talk to him and give him some food. Surprisingly, the man knew his Bible inside-out. And so, they struck up a conversation about the false religions I was involved in, for Tony was so distraught about how our marriage was being affected. The old man told him that although those cults were dangerous ground, no one was going to be able to convince me except God, through the cults themselves, which seemed to convince Tony to stop pressuring me to leave them, and to be more patient with me.

Strangely enough, God did allow me to be spiritually abused in those circles, so that I could learn where they were wrong, which sometimes makes me wonder if that homeless guy was an angel (Heb. 13:2)! It was also strange that he was allegedly seen two counties away in a church parking lot at the exact same time he was at our house! The man did say that he had visited many churches that did not uphold the true gospel of the Bible. I cringe at the thoughts of God's judgment on them (1 Pet. 4:17).

◊◊◊

Two years after we were married, I finally graduated from college, which had almost taken its toll on me. But God worked it all for good, through the extreme discipline, organization, research and writing skills that prepared me to fulfill His purpose for me as a Christian author to glorify His name.

He also enabled me to see through the secular sham that passes as education these days. And since my internship involved counseling at secular, government-funded organizations, I learned just how dangerous it was to mention the name of Jesus, Who is the *"High-est* Power," and how it was only acceptable to the world to mention a neutral *"high-er* power."

All of my college classes on psychology and human philosophy were just like being in the CoC. All of the New Age concepts of absolute autonomy, self-worship, self-improvement, self-esteem, self-help and self-will, paralleled perfectly with all of the CoC/Arminian concepts of freewill, self-determination, self-generated faith and the "divine spark of goodness" in fallen man. As the Bible reveals...such things may have a show of wisdom in *will worship* (Col. 2:23, emphasis mine)... *but are in fact, futile fallacies.*

After I graduated, God enabled me to home school the boys, at least long enough to try to undo some of the damage that had been done through the public school system, video games, church, etc. I began noticing how school book fairs had become nothing but witchcraft promos, and how TV was promoting filth and celebrity worship, while impoverishing and vilifying true gospel messengers. I became deeply convicted when I learned from Scripture that we are not to feed our minds with, approve of as entertainment or take pleasure in the sins of the world (e.g. Rom. 1:32).

So Tony and I agreed that it would be a powerful testimony to have a huge bonfire, where all seven of our children got to witness the burning of Harry Potter books, movies and other bad stuff that had kept worming its way into our lives. Naturally, some rebelled, but we stood firm on God's Word. And since the CoC had never taken a strong stand against any of it due to social sway and political acceptability, I was seen as a threat to its authority. So I was not only interrogated and ridiculed by the Board of Education, but also by some CoC leaders for being such a "renegade."

◊◊◊

As I continued to pray for God to show me the root of all my spiritual struggles, I found a book on my husband's desk, which had been loaned to him by a friend. Since he had never gotten around to reading it, I decided that I would. I had never heard of John Bunyan, and so, I confused him with the Paul Bunyan character we had learned about in school.

But once I started reading, I began to realize that I had providentially stumbled upon the answer to my prayers. What initially got my attention was the revelation of what *historic* Baptists believed and laid their lives down for, and how *modern* Baptists actually played a huge part in the spread of CoC heresies, due to side-stepping those unpopular Bible doctrines, in fear that confrontation would cost them something.

Though they were formerly stewards of the gospel, they brought disgrace upon the doctrines of grace, and lost strength when they ditched their reformed confessions of faith (e.g. 1689 Baptist Confession of Faith), which adequately articulated the gospel. Unconditional election, particular redemption, etc., had given them a solid foundation to stand upon.

But by reading what *original* Baptists formerly believed, I learned just how many doctrinal deviations had been slipping into their churches, which caused them a *huge* loss of respect, and had given the CoC so much leverage. I remember sermons in the CoC about how Baptists abused grace as a license to sin, and sadly, they were right (ironically the CoC did too, but in a more subtle way). This resonated as one of the main reasons most modern Baptists have had no power against the CoC and its proliferation.

I can remember how CoC preachers would often make fun of them for how some explained their subjective salvation experiences (being struck by lightning, hearing audible voices, etc.). I even own a short essay my grandmother wrote decades ago about her encounters with what she called "better-felt-than-told Baptists" who only seemed to be ignorantly driven by extreme emotionalism and self-delusion, with no evidence of new birth.[1]

Sadly, by becoming more "united" and less creedal, many modern, Baptist churches have been infiltrated by every wind of doctrine, which has been a major reason why the CoC has been largely left unchallenged today.

Due to a growing theological incompetency and a desperate need to still have conversions, many modern, Baptist preachers resort to emotional manipulation in order to produce superficial experiences and false professions of faith. But without a true, *spiritual* understanding of God and how He saves, one cannot experience the true God and Savior of Scripture.

Without creedal safeguards against heresy, an extreme emphasis is placed on subjectively *feeling* the Spirit, rather than biblical expositions on the importance of *spiritually understanding and believing the objective Word of God through illumination of the Spirit*, which is falsely called head knowledge by anti-intellectuals.... *who boast that ignorance is spiritual!*

This in turn, reinforced the CoC's faulty framework for justifying the use of natural, carnal reasoning to try to understand God's Word, rather than stressing fallen man's need for *supernatural* illumination of the Word, by the Spirit opening ones *spiritual* understanding (Rom. 8:7, 1 Cor. 2:14).[2]

By both groups focusing on what could only be weighed, measured and observed by the physical senses, the CoC gained momentum by arrogantly appearing to be so much wiser than the Baptists who seemed to be losing all sense of reason. The CoC's ability to make absurd doctrines appear reasonable, combined with the Baptists unreasonable compromise of reformed roots, contributed to the spread of CoC heresies. The conspicuous correlation between the rise of the former and the decline of the latter has been strikingly obvious.

So reading Bunyan's book, *Christ a Complete Savior: the Intercession of Christ*, marked one of the most significant milestones in my life of faith. It was also the starting point of helping my husband and me to finally come to terms with the fact that we had *both* been deceived by false religious notions. So after butting heads for years with knock-down, drag-out fights that led to back and forth tugs-of-war between legalism and license to sin, we were finally able to come together in like-minded peace with each other and with God through Christ, based on a balanced view of Scripture.

Although it was really hard to understand language from the 1600's at first, as I persevered, it was like being on a treasure hunt, finding precious gold in Scripture that had been hidden from me by false religion. In all honesty, until I read Bunyan, *I had never spiritually understood a true presentation of the gospel with such clarity!*[3] Then, after noticing the impact it had on my own life, my husband finally got into reading Bunyan too.

We then found that there had been a preacher in the 1800's who also loved reading his books. So I ordered *The Forgotten Spurgeon* by Iain Murray, to learn more about Charles Spurgeon, the "prince of preachers," who stood *strongly* against doctrinal compromise during the Downgrade Controversy. And his fight to the death against Arminianism, and the fact that most aren't doing so today, shed much light on why churches are in the shape they are in now. So this led us to seek out even more of his sermons.

As a result, my husband was truly converted to Christ and finally enabled to biblically re-evaluate the false, "altar call" experience of his youth! We both began to realize what we had been missing out on our entire lives. It was just so amazing how God led us to old sermons that actually expounded upon all the Scriptures that our churches never wanted to touch with a ten foot pole!! They had either ignored or glossed over those passages with flimsy interpretations that had only confounded, imprisoned and bound us from true, saving faith. But by God's grace, we never looked back.

Notes:

[1] For more examples of the CoC's mockery toward modern Baptists and what the CoC calls their "better-felt-than-told" concept of salvation, see: Allen Webster, *Why Would God Want to Save Someone Like Me?* Volume 20, Issue #2, pp. 1-3. Retrieved May 27, 2018 from: https://housetohouse.com/wp-content/uploads/2016/02/v20n2.pdf

[2] See: Alvin Jennings, General Editor, *Introducing the Church of Christ*, (Fort Worth, TX: Star Bible Publications, Inc., 1981), pp. 163-164.

[3] Also see: John Bunyan's excellent, well-known book, *The Pilgrims Progress,* which is a number one Christian bestseller, second only to the Bible.

Chapter 11

Blessed Assurance

"The Spirit Himself bears witness with our spirit that we are children of God" (Rom. 8:16, NKJV)...."that ye may know that ye have eternal life" (1 Jn. 5:13).

As the Holy Spirit kept graciously *guiding* me to Christ Jesus through faith, and *guarding* me from all of the CoC's false interpretations, by *directing* me deep into what Scripture actually conveys, I was finally able to start resisting the devils lies. For the first time in my life, all the pieces of the puzzle started to come together as God's Word shined with power into my heart, enabling me to finally perceive its beauty and cohesiveness (2 Cor. 4:6).

The love that then began to well-up within me for my Lord was so strong I could barely endure the strength of it. I remember being brought to tears when God finally gave me the blessed assurance that He accepted the righteousness of Christ on behalf of sinners like me, and that Jesus had been pursuing and rescuing me from slavery to sin and CoC lies all along.

Though I had been such a burned out, tangled mess of confusion all those years, God had been re-wiring me! He had even used sickness to draw me to Christ and to keep me in constant communion with Him, which revealed that they were sanctified afflictions rather than judgments. *"Before I was afflicted I went astray; but now have I kept Thy Word...It is good for me that I have been afflicted; that I might learn Thy statutes" (Ps. 119:67, 71).*

At the moment I realized these truths, I finally, wholeheartedly believed that Jesus had truly saved me. Needless to say, Jesus became precious to me as I perceived a peace in my soul that He had *always* loved me with an everlasting love, and that I was His forever. By the Lord giving me such strong consolation, I was finally able to know true, supernatural and eternal *"joy and peace in believing" (Rom. 15:13)*, without a terrifying fear of losing my faith and ending up in Hell! God saved me because Jesus is perfect, *Not* because my faith, repentance or knowledge of His truth was perfect.

God confirmed and comforted me in the fact that He had graciously delivered me from such paralyzing doubt and spiritual blindness. I was so thankful that He had revealed the true Christ of Scripture to me, and that He had been building my faith in Him all along, though I was unable to generate a single ounce of it myself. The Comforter came and bore witness with my spirit by graciously revealing to me through His Word that Jesus died for me, so that I *could* be granted the special graces of saving faith and repentance. For my Heavenly Father had been drawing me to Jesus all along!

God saved me and made His Word effectual in my life, for the Holy Spirit accompanies the Word and renders it productive in those who belong to Him, in those who've been granted *faith...which is the operation of God*, not the operation of humans. It is God Who gives the increase (1 Cor. 3:6).

And it was God, Who revealed to me through true expositions of His Word that He had enabled me to pray for faith in Jesus, and He showed me how He had been answering my prayers all along. He was the One showing me how bad sin is, how it affects every faculty of our being, and how I was completely helpless without the Savior, so that I could be truly humbled. And after I had suffered for a while, He gave me strong consolation of His mercy, by settling, strengthening and establishing me so solidly in the faith of Christ and the true gospel that He came to bear witness to (1 Pet. 5:10).

He revealed to me the true Savior, the true Jesus of the Bible, how He prays for those the Father has given Him, and how He loses none of them, because His intercession for them can never fail (Lk. 22:32, Jn. 17:9, Heb. 7:25). God showed me that Jesus only intercedes and pleads His blood for those He came to shed His blood for (Jn. 10:15); those given to Him by the Father (Jn. 17:6, 9). *"For He shall save His people from their sins"* (Mt. 1:21). Those who perish in unbelief are not His sheep, because the sheep He laid His life down for can never perish in unbelief (Jn. 10:28-29), because they have the *"faith of God's elect" (Titus 1:1).*

That's when the fear of Hell completely left me. By having the true Jesus revealed to me, I was finally able to trust such a trustworthy Savior, Who was actually able to save me to the uttermost, despite a natural inability to "cooperate!" I no longer had a reason to despair of His goodness and mercy, for He showed me that salvation is not based on my own goodness, but only on His. And this knowledge does not come by man's wisdom.

Through His Word He revealed to me the true gospel, how the true Jesus of the Bible was a *propitiation* for His people's sins; those God has chosen out of every tongue, tribe and nation. *Not for the Jews only*, which is why the word *world* is used to describe those He has died for (e.g. 1 Jn. 2:2). He was *their* substitute (1 Jn. 4:10). He died in *their* place. He bore *their* sins and took them upon Himself (Isa. 53:11, 1 Pet. 2:24). He bore the wrath of God upon Himself for *their* sins, so that His righteousness could be accredited to *their* account (2 Cor. 5:21). He paid *their* sin debt in full so that they'll *never* have to pay for them in eternal Hell (Heb. 9:26). This cannot be said for the *whole world*, or else *all* would be saved. This is why it's such a miracle that God has chosen to save *any*, for *none* deserve to be.

God also gave me the discernment to know what faith wasn't. Sincerely believing something doesn't make it true. Faith in a religious system of works, or faith in a religious system of license to sin, is not saving faith. He opened my eyes to the fact that doctrines of men had kept me from realizing that I needed to pray for faith in the sufficiency of Jesus' righteousness to save me, renouncing my own self-righteousness and my own delusions of false security in sin. My faith was not to be in a decision I had made (decisional regeneration), or in baptism (baptismal regeneration).

As Charles Spurgeon once said:

"A man who knows that he is saved by believing in Christ does not, when he is baptized, lift his baptism into a saving ordinance. In fact, he is the very best protester against that mistake, because he holds that he has no right to be baptized until he is saved."[1]

True regeneration precedes genuine repentance and faith, for these gifts of grace are what the Holy Spirit works within, not what He responds to. God showed me thru His Word, that a spiritual coming to Christ is not a physical act. *"Whosoever shall confess Me before men" (Mt. 10:32)* is not a call for public action in order to *become* a Christian. It is rather the natural outworking of a true Christian, whose nature has been supernaturally changed, from enmity against God, to love for God, and hatred toward sin.

I was finally enabled to read God's Word apart from the CoC's violation of certain texts that gave them the sense of works being the process whereby we become Christians. For instance, I could finally read John 15:8 to mean exactly what it means. *"Herein is My Father glorified, that ye bear much fruit; so shall ye be My disciples."* Fruit-bearing is the *evidence* of salvation, not the process that causes one to *become* a Christian. I could finally read Romans 10:13 to mean exactly what it says. *"Whosoever calls upon the name of the Lord shall be saved"...Not* the CoC's addition of baptism being how one calls upon the name of the Lord, which had discouraged prayer.

I could finally read 2 Peter 2:1 and see that the word "bought" there had nothing to do with Jesus' saving, blood purchase, but rather eludes to the fact that God's sovereign Lordship is over all people, even unsaved, false prophets and teachers that slip into the church. He even "bought" the *temporary* deliverance of many reprobate Jews from Egyptian slavery (Deut. 32:6, Jude 5).[2] It was also a comfort to realize that Jesus took upon Himself the sins of **every one** of the *spiritual* descendants of Abraham, and *not a single one* can ever be lost (See: Heb. 2:9, 16; 11:18 NASB).

The Holy Spirit also opened my mind to the truths of Scripture so I could see that faith is not an "energy force" that can be tapped into or worked up in our own power, for only He can change the heart and enable us to truly believe, repent and live for Him (true Holy Spirit regeneration).

The Lord *"gives us an understanding that we may know Him that is true, and we are in Him that is true, even in His Son Jesus Christ. This is the true God and eternal life" (1 Jn. 5:20).* By being given the knowledge of Who the true Christ really was, I was so taken with the love and mercy of God that I could barely contain myself. And He had begun this work in me by first showing me how bad sin corrupts our very nature, so that we can't rightly respond to the gospel unless God intervenes, grants faith, repentance and the ability to follow Christ (Rom. 6:17-20, 8:7, 1 Cor. 2:14, 2 Thess. 3:2).

By experiencing the merciful working of God upon my soul I finally realized that *God helps those who **can't** help themselves* (e.g. Isa. 64:6, Lk. 18:10-14). When I had been at the lowest point of my life, I realized it was then that God had been directing me to Jesus as my only hope of salvation.

I didn't realize I was eternally secure at that time, but once one trusts Jesus as their only hope, they are truly born of the Spirit, regenerated and transformed *at that very moment (Jn. 1:13).* Their lives are not perfection but headed in that direction *from then on,* in progressive sanctification, holiness and discipleship. And He showed me that's where I had been headed all along. *"Therefore, if anyone is in Christ, he is a new creation; old things have passed away; behold all things have become new" (2 Cor. 5:17).*

I finally had blessed assurance of salvation! It was a miracle to finally be able to believe that Jesus is a *complete* Savior Who didn't need my help in getting the job done, and that I am *complete* in Him (Col. 2:10). He did it all from start to finish! And by being so fully convinced, I became so content and satisfied in Christ that I was willing to endure any hardship for Him.

Though the natural tendencies of the flesh would always remain this side of Heaven, I was no longer dominated by sin, wildly swept along with the world or driven by perfectionism. I no longer felt defined by appearance or performance. Jesus revealed to me that the world's approval is actually a terrible sign of God's disapproval, for He said, *"Woe unto you, when all speak well of you! For so did their fathers to the false prophets" (Lk. 6:26).*

I took such comfort in knowing that I no longer had to be consumed with externals, for Jesus is my Sabbath rest (Heb. 4). And He speaks these words to all who truly seek refuge in Him: *"Come unto Me, all ye that labour and are heavy laden, and I will give you rest. Take My yoke upon you, and learn of Me; for I am meek and lowly in heart; and ye shall find rest unto your souls. For My yoke is easy, and My burden is light" (Mt. 11:28-30).*

I also learned that those who continue to live in an unbroken pattern of perpetual sin, *"according to the course of this world" (Eph. 2:2),* are also those that Hebrews 6 and 10 speak of. For by their own self-righteousness and/or by becoming desensitized and hardened in sin, they imply His sacrifice wasn't enough to save them or conform them to the image of Christ. Many also show by their legalistic works that they believe they must contribute to what Jesus already declared "is finished." And/or their lifestyle shows that they have no God-given power to prove their claim; they even think lightly of past sins, with no desire for Jesus to free them from their ongoing slavery to sin and worldliness. Either way they are unchanged.

Although the Bible states that *"there remains no more sacrifice for sins" (Heb. 10:26),* they imply that there is, by trying to appease God with their own works, rather than trusting solely in Jesus as the once and for all perfect sacrifice. Or they make excuses, by exploiting the truth that "no one is perfect," which implies that the merits of Jesus' sacrifice alone can't effectively change anyone. False professors of faith either imply that God's grace isn't enough to make them holier, or they imply that God's grace isn't enough to save without works being added to the equation. I learned that both license and legalism are two sides of the same heretical coin.

Those who are truly saved *"have put on the new man, which is renewed in knowledge after the image of Him that created him" (Col. 3:10). "That the righteousness of the law might be fulfilled in us who walk not after the flesh, but after the Spirit" (Rom. 8:4). "According as He hath chosen us in Him before the foundation of the world, that we should be holy and without blame before Him in love" (Eph. 1:4).* That Christ may be glorified in us.

Without these evidences that true regeneration has taken place, there can be no blessed assurance, but only a superficial, false security that makes excuses for sin, rather than grieving over it, fighting it and pleading for mercy through Christ. Christians can never reach sinless perfection this side of Heaven, but by God's grace they will have a tender conscience that will cause them to wage war on sin, rather than rest easy in it. *"Let everyone that nameth the name of Christ depart from iniquity" (2 Tim. 2:19).*

God leads His people in paths of righteousness for His name sake (Ps. 23:3). *"Therefore, having these promises, beloved, let us cleanse ourselves from all defilement of flesh and spirit, perfecting holiness in the fear of God" (2 Cor. 7:1).* I learned that the ability to truly "cleanse ourselves" is the fruit of the work God accomplishes in His people, for *"the blood of Jesus Christ His Son cleanseth us from all sin. (1 Jn. 1:7). "For we are His workmanship, created in Christ Jesus unto good works" (Eph. 2:10).* So we can draw near in *full assurance of faith* with a clean conscience, for He is faithful (Heb. 10:22).

He transforms people for His name sake and for the sake of godliness, so that they cannot continue in a perpetual pattern of sin. They can no longer in good conscience join a false religion or stay in one once they learn the truth. They can no longer in good conscience sit thru heretical Bible studies, for He calls them out. Though it takes them a while to discern the leading of their Savior, once they do, they will not be led by another spirit (Jn.10). They'd rather suffer *"without the camp, bearing His reproach" (Heb. 13:13).*

God is jealous of His worship, and commands that it not be mixed with false religion. *"For thou shalt worship no other god: for the Lord, Whose name is Jealous, is a jealous God" (Ex. 34:14). "Do we provoke the Lord to jealousy? are we stronger than He" (1 Cor. 10:21-22)?*

According to God's Word, Paul feared his people might *"put up with"* false teachers who proclaim a false Jesus and a false gospel (2 Cor. 11:1-4), because it would indicate that their mind had been corrupted and subtly deceived by the devil, even if they had so much as simply *tolerated* such. Paul grieved jealously for his people, for he knew that if they turned from the true gospel that he was giving them, they would turn to fatally deceived deceivers, and ultimately end up turning from God (2 Tim. 3:13).

Jesus said we cannot serve two masters (Mt. 6:24). We're either slaves to sin or slaves to righteousness (Rom. 6:19). There are no lukewarm in-betweens. This same warning is reiterated in 2 John vv. 9-11, which exclaims that we're not even supposed to give deceivers a *greeting* (in a way that would be approving their false doctrine), or we'll be *"a partaker of their evil deeds."* That's how *serious* God's pure worship is. Jesus revealed that those who worship Him *must* worship Him in spirit and in truth (Jn. 4:23-24).

Thankfully He rescues His people from all the messes they are born into or get themselves into, so that they can worship Him in truth. My own conversion is proof that God's sheep *will* be enabled to believe His truth and *will* be granted genuine repentance so necessary to escape deadly error.

Sometimes it's a slow, painful process, because doctrines of devils can take time to dislodge (Mt. 17:21). Many kick against the pricks of the heart for a very long time, but God has His way, for He cannot be hindered by any amount of so-called "freewill" (Acts 26:14-18). Jesus *actively* rescues His sheep and doesn't *passively* allow any to perish (Mt. 18:11-13).

Once the CoC stained lenses fell from my eyes like scales, I was able to devour God's Word through the right biblical lens. The Lord led me to such a deep, intense study of His Word and a profound spiritual union with Him in prayer, that I was finally able to express heartfelt love and gratitude back to my Savior for all that He had done for me. My conscience was finally purged from dead works so that I could serve the living God (Heb. 9:14)!

"God forbid that I should boast except in the cross of our Lord Jesus Christ, by Whom the world has been crucified to me, and I to the world." (Gal. 6:14, NKJV). I was no longer driven by legalistic fear and the impossible burden of trying to maintain my own salvation, while simultaneously trying to maintain the world's approval. So I was finally able to care for the souls of others. Like the woman at the well who left her water pot to proclaim the true Christ, after discovering His ability to satisfy her thirst (Jn. 4:1-42), I too left the water gospel that could never quench my spiritual thirst, to proclaim the true Christ, and to serve Him and others from a regenerated heart full of love and peace. For I finally understood and knew the true God and Savior!

"Let him that glorieth glory in this, that he understandeth and knoweth Me"
(Jer. 9:24).

Notes:

[1] Charles Haddon Spurgeon, Sermon on Baptismal Regeneration. Retrieved August 29, 2018 from: https://www.reformedreader.org/spurgeon/1864-02.htm

[2] For a deeper study of 2 Peter 2:1, see: John Owens, *The Death of Death in the Death of Christ,* (Carlisle, PA: The Banner of Truth Trust, 1999), pp. 250-256.

Chapter 12

Painful Persecutions

"Am I therefore become your enemy, because I tell you the truth?" (Gal. 4:16)

As all of the heavy CoC burdens were being lifted off of me, I began to manifest the Heavenly power and evidence of the gospel upon my soul by finally being able to love and forgive others, for I myself had personally experienced unconditional forgiveness and eternal peace through Jesus.

God's love even enabled me to go to my ex and his wife, to forgive them for all they had done, and to apologize for how I had reacted to it years ago. I also began praying for their salvation and sharing the gospel with them every chance I got, even as he was dying of cancer...taking his last breaths. For by a miracle of God's divine providence, the Catholic priest didn't show up in time to perform the sacrament of "Extreme Unction" or "Last Rites."

I also forgave my parents for disowning me and I apologized for ever rebelling against them. Since I'd been strengthened by the Holy Spirit in the knowledge of the true Christ and eternal God, I zealously labored to present Him to the conscience of others, so that they too could find joy in the truth. But, sadly, I soon found out that most did not share my enthusiasm.

As I continued to walk in the revelation of God's Word, with evidence and confirmation from Heaven that I belonged to Him, it became so obvious in my life that I also became a target for the witchdoctors and faith healers I had been involved with. When I shared the true gospel with them and encouraged them to re-evaluate their strange spiritual practices, they singled me out as being demon possessed, while those cheating on their spouses in those circles were still being "prophesied over" as having special spiritual powers, which was another real eye-opener for me!

My old friends were also some of the first to notice a change in me once I was strengthened in Christ. When my life was falling apart they were there, but once I found joy and peace in Jesus, they wanted nothing to do with me. Misery loves company. But the worldly, ungodly mindset that had once united us as friends was no longer there. They resented that I loved talking more about God than the latest gossip or my latest crisis. Some were even offended when I would express my desire to stand for the cause of Christ. For they were accustomed to following the crowd and were not willing to give up anything for Christ. And some were just simply annoyed when I would try to get it across that we all needed to make sure we were truly right with God through Christ, for they were like, *"been there, done that,"* and just wanted to get on with their lives and do their own thing.

If only they had realized, *"Faithful are the wounds of a friend; but the kisses of an enemy are deceitful"* (Prov. 27:5-6). But, sadly, instead of recognizing the true enemy of their soul, they turned on me, and so far, have remained a reflection of all that I had been before Christ saved and changed me. Though some continued to be "religious," the Bible was the last thing they wanted to talk about, unless it was just on a superficial level.

Those who are of the world love the pleasures of this life so much more and cannot relate to the severe chastening God often puts His people thru to wean them from the world. They resent when old friends are no longer interested in running headlong with them into worldly indulgences. But James said whoever is a friend of the world is an enemy of God (Jas. 4:4).

My CoC family also began to notice a change in me and most despised it. Since we were taught doctrine contrary to the truth of Jesus satisfying divine justice for the sins of His people, they were shocked and offended to find out that I believed Jesus had done just that for me.

So my faith in Jesus' righteousness as my only hope was assaulted with great force and fury. But since they were unable to biblically refute the truth that I shared with them, they resorted to plots to try to undermine my credibility. I was also accused of being prideful for believing I was saved. And even if that had been the case, it was all still a meaningless response to the gospel I shared, and was such a disgrace on their professed religiosity.

Then some, who seemed eager to learn the truth, were turned against me, which resembled the scenario in Acts 13:6-12, about those who were initially open to truth, but were turned against it. Even in Acts 17:13, the self-righteous Jews stirred people against the truth and those proclaiming it. No wonder my parents informed me that I was not going to be in their will.

If it had not been for Jesus' words, *"ye shall be hated of all men for My name's sake"* (Mt. 10:22), I would not have known why I had become a target for such hostility against the gospel of Christ. Thankfully, the shield of faith quenched all the fiery darts as Jesus gave me the strength to endure, by reminding me through His Word that He experienced the same. Even His own earthly relatives thought that He had lost His mind (Mk. 3:21; 6:4).

The ancient Pharisees were offended also, for like the CoC, they didn't want to be justified by faith in Jesus' righteousness alone either, for they too had faith in their own system of works. So I was not only considered a traitor, but was also treated as if I was completely ignorant of what the CoC actually teaches, because the veil was still over their eyes, making them unable to fully comprehend the heretical implications of their own beliefs.

For this reason, most of my CoC family (on both sides) has been cut off from me by their bondage to the church. And this is why they have been the hardest to reach. Because love for a false religious system is always characterized by antagonism on a personal level toward any who present the truth. CoC adherents often identify their dislike of the Christian message with the messenger themselves. For many, who are enslaved in false religion, to admit their religion is false seems equivalent to admitting God isn't true, for their system becomes a god to them. This is why it's typical for them to expel and shun those who begin to think independently, which can be very frightening to someone who is not willing to give up all for Christ.

This is also why so many remain in the system, even when they finally realize that it's wrong. *"Many believed on him; but because of the Pharisees they did not confess him, lest they should be put out of the synagogue: For they loved the praise of men more than the praise of God"* (Jn. 12:42).

Some just didn't want to risk all of the persecution they seen me going through. They cared more about family ties and careers. After all, it's hard to get and keep a high position and good reputation in an area dominated by a religiously abhorrent power structure if you are one that goes up against such ungodly conformity. So, many stay in the CoC, even after learning how blasphemous it is against the true gospel of Jesus Christ.

And Jesus is ashamed of those who are ashamed of Him (Mk. 8:38), for they *"have no root in themselves, and so endure only for a time. Afterward, when tribulation or persecution arises for the Word's sake, immediately they stumble"* (Mk. 4:17, NKJV). Many care more about people's approval than God's approval. And most just simply cannot come to grips with the fact that they've been deceived by false religion. This, however, is no excuse to play the victim, for it is voluntary rebellion against God, Who will still hold people accountable for their involvement and need for repentance.

Ezekiel 18 was also brought to my attention by a CoC member who said it proved that we should be able to conjure up faith, repentance and obedience to God *in our own power.* Of course those verses came as no surprise, since I too had struggled with them and many others when I was in the CoC. So I tried to gently get it across that God presents His impossible commands so that we would despair of ever being able to live up to His standards; so that confidence in our own self-sufficiency would be shattered in order for us to finally realize our desperate need for the Savior (2 Cor. 3:5). But they took it wrong and reprimanded me for giving up on myself! And when they condescendingly said that they would pray for me, I asked, "Why bother, if you don't believe God has to intervene in our lives?" Eerily, one could have heard the sound of crickets...*for they could not answer!*

Ezekiel 2:1-2 makes it clear that God grants His people what He commands, for He knows that we are helpless apart from His divine intervention. Ezekiel 18 is also a perfect example of how God deals with His people. He commands them to do the impossible. For instance, in vv. 30-32, He challenges His people to *"turn themselves"* and to *make themselves* a new heart and a new spirit. God tells them to do what He already knew they could never do apart from His divine intervention. Even in Ezekiel 3:7, He tells His prophet from the very start that these people would not listen, for they were hard-hearted. So I was asked why God even bothered telling His people what to do when He already knew they couldn't do it.

I showed them that by reading the whole book of Ezekiel, *in context*, the answer becomes obvious. God did this so His people would realize that they did not have the innate power to save themselves. And when His people accused Him of being unfair, He revealed even more of His glory by making it clear that He could destroy them all and still be just. Because, like all of us, they deserved the eternal consequences of sinning against their eternal Creator (Ezek. 18:25, 29). *"For whosoever shall keep the whole law, and yet offend in one point, he is guilty of all" (Jas. 2:10).*

But they rejected this great Christian truth and even became psychotic when I showed them that Ezekiel 36 makes it clear that God Himself has to grant a new heart and a new spirit. So I then tried to comfort them with the fact that God also shows that He is full of mercy and grace by revealing that He can change the most repulsive sinner in order to reveal His glory. And again, I went to vv. 26-27, to show that God tells His people that He is the

One Who gives a new heart and a new spirit. Even from the get-go, God showed them that they'd only have the power to obey His commands once He put a new heart and spirit in them, for He wanted them to know that the power was all of Him, not of themselves (Ezek. 11:19-20). For no one has power within their own fallen natures to do this. But these truths cannot penetrate the minds of those who are still tied to their legalistic roots.

Naturally, legalists refuse to give up anything they think they can bring to the table. But Ezekiel is just another beautiful reminder of how God's mighty power can triumph over our sin nature and make us partakers of His divine nature. Just as Jesus commanded Lazarus' dead body to come forth, He still commands sinners who are dead in sins and trespasses to do the impossible....to repent and believe the gospel. And the same power He gave Lazarus is the same power He gives His people to triumph today.

What's impossible for us is not impossible with God. By His grace, we must come to Him, confessing our helplessness; placing our trust in Him alone to give us the new heart and spirit that we so desperately need to be saved. And we must keep coming to Him; praying, reading His Word, worshipping and communing with His people, until we know beyond the shadow of a doubt that He has changed us and that we are forever His.

Thankfully, God helped me through a period of grieving over the loss of the worlds praise and approval as I was coming out of false religion. And rather than allowing persecution to draw me away from the gospel of grace back into perdition, God gave me the courage to suffer for His name sake.

He also enabled me to finally put all the pieces together that have kept me from ever clinging to CoC lies ever again, which had previously shipwrecked any possibility of saving faith in God and Jesus. But there are those who would rather be bound for Hell than to believe their religion is false. They'll often even say that they would never worship a God Who chooses His own, and will even accuse Him of being unrighteous for doing so, which Apostle Paul obviously anticipated when he wrote Romans 9.14.

This also happened with the multitude of superficial followers that turned away from Jesus once He let them know that the Father chooses His own and draws them to Him for salvation (Jn. 6:65-66). But in order to try to keep from being associated with these surface-level believers, the CoC takes the *drawing* here and tries to connect it with John 12:32, where it says Christ will *draw all men* to Himself when He is lifted up on the cross.

But the CoC's interpretation has Christ drawing all men without exclusion, which would make the entirety of Scripture non-sensical. The cross does NOT draw all people, for it is a stumbling block for some and foolishness to others (1 Cor. 1:22-24). Moreover, the CoC's eisegesis (reading into the text) begs the question as to why *all* the multitude were not drawn savingly to Christ, but only a select few who had been *"taught of God" (Jn. 6:45).* The answer is that Jesus didn't mean *all* without exception, but *all* without distinction of race, gender, status quo, works, etc. *"God is no respecter of persons" (Acts 10:34, Mt. 22:16)*, for He chooses His own apart from any earthly distinctions. Yet the CoC claims the opposite.

Thankfully, God helped me to understand why the CoC would always give lip service to God's sovereignty in everything, *except* in the salvation of His people. Strangely enough, it had limited God's freewill by teaching *the absurd impossibility that He "sovereignly forfeited His sovereignty" over human freewill.* Because false religion is fine with a surface-level faith that follows Christ for His earthly benefits as long as it's a superficial "freewill" following that can take personal credit for doing so. That's why its battle cry seems to ever be... *"We will not have this man to reign over us" (Lk. 19:14).*

"There is no doctrine more hated by worldlings, no truth of which they have made such a football, as the great, stupendous, but yet most certain doctrine of the Sovereignty of the infinite Jehovah. Men will allow God to be everywhere except upon His throne. They will allow Him to be in His workshop to fashion worlds and to make stars. They will allow Him to be in His almonry to dispense His alms and bestow His bounties. They will allow Him to sustain the earth...but when God ascends His throne, His creatures then gnash their teeth; and when we proclaim an enthroned God, and His right to do as He wills with His own, to dispose of His creatures as He thinks well, without consulting them in the matter, then it is that we are hissed and execrated [despised], and then it is that men turn a deaf ear to us, for God on His throne is not the God they love." (*Divine Sovereignty*, a sermon delivered by Charles Haddon Spurgeon on May 4, 1856, brackets mine).

God has gloriously preserved His complete freedom and sovereignty without giving up one ounce of it just because we have fallen from His glory. And Jesus is *willing* and *able* to save all who truly come to Him. Then His Word to them is: *"Behold, I send you forth as sheep in the midst of wolves: be ye therefore wise as serpents, and harmless as doves (Mt. 10:16).*

Chapter 13

Standing Alone at a Crossroads

*... "he that taketh not his cross, and
followeth after Me, is not worthy of Me"(Mt. 10:38).*

Soon after I graduated college and finished a year of homeschooling the boys, I ended up counseling in an ecumenical, *interfaith* organization that claimed to be Christian. But I soon found out the hard way that it was actually a "faith-based" catalyst for trafficking every wind of doctrine, which had created a melting pot for all false religions to come together.

So it was no wonder that I met up with others from the CoC there too, for all *consistently* Arminian religions are prophetically gravitating back to their roots through the Ecumenical Movement, led by Romanism. For the so-called "mother church" of Rome is the predecessor of their adulterated theology. And this is why they are all gradually ditching peripheral differences and uniting on the false "freewill" doctrine in a rampage against the *absolute* freedom of God, which they cannot tolerate.

There I encountered yet another diluted version of the gospel, with no emphasis on sin and judgment. So I met clients who had been coming there for years, who revealed to me that they had never been informed that those who practice fornication and adultery cannot enter God's kingdom (1 Cor. 6:9-11). One had even been living with someone else's husband for years, while still claiming to be saved! I found out the center had just kept boosting their self-esteem, reassuring them of salvation and handing them goods donated by churches that supposedly stood against such things!

Because, like many so-called "nonprofit" parachurches, they act independently from any authoritative oversight or discipline from the congregations they are wrenching resources from. But sadly, I also found that many of those who should be shepherding their flock, would rather put the unwanted off on parachurches, in order to focus more on "staff retreats," false or foreign missions, or on providing carnal programs that appease the goats that torment the true sheep in their churches.

So, as God strengthened me in the true gospel, I labored to hold forth Jesus Christ in all of His glory, and I prayed for the grace to discern, expose and remove all of the false supports that the world leans so heavily upon. I also ditched all of the psychotherapy that left clients even worse off than when they came in. And no wonder, for the standard seventy-one page *Volunteer Training Manual* devoted only two pages to a diluted gospel message, which was presented more as an afterthought than a priority.₁

So I biblically counseled unmarried couples who were living together, to either separate and abstain, or get married, based on what would honor God and their profession of faith, not merely what would be "in their best interests." Predictably, I was interrogated by leadership for sharing the true gospel, though their blood would be on my hands if I didn't (Ezek. 3:20). It was the typical, out-of-context *"judge not, lest you be judged"* scenario. And, ironically, I was being wrongfully judged as being judgmental!

Although Jesus did not come to judge the world during His incarnation, He came to proclaim that there would come a time when He *will* judge the world (2 Tim. 4:1). And this is why it's every Christian's duty to love others enough to let them know that His judgment has already been determined and that during this dispensation of grace He still offers escape from the penalty and judgment that sin is due (Jn. 3:18).

Yet when so-called faith-based operations leave out the truth about sin and judgment, it shows that they are not working under the operation of the Holy Spirit Who comes to reprove the world of sin, righteousness and judgment (Jn. 16:8). So they leave people with no reason to turn to Christ for salvation. Instead, they lead them to a false christ that praises self-esteem, cultivates pride and allows them to indulge in a sinful lifestyle.

The motto of false converts is, *"We are delivered to do all these abominations" (Jer. 7:10).* Some even try to compare apples to oranges by misusing Romans 14 or Colossians 2:21 as an excuse to indulge in illicit sins that have nothing to do with liberty of conscience issues. And one should *never* tempt God by trying to use the excuse that it's only His job to convict of sin, for He uses *means*...biblical correction, human accountability, etc.

However, conscience searing procedures are often performed through spiritually dangerous counseling and "prayer techniques" that are similar to occult practices and secular psychotherapy, which is highly encouraged in Arminian circles. But they are often "Christianized" under terms such as

"Soaking Prayer" contemplative meditation, etc., where one's *unconscious* or *subconscious* "needs" are brought to the surface, to expose causes of "unproductive behavior" that keep one from living up to ones "full-potential." So the main focus is always upon *self...* not God. And Scripture strongly warns against self-worship (e.g. Rom. 12:3, Phil. 2:3, 2 Tim. 3:2).

False religious systems promote the idea that one "gets in a bad situation" because their needs are not met, and portrays Jesus as a genie in a bottle. However, Scripture reveals that Adam, Eve and even Satan himself had everything one could ever ask for, and yet, they *still* rebelled against God! So Jesus let multitudes know that their only hope was for God the Father to draw them to Him *the true Christ*, to teach them that they needed eternal riches more than earthly treasures (Jn. 6:44-65). But superficial followers don't want to hear it and so they end up walking away (v. 66).

Scripture makes it clear that *sin* is humanity's problem, not "unconscious needs" or low self-esteem. The last thing we need is self-ascension. We tend to love ourselves too much, which is one reason we make bad choices. The *heart* (which is the seat of our conscience, thoughts, emotions and choices), must be made anew by a supernatural act of God, due to the effects of being spiritually deadened by sin. Although we don't have the ability to do this ourselves, it does not excuse us from being responsible toward God, for we are still *fully* conscious, self-aware and *actively* rebellious. He does not lower His standard just because we are fallen.

This is why we need the Savior, Who lived up to God's perfect standard of righteousness *perfectly*. Our rescue is not about *self*-realization of conscious or unconscious needs that must be "psychoanalyzed" or used as excuses not to be accountable to God for our *active,* self-centered sinfulness. Behavior modification only suppresses the truth in unrighteousness (Rom. 1:18).

Yet occult practices, such as "Sozo Prayer," are still being slipped into many churches and organizations, like the one I had become a part of. This type of regression therapy (as It's referred to in secular circles) was renamed Theophostic Prayer in 1996 by Ed Smith of *Campbells*ville, KY (the irony), in order to try to hide its psychotherapy origins. But he ended up having to adjust his "inner healing" ideas and pull his suspect training manuals off the market when *False Memory Syndrome* was occurring with clients. Sadly, damages were so severe that Sozo "counselors" today have to get clients to sign a disclaimer so that they will not be held legally liable.

The inner healing movement is founded upon the lie that one can use their imagination to hear from God. And the counseling techniques used to conjure up these experiences are the same ones used in the occult, mainly, "guided imagery" and "visualization." The mediators who assist these experiences are sometimes called "theo-therapists," in order to gain access within Christian circles. It is just another attempt to Christianize a man-made system based on false, psycho-therapeutic theories, which is another fulfillment of prophecy that the Bible warns about (e.g. Acts 20:28-30).

The mission of every born-again believer is to earnestly warn others of God's impending judgment on such practices, and to keep proclaiming the solid, theological foundation of the true gospel; so that those who *love the truth* will be able to discern a counterfeit gospel a mile away, which is all "theo-therapy" really is (2 Thess. 2:9-10). The shabby theology behind this form of psychology is a major cause of mental and spiritual damage. And, sad to say, many never come out of the deception once they've been fooled by the placebo effects that pop psychology produces.

When the Holy Spirit truly convicts us of sin, we are led to go to God for mercy, and to humbly ask Him for all we need to be saved. Only then can we truly comprehend by faith that Jesus' blood was shed to cover our sins and reconcile us to God. But the complicated methods and techniques of man have no power to spiritually transform anyone, no matter how sincere the motives. But the power of the *true* gospel does (Rom. 1:16, 2 Cor. 11:3). Because the true gospel of God's grace, and those who proclaim it, are the means that God has ordained to set His people free.

True Christianity is the only religion in the world that's based solely on salvation by grace alone, through faith alone, in Jesus alone. All others are centered upon externals rather than inward change. In fact, every false religion in the world is built upon that same legalistic foundation. The only difference is that they all just build upon it *differently;* depending on what each sect thinks are the most important externals *"for obtaining full salvation."* Some think it's snake handling, some think it's baptism, and others think it's wearing certain clothes or choosing certain types of transportation. Then again, some think it's "deliverance techniques."

"Beware lest any man spoil you through philosophy and vain deceit, after the tradition of men, after the rudiments of the world, and not after Christ" (Col. 2:8). Salvation is of the Lord and He finishes the good work He begins

in His people, so that they don't have to be made complete and whole by their own efforts or the works of a "theo-therapist" or "life coach" (Ps. 37:39-40, Phil. 1:6). Those who are born again by His Spirit *"are complete in Him, which is the head of all principality and power" (Col. 2:10).*

Humanistic psychology is based on the godless imaginations of atheists, such as Sigmund Freud, who, like most unswerving Arminians, *hated* the absolute sovereignty of God and the biblical concept of sin. Though the CoC claims that confessions of faith (or creeds) are nothing more than man-made opinions, it has the audacity to incorporate into its ministries, the unbiblical opinions of *pseudo-science*, which is defined as: "a system of theories, assumptions, and methods erroneously regarded as scientific."[2]

The Bible warns against *"science falsely so-called" (1 Tim. 6:20)* and tells us to avoid it. True science can be measured, studied, tested, repeated, observed and verified. Yet--

"Psychotherapy escapes the rigors of science because the mind is not equal to the brain and man is not a machine. The actual foundations of psychotherapy are not science, but rather various philosophical world views, especially those of determinism, secular humanism, behaviorism, existentialism, and even evolutionism. Its influence has not been confined to the therapist's office, for its varied explanations of human behavior and contradictory ideas for change have permeated both society and the church."[3]

It is a solemn, Christian duty to warn others of *God's* judgment, and to discern between good and evil according to His truth, which is based solely upon the objective Word of God, not the subjective experiences and opinions of man that are slyly designed to explain away sin.

It's expected that secular organizations will fall in with the world, but those who bear the title "Christian" have a stewardship to uphold, and *"it's required of stewards that one be found faithful"* (1 Cor. 4:2), not to a political or secular worldview, but to a biblical worldview.

If we are going to be faithful Christians, we must *"try the spirits,"* due to spiritual wickedness in high places (Eph. 6:12, 1 Jn. 4:1). We must even be willing to leave high positions for the sake of Christ. And we need to know exactly what people mean by what they say. Because even though they use the same Christian terminology, the words mean something totally different to other so-called "faiths" that promote secular salvation.

"The enticement of the "all truth is God's truth" fallacy is that there is some similarity between biblical teachings and psychological ideas. But similarities do not make psychology compatible with Christianity. They only emphasize the fact that the systems of psychological counseling are religious rather than scientific. Just as the various world religions include glimpses or elements of truth and just as Satan's words to Eve in the Garden contained some truth, so do psychological opinions of men."[4]

Christianized secularism is hostile to the gospel, for it takes snippets of truth from Scripture and pulls them out of context to make it seem as though God approves of "bringing Heaven to earth" through social and political reform, rather than *bringing people to Christ* through the gospel. This is why biblical exegesis is *so crucial,* for Jesus taught us to **affirm** in prayer that... *God's will is being done on earth, just as it is in heaven* (Lk. 11:2), not man's will to play God in people's lives. Pretending to *"be Jesus to people"* can no more change a person's heart than a leopard can change its spots (Jer. 13:23).

God's will is *already* being accomplished on earth, and His kingdom is *Not* of this world (Jn. 18:36). His people are also *in* the world, but not *of* the world. And as workers of His kingdom, we are commanded to judge with righteous judgment, according to God's will revealed in His Word (Mt. 7:6; 15-20; 23:1-36, Titus 1:15-16). So for these reasons, I had a private meeting with some leaders of the interfaith organization. For after many months and much prayer, God enabled me to discern what was really going on there.

So I asked them several different times (to try to give the benefit of the doubt) if they believed Jesus was God in the flesh, and they absolutely and evasively *refused* to answer, which confirmed what God had been showing me through His Word (1 Jn. 4:2-3). To my complete dismay, they would never directly answer the question, but would only acknowledge Him as the Son of God, which even the devil and almost every false religion will affirm.

But since they were aware of the fact that *no one can say Jesus is the Lord, except by the Holy Spirit (1 Cor. 12:3),* they made sure to give lip service to the fact that Jesus is Lord, just as many other cults will deceptively do. For example, some Word of Faith teachers will *say* He is Lord, but then turn right around and reveal the *real* "Jesus" they are serving, by claiming he was born again in Hell.₅ Some *will* even say *their* Jesus is God in the flesh, but only because they believe all people are gods! They can be so tricky!

But despite such obscurity, it still became increasingly clear that they were *not* talking about the Jesus of the Bible, for when I asked whether or not they would allow Mormons or Jehovah's Witnesses (who also believe in a different Jesus) to *spiritually* counsel clients, they said that they definitely would! That alone confirmed the organizations heretical, ecumenical agenda. It also explained why there had been such hostility against the exclusive claims of Christ and the true gospel. So much so, that cart loads of CoC, Word of Faith and every other wind of doctrine was being brought in to supersede all of the gospel tracts, videos and books that I had donated.

So in tears, I told them that I could no longer in good conscience work there and support the social engineering of such a destructive agenda against the true gospel. Although I had gone to college for seven long years just so I could go into that line of work, I had to count the cost of following Christ. So by God's grace, I was done with lesser things and was finally willing to venture all for *"the one thing needful"* (Lk. 10:41:-42).

The Lord had changed my entire worldview from that of a social, pseudo-science perspective, to a biblical perspective that could never again allow me in good conscience to compromise the truth under the false pretense of *"bringing heaven to earth,"* which would ironically mean no evangelism on earth, for everyone in Heaven is already saved! I could no longer in good conscience substitute social reform for the gospel, because Jesus encouraged gospel proclamations, not just "lifestyle demonstrations."

Only by knowing the true gospel and the true Christ of Scripture can we realize that He is worth giving up sin for, worth giving up our own will for, worth giving up careers and wealth for....worth giving up *everything* for!

"But what things were gain to me, those I counted loss for Christ...I count all things but loss for the excellency of the knowledge of Christ Jesus my Lord: for Whom I have suffered the loss of all things, and do count them but dung, that I may win Christ, and be found in Him, not having mine own righteousness, which is of the law, but that which is through the faith of Christ, the righteousness which is of God by faith. That I may know Him, and the power of His resurrection, and the fellowship of His sufferings, being made conformable unto His death; if by any means I might attain unto the resurrection of the dead" (Phil. 3:7-11).

Notes:

[1] To learn more about this resource go to:
https://222.carenetu.org/library/caringfoundations/about/
---Also see: George Grant, *Third Time Around: A History of the Pro-Life Movement from the First Century to the Present,* (Brentwood, TN: Wolgemuth & Hyatt Publishers, Inc., 1991). Page 126 reveals where the CoC system went wrong on the abortion issue. His book also reveals how the pro-life movement went completely off the tracks when it ditched true Christianity and began pushing a Romanist, social and political gospel. Thus, it became a wicked force against true Christians who want to condemn and abolish abortion from being sanctioned under law.

Also see: EndAbortionNow.com---A Christian movement that offers adoption and exposes the political, pro-life stance led by Rome which claims many "victories," but in reality, it has only exacerbated the problem and has become an even worse enemy against Christians than pro-choicers, because it lumps true Christians in with the hateful Westboro Baptist type. It also exposes how many Crisis Pregnancy Centers subtly marginalize and criminalize Christians who lovingly proclaim the *true* gospel to hearts that have been hardened by the sanctioning of abortion under law.

Rome's repulsive facade even exploits people's emotions through "Christian" movies, such as *Unplanned (*Abby Johnson is actually Rome's *controlled opposition*), where we are falsely portrayed as judgmental. It also strips resources from local churches in order to rally for ultra-sounds, CPC funding, etc...but NOT for the abolishment of abortion! It claims that a better option is to come along side the murder-minded without being "judgmental." As a result, it emboldens hearts to do even more evil, by catering to felt needs, rather than spiritual needs through the *true* gospel. By not warning people of their accountability to God, and by not criminalizing murder, it dishonors God and does way more harm than good (Eccl. 8:11, Rom. 13: 1-4, 1 Pet. 2:13-14). See Rome's YouTube channel, EWTN, for more evidence. Also see Justin Peters' blog at: https://justinpeters.org/2015/09/war-room-a-review/ on the spiritual dangers of the so-called "Christian" movie industry, which tugs at people's heart strings instead of leading them to the true gospel.

[2] *Websters New Collegiate Dictionary*, (Springfield, MA: G. & C. Merriam Company, 1974).

[3] Martin and Deidre Bobgan, *Prophets of Psychoheresy I*, (Santa Barbara, CA: EastGate Publishers, 1989), pp. 24, 25.

[4] *Ibid.,* p. 332.

[5] See: CAnswersTV YouTube channel playlist entitled, "Dealing with Phony Word-Faith TV Preachers (TBN) & King James Onlyites at:
https://www.youtube.com/playlist?list=PL2CDA855486B09128&feature=plcp

Chapter 14

"Politically Correct" Theology

"He who trusts in his own heart is a fool" (Prov. 28:26).

Recently, a local "Church of Christ" sign stated: "The pulpit is no place for politics." Yet, ironically, a few weeks later the same sign stated: "Choice not chance determines our destiny," which revealed a type of political theology, because in politics a person is voted into office. The candidate plays no part except for offering themselves for election, while voter's make their independent choice. So the irony is that by promoting such lies, the evil spirit behind the CoC system portrays Jesus as a passive candidate for election, as if we are to just campaign to win votes or random "decisions for Christ," which would also ironically imply that the results *are* by chance! [1]

One of the CoC's favorite worn out cliché's is that "God votes for you, the devil votes against you, and which way you vote determines where you will go."[2] This is one way it promotes a "general election," where all are given an "equal chance," for it hates the biblical doctrine of *unconditional* election, which glorifies *God's* sovereign choice (e.g. Rom. 8:33; 9:11, 1 Pet. 1:2).

According to the *true* gospel, we can't vote God's Son into office as our Savior. On the contrary, we are at His mercy, for all of our natural attempts to gain favor with God are futile. Furthermore, Ecclesiastes 9:11 reveals that, *"the race is not to the swift, nor the battle to the strong, neither yet bread to the wise, nor yet riches to men of understanding, nor yet favor to men of skill; but time and...chance happens to them all."*

Amazingly, God is sovereign over choice *and* chance, for they are both included in God's divinely ordained means for bringing about His purposes (e.g. Prov. 16:9, 33, Ps. 37:23). Even the very hairs on our head and the days of our life are all numbered and ordered by God (e.g. Mt. 5:36; 10:30, Job 14:5). Or else He wouldn't be God and He wouldn't be all-knowing.

Yet fallen humanity would rather have the upper hand, call all the shots and make all the decisions. Although they constantly fight for their political right to "choose," they have the audacity to suggest that the sovereign God of the Universe doesn't even have the right to choose His own Bride (His Church, His Body, the Elect).₃

God has clearly chosen those who are able to approach Him, for He's the One Who has enabled them to do so (e.g. Ps. 65:4). Our destiny doesn't ride on us, or else we'd be captains of our salvation and masters of our own souls (Heb. 2:10). In other words, we'd be God. But thankfully we're not! Or else we would have no hope at all, which is why God's eternal plan of redemption reveals that He alone is God, and that Jesus is an actual, powerful Savior based on His promises, not a powerless, "potential" Savior.

Jesus isn't passive as His Word goes forth. He *actively* works with and through His Word, while visiting sinners with salvation by working faith in them and drawing them in mercy to Himself. Far from just standing by, while watching His people "freely" choose Hell, Jesus lovingly pursues and *rescues* His lost sheep (Mt. 18:11-14), by delivering them from the bondage of sin. He never leaves them to their own "freewill," which is nothing but "freedom" to choose evil and reject God, which is not true freedom at all.

God's free grace enables us to love Him more than sin, for whoever the Son sets free is free indeed (Jn. 8:36). His blood doesn't potentially save, based on our "choice," but effectually saves, based on His promise. Not so we'd become robots, but so we could know the joy of *true* freedom, which isn't the ability to choose good *or evil*, or else God Himself wouldn't be free, for He can't choose to be evil. True freedom is the God-given ability to hate evil and to love Him Who is completely free because He is completely sinless. So, indeed, God does set before us life and death (Deut. 30:19). But only when the Holy Spirit applies the benefits of Jesus' sacrifice to one's life, can one *choose life* by truly believing, repenting and obeying the gospel.

But since these truths were missing in the CoC, it's no wonder we were duped into the "bringing heaven to earth" agenda to institute subjective morality. Because we didn't understand that only God can transform people's souls, change hearts and renew minds, not social reform. Making the world a better place for heathens to go to Hell from... *is not the answer.*

"When believers become confused about what God has called us to do—when they make moralizing society their top priority—they abandon their true mission. When the church elevates the pursuit of cultural morality above the biblical mandate to proclaim the gospel, it essentially forfeits its distinctive voice and takes its place among a myriad of lobbyist groups and political parties peddling earthly agendas. Heaven's agenda is summed up in the Great Commission; it is the task of evangelism, not political and moral reform."[4]

This reminds me of another photo that I obtained of a local CoC sign that said: "The Great Hope of Society is Individual Character." I could barely believe my eyes! But it should not have surprised me, for secular humanism is the driving force behind false religious systems that don't uphold the true gospel, which makes any mutual mission with them absolutely impossible without compromising the truth and dishonoring Christ.

Jesus is the great hope of society...*Not* mankind! Christians are to be united by believing and trusting in the *true* Jesus of the Bible and *"all the counsel of God" (Acts 20:27)*, not just a narrow focus on a "common cause" at the expense of truth. However, a tower of Babel is being re-built, where "unity" with falsehood is taking center-stage over and against a reverent fear of God, Who happens to hate false doctrine (Rev. 2:15). A narcissistic society where self-esteem or "individual character" takes precedence over Christ as our only hope... is a *hopeless society!*

All one has to do is look at the roots and fruits of behavior modification to see that it is *Not* "the great hope of society." Though the CoC bears the name of Christ, it denies Him by emphasizing self-love, rather than self-sacrifice. Scripture is clear, that to truly love our own soul we must hate sin. Those who love sin are actually hating their own souls (Prov. 15:32, 19:8). And so, to truly *"love others as ourselves,"* we must warn them about sin.

It's no coincidence that abortion rates have skyrocketed since the so-called pro-life movement, headed by Rome, began to propagate its false gospel and political theology to abortion-minded women, dealing with them as victims, rather than those who want their child killed, while women who hire hit-men to kill their husbands are still rightly prosecuted as murderers.

Even atheists have the audacity to borrow from the Christian worldview to say rape is wrong and that females have rights (*unless* they are in the womb of course). Many ignorantly think that it is okay to kill a baby if it's conceived through rape, or they think baby killing should be "safe." But one must ask... should rape also be made safe for the rapist? Of course not! How ridiculous! Yet this is how inconsistently insane secular moralism gets, for it is not built upon the Scriptural consistency of absolute truth.

From God's point of view, no one will be considered victims of circumstance on judgment day, for all have fallen short of His glory and will be held accountable for their own sins....*unless Jesus has rescued them.* However, when religious racketeers portray Jesus as an "inner healing tool" for "victims," or when His unique nature and Deity is downplayed, denied or usurped by those who would rather dethrone Him and exalt their own "freewill".... *the natural outcome is complete lunacy!*

This is why there is now a collective banner under which biblical churches across the nation are uniting against Rome's false gospel and false pro-life party that sinfully sells "indulgences" to women who commit murder. True Christians are calling abortion what it really is. And instead of fostering a victim mentality, they are calling murderers to repentance, so that they can be directed to Christ as their only hope of walking in newness of life and the true joy of God's forgiveness. Because so-called "Crisis Pregnancy Centers," headed by Rome, have been nothing but a complete failure, by contributing to the problem with a false gospel that exalts self-will over God's will.

True forgiveness can only be found in the *true gospel*, not a false one that says we can have our "best life now," which prompts women to pursue personal goals at the expense of another. The gospel of Christ, laying His life down for His people, is what prompts them to reciprocate and lay their lives down for others. The power of the *true* gospel keeps women from aborting, inspires parents to raise godly children and brings God glory...*Not* "individual character." "Let God be true, but every man a liar" (Rom. 3:4).

Notes:

[1] Allen Webster, *If Jesus Was Running For President Would He Win?* Volume 21, Issue # 5, pp. 1-2. Retrieved May 3, 2018 from: https://housetohouse.com/wp-content/uploads/2016/09/v21n5.pdf

[2] Flavil Yeakley, *Why They Left*, (Nashville, TN: Gospel Advocate Co., 2012), p. 159.

[3] For proof, see: Allen Webster, *Why Would God Want to Save Someone Like Me?* Volume 20, Issue # 5, pp. 1-2. Retrieved May 3, 2018 from: https://housetohouse.com/wp-content/uploads/2016/02/v20n2.pdf

[4] John MacArthur, *Can God Bless America?* (Nashville, TN: The W Publishing Group, 2002), p. 85.

Chapter 15

Ecumenical Anarchy

"Ye cannot drink the cup of the Lord, and the cup of devils: ye cannot be partakers of the Lord's table, and of the table of devils" (1 Cor. 10:21).

Many politically controversial organizations, such as "Crisis Pregnancy Centers," are headed mainly by the Roman Catholic Church, and have only a Christian front, with a fully political agenda.[1] Some even seem sincere in their motives, but only give lip service to the gospel, while striving endlessly to maintain the public image of their "ministry," just so they can get financial support from local churches. Some are even experts at using Christian terminology, but in practice it's something else altogether.

This is where godly discernment is needed. Although the pro-life stance is Christian-based, not all of its supporters and outreaches are. So, many churches may be unknowingly funding a political and possibly interfaith, ecumenical agenda, thinking they are donating their time and money to a purely Christian cause, when it is actually a waste of the churches resources.

"Our energies should not be spent just trying to make sinners better people. We need to be telling them the solution to sin and the way of salvation." "Moralism is a religion devoid of theology. For the most part, the Religious Right in America has nothing to do with theology. That is by design. The Religious Right is a coalition of people who share a basic political conservatism but often have little in common theologically. So they avoid dealing with theological issues. Consequently, many people in the movement are ignorant of sound doctrine, ignorant of the Scriptures, and even ignorant of the true God. They are trying to accomplish something that has no theological underpinnings. I'm concerned about efforts at morality that are not undergirded with sound theology and driven by a concern for the glory of God. Such efforts are doomed from the start, because they don't have either the right motive or the right goal."[2]

Only the true gospel has the power of God to save. Yet pressure from the world and advocates of "tolerance" (who are ironically *intolerant* of Bible-based Christianity) are forcibly causing many religious organizations to compromise their stance on truth. They've been backed into a corner to conform to a progressively, morally declining society in order to "serve" the public without offending. Jesus *is* the Rock of offense; so naturally, there will be those who are offended because of His exclusive claims in such an inclusive world (Rom. 9:33). His way is so narrow that there is no room for legalistic luggage. Jesus said, *"Enter ye in at the strait gate; for wide is the gate, and broad is the way that leadeth to destruction, and many there be which go in thereat; Because strait is the gate, and narrow is the way, which leadeth unto life, and few there be that find it"* (Mt. 7:13-14).

Outwardly, many seem to be doing good works, but the corrupt fruits of false doctrines and false political narratives that distract from the gospel will always begin to manifest when closely inspected and confronted. The good fruits that the Pharisees thought they had were not *"fruits worthy of repentance,"* for they came from a bad tree that was not made good by God. The bad tree in the Garden, with fruit that was *"pleasant to the eyes,"* was just a superficial illusion. So it is today with many who claim to have proof of their validity due to the supposed good fruits they produce.

Jesus said to *"Judge not according to appearance, but judge righteous judgment" (Jn. 7:24).* He also said that we will know others by their fruits, which includes their heretical doctrines. Although a heretical use of biblical terminology creates a veneer of "appearing good," it is rotten to the core.

This is one reason Arminianism is so dangerous and why those who follow it are perfect prey for re-absorption back into Rome. No wonder so many CoC members and ex-members are now trying to fill a spiritual void by becoming affiliated with ecumenical churches, organizations and crusades. And those who try to stand against such unholy alliances are often accused of being "divisive." When in fact, Jesus is the One Who does the dividing (Mt. 10:34-36). For we are only to be united on the true gospel.[3]

But in order to blur the lines of distinction, neutral catch phrases are often used to try to excuse being "united" on false doctrines. For instance, the phrase, "It's about a 'relationship' with God, not theology," leaves out the *theological* fact that our only hope of having a *right* relationship with God is through saving faith in the *right* Jesus and the *right* gospel! Whenever a religious group claims to have "Christ, not creeds" (like the CoC does), it is not being honest and is creating a Christ of its own.

And the neutral catch-phrase "higher power," becomes whatever one wants it to be. So if someone claims that their "higher power" is Jesus, they may still be grudgingly tolerated, *but only* if they accept other peoples "higher power" too, even if it's the Pope or the devil! Because the devil doesn't mind if we serve God as long as we serve him too. But God says we have to choose one or the other (Mt. 6:24, 1 Cor. 10:21, 2 Cor. 6:14-17).

And, sad to say, time is proving that the CoC is progressively choosing what is most *consistent* with its theology. For example, CoC author, Flavil Yeakley, encouraged people to look to the Mormons on how to evangelize, and even promoted the likes of globalist infiltrators, such as Rick Warren and Peter Wagner, who've both been Pope sympathizers and major leaders in the ecumenical "Church Growth Movement." So, naturally, Yeakley also endorsed the ecumenical "relationship, not theology" scheme. [4]

No wonder all of Yeakley's books and articles have been a pitiful attempt to explain the mass exodus that's occurring in the CoC via the ecumenical movement. He tried to prove that they can still hold to their theology while learning from and sympathizing with other "faiths." Ironically...*he was right!* Because the CoC's basic theology is the same as all other man-made religions, and can unify with them without losing its former essence.

"Although the strict-going Campbellites (the "Church of Christ" brand) consign everyone to Hell but those within their church, their basic theological views are identical with those of Roman Catholics, Episcopalians, Lutherans, Methodists, Russellites {Jehovah's Witnesses}, Mormons, Seventh Day Adventists, Holy Rollers {Pentecostals}, and other Arminian groups. All of these groups hold to free-willism, the general atonement, falling out of grace, and the necessity of works (including baptism) for salvation. They all deny election, predestination, particular redemption, effectual calling, salvation wholly by grace, and the security of the believer. So Campbellites are not so different as they would have us believe. Their views are merely dressed in ecclesiastical garments of a different style. When you strip the Romanist and the Campbellites and look at their basic positions, you see that they are really "birds of a feather" (Brackets mine and Emphasis his). [5]

This is why they can drop all of their peripheral differences and merge on the basis of their common Arminianism, and especially upon the natural outcome of *consistent* Arminianism, which is sacramental salvation through baptismal regeneration. So the CoC's heretical Campbellite soup has all the ingredients necessary for coming full circle to the supper table of intimate interconnectedness with the ecumenical movement headed by Rome.

But a *crucial* point needs to be clarified here. While there are *zero* reformed Roman Catholic churches, *zero* reformed Campbellite groups, *zero* reformed Kingdom Hall's, *zero* reformed SD Adventist churches, *zero* reformed Mormon temples or any other cults, there are *some* Lutheran churches, *some* Methodist churches, etc., that are actually reformed. Yet there are *many* Baptists, *many* Presbyterians, *many* Anglicans, etc., that were *originally* reformed, but became Arminian to the core. And still, this is not to say that every Arminian *individual* is lost, for some in *every* sect are *inconsistent* enough (by God's grace) *to live above their theology*, with true, saving faith in the true Jesus, which soon becomes evident in their life.

With that said, interfaith agendas involve the idea that all roads lead to Rome, where *different* "faiths" can come together for a common cause; the first steps to forming a one-world religion. However, true believers are to be "contending for *THE* faith *once delivered to the saints*" (Jude 1:3), not a *different* gospel, a *different* Jesus or a *different* faith, which is why we're *commanded* to examine ourselves to see if we're in the *true* faith (2 Cor. 13:5). Although many claim to be believers (just as demons do), *true Christians* are those who believe and *love* the truth about Jesus; how He saves and the true gospel He came to proclaim. False religion, on the other hand, redefines what biblical truth really is, in order to suite its own agenda.

In order to market itself as Christian, it must claim to believe in the same biblical characters, but the *representation* of the characters is completely foreign to Scripture. For instance, Mormons portray Jesus as a created brother of Lucifer, Jehovah's Witnesses portray Jesus as Michael the created archangel, and Roman Catholic priests present Jesus as a wafer! [6]

This is not to say that we have to know all of the cults beliefs, but we must know enough to be able to say along with Apostle Paul, *"Being crafty, I caught you with guile" (2 Cor. 12:16).* To be biblically frank, we must be able to expose wolves in sheep's clothing and recognize counterfeits by studying what true Christianity really is, *Who* the three Persons of the Godhead really are, *what* they have accomplished concerning eternal salvation and *how* they save....*all according to God's Word*. Because just like the CoC—

....."Rome does say the final solution for sin is to be found in the person and work of Jesus Christ, but this is nothing but cosmetic fluff. Mormons can say the same, as can the Jehovah's Witnesses and a myriad of other religions which have Christ as a "touchstone" to their peculiar forms of religious rituals. But this has nothing in common with the gospel of Jesus Christ....superficial commonality does not equate with a proper assessment of the Gospel of Jesus Christ" [7]

Although most CoC's, like Romanism, will affirm some basic Christian doctrines (e.g. the virgin birth, the incarnation, etc.), they still have a *different* gospel, which puts them completely at odds with biblical Christianity no matter how many other things they get right.

Their baptismal regeneration formula is ecumenisms lowest, common denominator for bringing all false religions together, for it can be easily used to blur the lines of distinction when combined with mystical methods that seem religiously neutral. As a classic example, the heretical implication that baptism is some kind of spiritual portal to the supernatural realm, where one can allegedly come in contact with Jesus' blood and be born again...creates a strong delusion and "connection" with other religions.

This is one reason the Word of Faith movement birthed the "River" cult, which also places a tremendous amount of emphasis on water as a means of entering worldwide "unity," "revival" or "rebirth."[8] It is heavily involved in ecumenism, for baptismal bridges are being built across many waters, to re-channel all apostate churches back into the polluted sea of Rome.

Before I left the WoF cults, I began to get a sick feeling in the pit of my stomach when they began constantly talking about how a "river" was getting ready to "open up" that would bring revival. One leader even said a river had opened up near the pulpit and that anyone could come up and "dive in" to get healing. But by God's grace, I was enabled to finally resist pressure from the pulpit, while watching most of the group go up to swim in that polluted river of deception. I witnessed bizarre manifestations: people falling flat on the floor in a trance, screaming, shaking or speaking gibberish.

I had already had my share of those kinds of experiences and learned the hard way that they are nothing to play around with, due to the demonic activity involved. The same things would happen when they would have foot washing ceremonies, all because of the suggestive emphasis placed on a mystical "operation of God" that would supposedly occur in water. Not only did Christ rescue me from the "Church of Christ"... *He also delivered me* *from "deliverance ministries"*₉ and kept me from falling for yet another "water gospel," where mystical suggestions cause strong delusions.

Pagans use water rituals as a very suggestive means of convincing people that they have entered "transcendence." The physical experience of having your whole body immersed in water, combined with false ideas of what its purpose is for, creates a powerfully suggestive substitute for the gospel that the devil works through, in order to convince people of a false conversion.

This is what makes the false, baptismal regeneration doctrine the perfect catalyst for bringing in the one world religion of Anti-Christ. It is used as a means to soothe a guilty conscience and to "consolidate faith." To put it candidly, it creates a *contrived faith,* not the *gift of faith*, which can only come from God by virtue of Jesus' perfect sacrifice. It makes baptism out to be something we are given to *do* ourselves, *to save ourselves*. Ironically, this is how the CoC attempts to take the mystery out of how God saves.

The CoC's perception of baptism is not only shallow and misleading; it teaches that a *physical* performance can produce *spiritual* conversion, which is a contradiction of terms. It's also an insult to the atoning sacrifice of Christ, for it teaches the Romanist doctrine that one can be reconciled to God through the portal of baptism, rather than *directly* through Christ.

Although there are many ways to Hell, there is only one way to Heaven, which is why Jesus said, *"I am the way, the truth, and the life: no man cometh unto the Father, but by Me"* (Jn. 14:6). He never even gave the slightest impression that He opened a baptismal door to Heaven as an initial entry point to God....*for Jesus said that* **He is the door** (Jn. 10:7)!

No matter how deceptively convincing it may be... *the "Church of Christ" rejects Christ*, for it injects idolatry and mysticism into baptism when it promotes it as a way to Heaven, just as Romanism and other pagan religions do. As a sad consequence, its sincere captives are sincerely wrong, for their heretically unreliable system is causing them to be perfect candidates for re-absorption back into that "ancient gospel," which claims that—

"All who have been properly baptized are put in some, though imperfect, communion with the Catholic Church."[10] "Vatican II has found the soft underbelly of state churches and starkly liberal Protestant denominations. This soft belly is the age old heresy of baptismal regeneration."[11]

Notes:

[1] See: Robert M. Zins, Th.M., *On the Edge of Apostasy: The Evangelical Romance with Rome,* (Huntsville, AL: White Horse Publications, 1998), p. 251. "Care-Net is a national umbrella organization that serves the Crisis Pregnancy Centers (CPC's) nationally. Care-Net endorses Roman Catholicism as an alternate worshipping community and has no qualms with staffing **evangelically funded CPC's with Roman Catholic workers."** (Emphasis mine)

[2] John MacArthur, *Can God Bless America?* (Nashville, TN: The W Publishing Group, 2002), pp. 86, 88 and 89.

[3] For a classic example, see: Charles Simpson, *Inside the Churches of Christ,* (Bloomington, IN: AuthorHouse, 2009). Though he came out of the CoC, without a solid foundation to ground him in the truth, like many, he ended up going "from the frying pan into the fire." Sadly, he was still ungrounded when he wrote his book, which promotes infiltrators: Billy Graham, James Dobson, Beth Moore, Rick Warren, 12 step secularism, Southern Baptist ecumenism, easy-believism, etc. These are common pitfalls for those who leave just so they can be worldlier than ever. And it's a terrible witness to those still in the CoC who desire the ability to live more holy, not more sinful! This is why we must first make sure that we don't still have a log in our own eye, before trying to take a splinter out of someone else's eye (Mt. 7:1-4).

[4] Flavil R. Yeakley, Jr., *Why They Left,* (Nashville, TN: Gospel Advocate Co., 2012), pp. 86, 155 and 202. Throughout his book, Yeakley spilled forth CoC Arminianism and how it relates to ecumenism and psychology. See Appendix 2 for a more in-depth review of his book.

[5] Bob L. Ross, *Campbellism: Its History and Heresies,* (Pasadena, TX: Pilgrim Publications, 1981), p. 85.

[6] See: Dr. Walter Martin, *The Kingdom of the Cults,* (MN, Minnesota: Bethany House Publishers, 1997).

[7] Robert M. Zins, Th.M., *On the Edge of Apostasy: The Evangelical Romance with Rome,* (Huntsville, AL: White Horse Publications, 1998), p. 46.

[8] For more detailed information on the "River Movement," see: Kevin Reeves, *The Other Side of the River,* (Silverton, OR: Lighthouse Trails Publishing, 2007).

[9] *Jesus Delivered Me! ....from "Deliverance Ministries"* is the next book I'm working on, in order to go deeper into what's really going on in that movement.

[10] *Vatican Council II*, Volume II, Austin Flannery, General Editor, (Northport, NY: Costello Publishing Company, 1992), p. 455.

[11] Robert M. Zins, Th.M., *Romanism: The Relentless Roman Catholic Assault on the Gospel of Jesus Christ*, Fourth Edition, (Charlotte, NC: A Christian Witness to Roman Catholicism, 2010), p. 224.

Chapter 16

The Falling Away

... "that day shall not come, except there come a falling away first, and that man of sin be revealed, the son of perdition"
(2 Thess. 2:3).

As I was proofreading the last chapter, I providentially came across a newly released book, *Why We Stayed.*₁ It's a compilation of essays by high ranking "Church of Christ" advocates. And though I'm sure it was not their intention, they have not only confirmed what I've written in this book, but have gone above and beyond to reveal that their movement is merging with the one-world religion of Anti-Christ led by the Vatican, at an alarming rate that's even more staggering than previously thought.

Since knowledge has increased in these last days, just as Daniel prophesied, there has been a mass exodus from the Stone-Campbell movement. Consequently, many are going to and fro, trying to find a solid, spiritual foundation to cling to (Dan. 12:4). While many of God's people are being drawn out of the CoC into true communities of faith, those who have the regrettable persistence to stay are finding themselves in league with Rome and the moral and social decay that inevitably follows.

The highly publicized Kentucky Clerk, Kim Davis (an Arminian who didn't even have a biblical view of the Trinity), was used as *controlled opposition* by the Vatican, to get millions to buy into a false, political narrative that skewed true Christianity by having it "championed" superficially. No wonder the Pope met with her privately to encourage her to "stay strong" and to give her rosary beads to *strategically* display on all media outlets.

Rome has always been notorious for creating civil chaos and utilizing what's known as the "Hegelian Dialectic" (summed up as *problem, reaction, solution)* so that it can come on the scene pretending to be the one that can bring "order." So it's no wonder *Why We Stayed* reveals that CoC's are now involved in Jesuit initiated, third-wave feminism and gay activism (pp. 27, 130-132 and 173), which are so manifestly evil. And yet, they are *"halting between two opinions" (1 Kgs. 18:21),* while admitting that their loyalty to the CoC borders on folly (p. 153). On the back cover they stated as follows:

"The Church of Christ, at this present hour, is host to a multitude of frustrated and disenchanted ministers and scholars. From the inside of ministry, the veneer of our movement disappears and the blemishes take center-stage. Discouragement is common. In response to this state of affairs, we asked an eclectic cast of authors, ministers, and scholars to answer the question, "Why did you stay within our movement?" The result is a diverse set of answers which we hope will create some hope for the future of our people."

And within this "diverse set of answers" we find one common theme; a willingness to drop side issues, while keeping the CoC's two main pillars intact: the *doctrine of man's absolute autonomy and universal atonement*. For these are the necessary components for its sacramental system of salvation to remain intact for ecumenical integration into an ever evolving "hive-mind hybrid" that will be neither Catholic nor Christian.

This great "falling away" of all harlot churches into the hands of their predecessor must be fulfilled (2 Thess. 2:3, Rev. 17:5). As the Lord has spoken: *"Every plant, which My heavenly Father hath not planted, shall be rooted up, Let them alone: they be blind leaders of the blind. And if the blind lead the blind, both shall fall into the ditch"* (Mt. 15:13-14).

This is why we find in their literature, the exaltation of spiritually blind leaders, such as: Catholic, mystic priest "John of the Cross," mystic Julian of Norwich (p. 125), Catholic, mystic monk Thomas Merton, Catholic priest Henri Nouwen (p. 134) and St. Francis of Assisi (p. 153).....all of whom many "Church of Christ" leaders are now calling "spiritual surrogates" (p. 125).

As another consequence of their *consistent* Arminian theology, they are calling ecumenical leaders in their movement "matchmakers of sacraments" (pp. 128-133). On page 135 we even find this stunning statement:

"God's used Churches of Christ through sacraments, saints and surrogates to lead me nearer and nearer to that final and ultimately soul-fulfilling wedding with Christ."

Sadly, they do not realize that it is a *false* christ that they are being led to, through sacramental salvation, mysticism, Catholic "saints," monks and ecumenical "surrogates." So it's no wonder the last chapter of their book resembled the Romanist practice of *Necromancy* (invoking special graces from the dead), which is actually communication with demons *who pose as the dead,* and God condemns it (Deut. 18:9-12).

Eerily similar to the wicked diviners of old who would consult with images (Ezek. 21:21), their book featured pages worth of spiritual inquiry involving a portrait of CoC founder Alexander Campbell! It even glamorized and quoted "poetry" by Vachel Lindsey, who was a mentally ill vagabond who claimed to be a prophet of Alexander Campbell! Tragically, his misguided zeal led him to commit suicide by ingesting Lysol (pp. 167-175).

This is what happens when heresy takes root and spreads like cancer (2 Tim. 2:17). And this is why creedal safeguards are needed to protect against such unbiblical insanity. While CoC supporters admit that their "mottos" are actually their creeds (p.50), they still try to claim some common ground with reformed creeds, in order to still try to be accepted within Christendom.

Yet their minimalist approach agrees only upon some bare basics that even Romanism agrees upon, such as the virgin birth, Jesus' bodily resurrection, etc. But, as usual, they dared not go over all of the essential points they *disagree* on concerning reformed confessions of faith. For all throughout their entire book they have had to reluctantly admit that they can no longer try to biblically back up their reasons for differing when it comes to the gospel. However, instead of repenting and abandoning the faulty foundations of their theology, they took a philosophical approach:

"Rather, as I gradually learned to recognize the idiosyncrasies, inconsistencies, and occasional fumbling, my reaction has tended to be simply, *c'est la vie*---what else is new?" (p. 152)

Instead of turning to the true Christ and the true gospel of Scripture, they are becoming desensitized and hardened in their errors. As a result, they have resorted to a pitiful attempt to dodge the real issues, while pleading for ecumenical "love and tolerance," despite the Bibles warning against tolerating those who teach false doctrine (e.g. 1 Jn. 4:1, Rev. 2:14-16, 20).

Since CoC proponents are no longer able to defend their errors due to an ever growing database of information exposing their movement, they have had to resort to "damage control" in order to try to "save face" and cover their tracks. By taking lessons from "spiritual surrogates" all these years, they've learned how to employ a very subtle form of trickery involving double-talk that can be affirmed by either side.

For instance, while now claiming they believe *justification is by faith alone* (p. 44), they refuse to define exactly what those terms mean in their movement. Because the evil spirit behind the CoC system makes the terms faith and baptism interchangeable. No wonder its enthusiasts included a "disclaimer" in fine print at the bottom of the very next page (45), along with an appeal for tolerance, despite their "high view of baptism," which happens to be a view that is in direct opposition to orthodox Christianity.

The CoC version of faith is that baptism is the *instrumental cause* of salvation and that justification is an *ongoing process* that involves more and more "obedient acts of faith." Its fatal failure to teach the true nature of saving faith causes its members to confuse justification with sanctification.

But the Christian understanding of *justification by faith alone* entails an instant justification, based solely upon faith in Jesus' *perfect* obedience unto death, not our own *imperfect* obedience. True Christianity distinguishes the difference between justification, which is instant, and sanctification, which is where one is set apart by God for the *ongoing process* of being conformed to the image of Christ; a working out of what God works within (Phil. 1:6).

Although the CoC is now claiming to hold *"justification by grace through faith"* (p. 147), its fatal understanding of these terms is that one is justified on account of grace imparted through baptism, when performed in faith. This is why its operatives can turn around on the very next page (148) and claim to have common ground with Romanism concerning their heavy emphasis on the importance of baptism *literally* "for the remission of sins."

And, like Rome, they employ the use of double-speak throughout their book in order to accommodate both sides of the issue. Accordingly, their language has created a type of "middle ground," which they are desperately pleading for (p. 50). While CoC's have always been reluctant to admit to their sacramental system of salvation, they are gradually feeling safe enough in such a corrupt society, to finally "come out of the closet"---

"I have often heard it expressed that the person being baptized comes into contact with the saving blood of Jesus through water baptism. In this way we are sacramental, that is that God works in a mysterious way through the waters of baptism, even if we rarely use the terminology" (p. 64). "Among us, a person has room to view baptism in a sacramental way that is appealing even if some might shy away from the word sacrament itself" (p. 68).

Although many CoC supporters are still claiming not to believe in baptismal regeneration, their language betrays their claim. And since there are those who are finally breaking through their heretical language barrier, they have no choice but to try to "up their game" with statements such as this:

"While our language about salvation can be overly focused on baptism, our robust baptismal theology among 'Evangelicals' is a great strength" (p. 68, emphasis his).

Again, we read of the new ecumenical phase that the CoC is entering upon:

"Churches of Christ are in a unique position to share their theology and experiences with people who are open to learning more about baptism and the Lord's Supper. Although there may be certain aspects of our past we are not fond of, now is the time to embrace our heritage and begin to have conversations with others who are intrigued by our *unique* beliefs" (p. 78, emphasis mine).

This is why CoC's are now involved in ecumenical "dialogue." So, although they are grudgingly admitting to the shady past of their "restoration heritage," their movement has not turned to the true gospel of Jesus Christ. Instead, it has only switched gears in order to take their theology to its ultimate destination. Because they are now realizing that they are living in a time where their "sacramental *uniqueness*" actually qualifies them to be on the cutting edge of the ecumenical movement, where all false religions are building a kingdom that they will eventually have to hand over to the Beast that has led them into error, in order to fulfill Bible prophecy (Rev. 17:17).

As a final note here, I need to make it very clear that as an ex-CoC member myself, I can honestly say that the absolute worst way to try to reach a CoC captive, is to try to convince them that they should be open to more false religion and more worldliness, for many of them truly desire to be able to please God and live a holier life, not a worldlier life than ever!

One must choose their battles wisely and never try to get them to be more open to worldliness, or else it will be a losing battle that will only convince many of them even more that they should stay in bondage. The focus should *always* be on how fallen we are and how much we need the righteousness of Christ imputed to us by virtue of God's grace, *never* on how we should be more open to worldly seduction and sinfulness. That is so harmful and it is *NOT* walking in wisdom and love towards them (Mt. 10:16).

I've heard and read the testimonies of some who have left cults, and they often seem to be about how they then felt liberated to do all kinds of sinful things, which revealed that they were still in the mindset of thinking God's moral law is restrictive, rather than instructive on how to be more like the Savior. It also reveals that some only leave legalistic cults just so they can feel free to live a worldlier lifestyle than ever. And that becomes a terrible witness to those who are still in the cults. Sadly, it makes many even more afraid to leave than ever... in fear that they too may turn out like that!

It just goes to show that just because someone leaves a cult it does not necessarily mean that they are right with God. A worldly lifestyle is not good evidence that one has truly been rescued by Christ, but reveals a mindset that still thinks godly living is all about rule keeping, rather than true obedience from the heart, which only comes about after one has been resurrected to new spiritual life by the quickening power of the Holy Spirit.

So just in case someone reads this book in hopes that such sinful motives for judging the CoC or any other legalistic cult will be justified in their abuse of God's grace as an excuse to live like the devil….think again! For this is where the *biblical* use of "judge not lest you be judged" comes into play.

Both legalism *AND* license are two sides of the same ditch that essentially denies Jesus. If we are truly following Christ, we can then be obedient to His command to "judge with righteous judgment." If not, we can have no real discernment at all and will have ruined our witness to the world by becoming like the world and like salt that has lost its flavor (Mt. 5:13).

Notes:

[1] All book references in this chapter are taken from: Benjamin J. Williams, General Editor, W*hy We Stayed*, (Los Angeles/London: Keledei Publishers, 2018). Also see: https://www.youtube.com/user/LizziesAnswers --concerning the mass exodus from the CoC into Roman Catholicism. In her YouTube videos she reveals the growing trend of CoC members being led into Romanism, especially the younger generation. It is truly heartbreaking. However, the truth remains, that there will always be true *followers* of Christ, just as there will always be *"fall-a-wayers"* from Christ.

Part 3

Believing a False Gospel Leads to Eternal Damnation

Chapter 17

The Water Gospel

"But though we, or an angel from heaven, preach any other gospel unto you than that which we have preached unto you, let him be accursed" (Gal. 1:8).

Alexander Campbell was at the headwaters of the "water gospel," for he laid the groundwork for the very first "Church of Christ." Since then, this religion has been marked with an inbred authority structure based on the "ancient gospel," a man-centered, *synergistic* concept of salvation, which the Bible calls "another gospel." It is so contrary to God's way of salvation that He places it and those who promote it under a divine curse (Gal. 1:6-8).

True salvation is a *gift* from God (Eph. 2:8-10). It comes solely by His grace (unmerited favor), not by personal righteousness or works. Baptism is a *work of righteousness* that only Jesus fulfilled perfectly (Mt. 3:15). The Bible makes it clear that we can only be saved by God's mercy alone, *"Not by works of righteousness which we have done"* (Rom. 4:5, Titus 3:5). Yet the CoC makes baptism and regeneration synonymous, which alters the true, biblical meaning of both. This, in turn, causes its ministers to believe that preaching about baptism is the same thing as preaching about Jesus.[1]

It cannot be stressed enough, just how *crucial* water baptism is to the CoC's sacramental system of salvation. Water baptism is *everything* in this religion. In the CoC, *baptism* is faith; *baptism* is repentance; *baptism* is obedience; *baptism* is salvation; *baptism* is how one receives and accepts Christ; and *baptism* is even how one calls upon the name of the Lord!

To put it more precisely, the CoC makes everything in the Word of God dissolve into water![2] This is why its preaching is peppered with references to water, in order to induce a false and unbiblical obsession with baptism as the only way to even have a fighting chance at obtaining salvation.

Though Jesus Himself never taught such a thing, this warped "water syndrome" is the one thing that all CoC's agree upon and show severe symptoms of, for it's the most consistent, inevitable result of the two foundational pillars of their sacramental system of salvation: *autonomous freewill and universal atonement.* Without these, all CoC's would collapse.

"Arminian Evangelicals may not like to hear this but the fact is inescapable. The Catholic religion is able to build an *autosoteric* (self-salvation) system because it builds upon the unscriptural foundation that Adam's sin did not impair the will from choosing God. The Catholic also posits an unscriptural "given" that the death of Christ redeemed everyone in the world."[3]

This is also why the CoC is able to build an *auto-soteric* system. And by adding baptism *literally* for the remission of sins (which must be administered by a CoC member) as a *requirement* for salvation, *it makes the sovereignty of its system all the more essential*. But Scripture in no way bears this assertion out. By trying the spirits behind this doctrine, as we are expressly urged to do, it becomes obvious that it is not biblical (1 Jn. 4:1).

Two signs of deceiving spirits are when "contradicting and blaspheming" of God's Word occurs (Acts 13:45). But the CoC is notorious for "yes, but" explanations for these occurrences. For example, it will *seemingly* agree that it's not works that save us, but then turns right around and contradicts that statement by *cleverly* making faith and baptism synonymous "passive works," in an attempt to avoid the Bible's condemnation of works salvation!

The reasoning behind this is a twisting of Scripture. Another example is when the spirit behind the CoC system contradicts itself by falsely claiming that the thief on the cross was saved without being baptized because he was still under the Mosaic Dispensation.[4] At the same time, it also claims that Jesus told Nicodemus (who was ironically still under the Mosaic Dispensation) that he must be born again by being water baptized (Jn. 3:5)!

So one must wonder....why the double standard? Besides, baptism isn't even mentioned there, which is embarrassingly ironic, for the CoC system prides itself in being "silent where Scripture is silent." Yet here, it makes Scripture say something that it doesn't! John chapter 3 doesn't even mention baptism in the *entire context*... the CoC has to insert it!

The CoC inserts the word baptism into *many* passages that mention water. It automatically assumes that whenever the word "water" shows up in the Bible it automatically means baptism. However, all throughout Scripture water often refers to the Holy Spirit. In John 3:5, many Greek translators prefer "water *EVEN* the Spirit." And, in John 7:38-39, Jesus even said, *"He who **believes** in Me...out of his heart will flow rivers of living **water**.*

*But this He spoke concerning the **Spirit**, whom those **believing in Him** would receive" (NKJV, emphasis mine).*

Besides, Jesus would not have reprimanded Nicodemus for not knowing about Christian baptism, for it had not even been instituted yet! However, Nicodemus *would* have been very familiar with water being symbolic of the purifying agency of God's Spirit in the Old Testament (e.g. Ex. 30:18, Deut. 21:6, Ezek. 36:25). The New Testament parallel is that *the Holy Spirit* is the regenerating and purifying agent, and the *"water of the Word"* is the instrument that He uses to guide His people to Jesus Christ, and whereby all of God's graces are called into exercise (Eph. 5:26, Heb. 4:12, 1 Pet. 1:23).

The CoC system has never been able to prove that John 3:5 means water baptism, or that there is a biblical mandate for summoning the Spirit of God in baptism to literally wash away sins. The context reveals that regeneration is God's sovereign act, not ours, for the Spirit is free to quicken *whomever He wills* (Jn. 3:8; 5:21). Scripture never reveals that baptism or baptismal mediators can ever *cause* the Holy Spirit to wash away someone's sins.

To truly be *born again*, one must be *born from above*. The Greek word "again" in John 3:5 has two possible meanings. The first one is "again" and the second one is "from above." Nicodemus made the mistake of thinking it was the first one, but Jesus corrected him by making it clear that He was referring to *spiritual* birth. God's people are *"born again, not of corruptible seed, but of incorruptible, by the Word of God, which liveth and abideth forever"* (1 Pet. 1:23), *"with the washing of water by the Word"* (Eph. 5:26).

Yet the CoC falsely teaches that the Holy Spirit comes down out of Heaven to regenerate a person when baptism is performed. But the Spirit *cannot* be called down to regenerate a person through the manipulations of a sacrament, neither can one channel a "Jesus encounter" in the waters of baptism….*unless it's a false Jesus!* The CoC's false gospel of salvation has one being "born from below" in the *womb of water...* by another Jesus!

Eerily akin to Romanism, the CoC not only injects mysticism into baptism, it promotes it as a requirement for salvation that turns the one who administers the "requirement" into a human mediator, which is blasphemy!

There is only one mediator between God and man, Christ Jesus (1 Tim. 2:5). Only He can administer what's necessary for us to be saved, for He has obtained our redemption and all of the spiritual blessings that accompany salvation (faith, repentance, obedience, love for God and others, etc.).

The heretical and hidden creeds of the CoC concerning baptismal regeneration stem from Romanism, which is why it is so careful not to call it what it is. For even more proof, here are just a few citations from the Roman Catholic Catechism that coincide with the CoC's unwritten creeds:

- "The sacraments of the New Covenant are necessary for salvation" (#1129, p. 292).
- "Baptism is necessary for salvation.... The church does not know any other means other than baptism that assures entry into eternal beatitude" (#1257, p. 320).
- "By baptism all sins are forgiven, original sin and all personal sins, as well as all punishment for sin" (#1263, p. 321).
- "The Church bears within itself and administers the totality of the means of salvation" (#868, p. 230).

These perfectly correspond with the CoC doctrine of church authority. Like Romanism, the CoC has a sacramental system that can only be accessed through its church. And though it has always tried to hide the origins of its doctrine, its more modern literature actually lets the words "divine absolution" slip out. The CoC teaches that the apostles offered *divine absolution* by offering to baptize people![5] This is paralleled in Romanism, which holds that only its priests (through apostolic succession) have the authority to grant "divine absolution" of sins. This is blatant blasphemy!

Like Romanism, the CoC takes John 20:23 out of context and makes it out to mean that only its leaders have the authority and power to grant or withhold divine pardon! But the truth is that Jesus has made His people ambassadors to *proclaim forgiveness through faith in His name*. Thus, sinners can receive forgiveness *directly* from God *through faith*, rather than having to avail themselves of a Catholic priest or a CoC mediator. They do *Not* have to go through "layers of clergy" or "layers of laity" to get to Jesus!

Divine absolution and baptismal regeneration are Roman Catholic doctrines, with the sole purpose of exalting man over God, which reveals a spirit of antichrist. In this respect, the CoC never completely broke away from Romanism, and will therefore eventually be re-absorbed back into it. In fact, it is already happening one member at a time.

The Roman Catholic YouTube channel, *"The Journey Home,"* reveals that it's now occurring at a rapid pace. Interestingly, Bruce Sullivan, a former "Church of Christ" preacher in Kentucky, gave his testimony on the show. He said the CoC had "bridges to Rome" that paved the way to the "mother church," such as baptismal regeneration, "faith working by love" and the concept of an *institutionalized* church body. No wonder the CoC and the Roman Catholic Church both claim to be the *visible* body of Christ.[6]

Mr. Sullivan concluded by saying that "Churches of Christ" are just a "watered-down Catholicism," which is why he wrote a book on how *"Christ In His Fullness"* can only be found in the Catholic Church. To be exact, if CoC members want to be *fully* consistent with their theology, they would have to take it to its logical conclusion....which is Romanism. For the "fullness" of the CoC's false christ can only be found there. This is why the CoC can only rebuke peripheral issues in Romanism, such as *infant* baptism, rosary beads, etc. Because, if it exposed the two foundational pillars of Romanism: *the absolute freedom of man's will and universal atonement,* it would also expose itself as a false religion built upon sinking sand!

"The Arminian jettisons the Catholic system while retaining the same two pillars, i.e., freedom of the will and universal atonement of Catholic theology! Thus, in critically critiquing the Catholic religion, we are left with short-handled hoes and dull shovels if we try to correct the Catholic error with something that is at base Catholic! The Catholic apologist is well aware of this and that is precisely why he picks on the evangelical Arminian. He knows the Arminian at heart believes in *autosoterism.*"[7]

In his ebook, *What Must the Church of Christ Do to Be Saved?*—Leroy Garrett drove the final nail in the CoC coffin when he stated:

"I am saying that for the Churches of Christ to be saved they must have their own Vatican II. What is remarkable about Vatican II is that it set in motion some of the very changes the Churches of Christ must make. That may be because there are striking similarities between the two churches" (p. 58). "If the Roman Church has its written creeds we have had our own unwritten creeds, and unwritten ones can be even more coercive and domineering than written ones" (p. 62). "In unwritten creeds people make up their rules as they go along, tailoring the creed to fit the occasion or the one "to be marked"---"we have made creeds of our opinions." (p. 199) (SCMe-Prints@stone-campbell.org., ©2010).

Notes:

[1] For a classic example, see: Benjamin J. Williams, General Editor, *Why We Stayed*, (Los Angeles/London: Keledei Publishing, 2018), p. 65.

[2] See: Allen Webster, *They That Gladly Received His Word Were Baptized,* Volume 17, Issue # 5, p. 1. Retrieved May 3, 2018 from: https://housetohouse.com/wp-content/uploads/2016/02/v17n5.pdf

[3] Robert M. Zins, Th.M., *Romanism: The Relentless Roman Catholic Assault on the Gospel of Jesus Christ*, Fourth Edition, (Charlotte, NC: A Christian Witness to Roman Catholicism, 2010), p. 78. The word *auto* means *self*. *Soteriology* refers to the theology of *salvation*. When you put the two together you have auto-soteric (self-salvation).

[4] Allen Webster, *The World's Most Popular Thief*, Volume 18, Issue #1, p. 1. Retrieved March 3, 2018 from: http://housetohouse.com/wp-content/uploads/2016/02/v18n1.pdf

    Also see: Floyd Chappelear, *The Righteousness of a Thief*, Volume 21, and Issue #4, p. 4. Retrieved May 3, 2018 from: https://housetohouse.com/wp-content/uploads/2016/06/v21n4.pdf

[5] Allen Webster, *What Does the Church Have to Offer Me?* Volume 18, Issue # 2, p. 1. Retrieved March 3, 2018 from: http://housetohouse.com/wp-content/uploads/2016/02/v18n2.pdf --Here CoC literature states as follows: *"Offering divine absolution, Peter responded, "Repent, and be baptized every one of you in the name of Jesus."* On the same page it mentions how this is part of *"God's paint by the numbers plan,"* and that... *"the Church of Christ offers the same 'benefits package' today."*

[6] EWTN Global Catholic Television Network, with host Marcus Grodi, *Interview with Bruce Sullivan - Former Church of Christ Minister.* Retrieved May 3, 2018 from *The Journey Home* YouTube channel: https://www.youtube.com/watch?v=Ev40dzl-35o

[7] Robert M. Zins, Th.M., *Romanism: The Relentless Roman Catholic Assault on the Gospel of Jesus Christ*, Fourth Edition, (Charlotte, NC: A Christian Witness to Roman Catholicism, 2010), pp. 78, 79.

Chapter 18

Fatally False Interpretations

"[The Scriptures] in which are some things hard to be understood, which they that are unlearned and unstable wrest {twist}, as they do also the other Scriptures, unto their own destruction" (2 Pet. 3:16, brackets mine).

The CoC system reads into Bible passages its own erroneous, sacramental interpretations. For instance, it claims that the word "and" in Mark 16:16 is a coordinating conjunction, which would make the verbs baptism and belief of equal importance. But it commits a *negative inference fallacy* here, for the verse does *Not* say, "he that is *not baptized* will be damned," but it *does* say, "he that *believeth not* shall be damned." (Emphasis mine)

Scripture *never* says one can't be saved unless they're baptized. Yet it *does* make it clear that one cannot be saved unless one *believes* (e.g. Jn. 3:18, 36; 6:53-54, 8-24). When the Philippian jailer asked, *"What must I do to be saved?"*-- Paul answered, ***"Believe** on the Lord Jesus Christ, and thou shalt be saved (Acts 16:30-31, emphasis mine)*. And one can only have saving faith if they have been *directly* regenerated by the Holy Spirit, through His Word, not *indirectly* regenerated through baptism (Titus 3:5).

In 1 Peter 3:20, Noah's family was *"saved **by** water"* only in the sense that the reality of their salvation became obvious *through* the trial of water, for they were enabled by God to pass safely *through* the destructive waters by being in the Ark, which represented Christ. The word **"by"** in this verse is translated **"through"** in the original Greek. The water itself was a means of God's judgment, *not* a means of salvation! Yet the CoC could grasp for straws here and say "the ark couldn't have floated without the water."

But, the fact remains, the water itself didn't save, or else those outside the Ark would have been saved! Peter even says here, baptism does not put away the filth of the flesh (v. 21). And a symbol cannot *literally* purge a guilty conscience. It can only be an outward sign of what's already occurred inwardly. There is no such thing as baptismal regeneration. Baptism, in no way, shape or form, effects what it signifies. Yet the CoC claims that it does.

But, in reality, the Ark was a figure of Christ; it was a *figure* of the true, whereas faith was the substance. Today, baptism is a *figure* of Jesus' death, burial and resurrection; it is a *picture* of the true, whereas faith is the substance (Heb. 9:9, 14, 26; 11:1, 7). Baptism is the outward response of a conscience that has been purified by faith in Christ and what He has accomplished in the believer who identifies with Him in baptism. All who savingly believe in Christ have *already* been baptized by the Holy Spirit into His death *spiritually* (1 Cor. 12:13). They, like Noah and his family, have passed safely *through* the waters of sin and death.... *in the Ark of Christ*.

Still, the CoC goes to great lengths to exalt man and his own works by performing a play on words that is straight from the Campbellite recipe book. For example, it twists Acts 2:38 to mean that people are baptized "in order to get," remission of sins, rather than baptized "because" their sins are *already* remitted by grace thru faith in the efficacy of Jesus' blood (Heb. 9:22). The CoC teaches that baptism is literally "for" the remission of sins.

Yet if baptism *literally* saves then there would be no need for the CoC's "second laws of pardon." This highly spiced dilemma creates a double-bind for the CoC system that cannot be escaped by any amount of soupy, Campbellite word play. Baptism is indeed a command, but so is "love thy neighbor as thyself," and "be ye perfect." But the CoC has singled out the command of baptism as a means of salvation, because baptism is a *much easier* command to perform... *especially* since it's only a one-time event!

No wonder the spirit behind the CoC system slyly slithers in the easy and shady salvation of baptismal regeneration, for the shadowy implications of sacramental salvation are ever so subtle. And, by doing so, it causes an extremely unhealthy and unbiblical obsession with Acts 2:38....making it out to be the whole gospel. No wonder so many CoC members have it engraved on their tombstones! This is why I've included an entire biblical *exegesis* of this verse in Appendix 1, which exposes the CoC's unbiblical *eisegesis*.[1]

Interestingly, Matthew 3:11 uses the same Greek word (*eis*) in connection with baptism as Acts 2:38. And clearly it can't mean "in order to get" repentance, for John told the Pharisees they had to first *"produce fruits worthy of repentance,"* like the Ethiopian, Saul, Cornelius, his family and thousands of others did in Acts, AFTER God had purified their hearts by faith and AFTER God had granted them the Holy Spirit, Who *spiritually* baptized them into Christ (Acts 15:8-9), BEFORE they were *physically* baptized in water to represent what had *already* been arranged by God the Father, accomplished by God the Son and applied by God the Holy Spirit!

Yet the CoC will protest. For example, it teaches that Cornelius, in Acts 10, was told that he must do something *to be saved* (v. 6). And it takes this "something" to be baptism. But the context shows that he had *already* been accepted by God *through faith (v. 4)*, for he had already been *effectually directed* by the Spirit to fear God, pray and do righteous works (v. 35), Who then *effectually guided* him to Christ at the appointed time and *effectually moved* him to be water baptized as a testimony. So this begs the question...did Cornelius *do* something to *cause* God to do all of that? Who moved who? The answer is in His Word (e.g. Prov. 16:9; 20:24, Jer. 10:23).

Even in Acts 11:16-18, Peter describes what God had done in Acts 10, and there's absolutely no mention of water baptism saving anyone, but only of Holy Spirit baptism into the Body of Christ *through faith*. And yet, his audience *still* glorified God for **granting** the Gentiles *"repentance unto life."*

The CoC says that "God's Spirit is only given to those who *in faith obey Christ*."₂ So let's carefully evaluate this statement. First of all, they cannot obey Christ *acceptably* unless they first have the Holy Spirit enabling them by grace through faith. For *"without faith it is impossible to please Him" (Heb. 11:6)*. Secondly, it has been demonstrated in earlier chapters, time and time again, how the CoC redefines the biblical term "faith." Remember, to the CoC, "faith" literally means obeying the water gospel, whereas the Christian position is that true, biblical obedience to the gospel is faith itself.

The irony is that if any of the CoC's "proof texts" truly meant that baptism *obtains* remission of sins and repentance, then they would have to confess that no one needed that more than the Pharisees, yet John refused to baptize them! To be consistent with the water gospel, they would also have to confess that the Israelites were baptized "in order to get" Moses to be their leader, rather than "because" he had already led them out of Egypt. For the same Greek preposition (*eis*) is used in conjunction with baptism in 1 Cor. 10:2. The Greek word (*eis*) "for" **or** "unto" is to be understood as "because of" **or** "in reference to".... *when it comes to biblical ordinances.*

Take Luke 5:12-14 for example; Jesus literally cleansed and healed the leper *before* He told him to go through an ordinance "for" (*eis*) cleansing:

"And it came to pass, when He was in a certain city, behold a man full of leprosy: who seeing Jesus fell on his face, and besought him, saying, Lord, if Thou wilt, Thou canst make me clean. And He put forth his hand, and touched him, saying, I will: be thou clean. And immediately the leprosy departed from him. And He charged him to tell no man: but go, and shew thyself to the priest, and offer... *for {eis} thy cleansing,* {which Jesus had already performed} according as Moses commanded, **for {eis} a testimony** unto them" (Lk. 5:12-14, emphasis and brackets mine).

Carefully note that the man's offering *did not heal him*, but was only an external ordinance to testify that he had *already* been healed. The ordinance was *"for a testimony."* In the same way, baptism *does not save*, but is only an external ordinance to *proclaim and testify* that one has *already* been assured of salvation inwardly (by the Holy Spirit bearing witness with their spirit), based solely on faith in Jesus' offering of Himself on their behalf. The same Greek word *"for"* (*eis*) is used in Acts 2:38:

"Then Peter said unto them, Repent, and be baptized every one of you in the name of Jesus Christ *for {eis} the remission of sins,* and ye shall receive the gift of the Holy Ghost." (Emphasis and brackets mine)

So Scripture clearly shows that Jesus *first* cleanses, heals and saves. Then, a believer is to go through a *figurative* ordinance "in reference to" what Jesus has already *literally* accomplished in them. Old Testament, sacrificial ordinances were "for" (*eis*) thy cleansing---"in reference to" Jesus' future sacrifice of Himself on behalf of that person. Whereas New Testament ordinances are "for" (*eis*) remission of sins ---"in reference to" what Jesus has already accomplished on behalf of that person.

Notes:

[1] Robert Meyers, General Editor, *Voices of Concern*, (Saint Louis, MS: Mission Messenger, 1966), p. 104—"The teaching of the Church of Christ is based upon a superficial interpretation of the Bible and is fundamentally in error. This is true with reference to the nature of God, Christ, the Bible, the Church, man's mission in the world, and many other issues having both theological and social implications."

[2] Alvin Jennings, General Editor, *Introducing the Church of Christ*, (Fort Worth, TX: Star Bible Publications, Inc., 1981), p. 164. This is discussed further in Appendix 2.

Chapter 19

Baptismal Regeneration is a False Gospel

"Through Thy precepts I get understanding: therefore I hate every false way"
(Ps. 119:104).

So now that we've explored some of the CoC's contradictions concerning baptism, let's just briefly go over some more of its assumptions, such as the thief on the cross "probably" getting baptized by John earlier, or that Jesus was "probably" preparing Nicodemus to be baptized after the New Covenant was established, and the ridiculous assumption that Jesus could only directly forgive sins *then* because He was still on earth. Because these false assumptions demonstrate how grasping for straws will occur whenever one tries to prove that baptism or any other act saves us.

If the thief on the cross was saved because he was earlier baptized by John, then that would still throw a huge monkey wrench into the whole CoC system. For it admittedly teaches that John's baptism was obsolete *after* Jesus' death. And the thief died *after* Jesus! Scripture reveals that the two thieves had their legs broken in order to speed up death, but *not* Jesus, for He had *already* died! So the thief on the cross was no longer under the Mosaic dispensation right before he died. Jesus died *before* the thief, so the New Covenant was immediately in force upon the thief *before* he died!

"For where a testament is, there must also of necessity be the death of the testator. For a testament is of force after men are dead; otherwise it is of no strength at all while the testator liveth" (Mt. 26:28, Heb. 9:16-17).

It just goes to show, that unless God, through His Word, has convinced a sinner how badly sin corrupts, they won't realize their desperate need for the Savior, and will be fooled into believing they can, by their own corrupt "free" will, choose salvation by doing something. Apostle Paul clearly warned that we need to be sure that we believe the true gospel, not one that causes a fall from grace into work-righteous legalism (Gal. 1:6-10).

Adding requirements other than faith in Jesus' perfect sacrifice, becomes works in disguise, which is why false doctrines are so tricky. Jesus' blood didn't just make His people "savable" depending upon their actions.

His blood *literally* saves them, based on His work, His grace, His mercy, His will and His choice (Jn. 1:13, Rom. 9:16, 18, Heb. 9:12).

The true gospel is a call to faith in the righteousness of Christ alone and to full, confident assurance in His blood atonement for sins as our only title to Heaven. Baptism is a pure act of obedience that *God works in us to do*, AFTER God has purified and cleansed our hearts *by faith* (Acts 8:37; 15: 8-9, Phil. 2:13). But if one is baptized in order to *get* saved, then it becomes an impure, meaningless and defiled work of the flesh that God has no part in.

An unregenerate act that attempts to appease God's wrath, instead of believing Jesus has already done that for us, becomes a witness against us. So unless God first purifies our hearts by faith, nothing we do will be pure in His sight (Titus 1:15). It is dangerous ground when one tries to go through an outward performance in order to try to bribe God into saving them, for that is an abomination to Him!

A fatal blow to baptismal regeneration is that Paul made a crystal clear distinction between the gospel and water baptism (1 Cor. 1:17). And he revealed that he begot believers through the gospel, *Not* through baptism (1 Cor. 4:15). Yet if we went by the CoC interpretation, Paul would be saying that he was thankful that no Corinthians were saved!! (See: 1 Cor. 1:14)

As usual, the evil spirit behind the CoC system creates an irreconcilable contradiction, by promoting baptism as the gospel. But to try to weasel out of this, it suggests that Paul was just thankful that he hadn't personally baptized the Christians at Corinth because they were calling themselves by the name of the person who had performed their baptism. But this lame excuse makes Paul out to be a tease who tells them that they can only be saved by water baptism... *but then withholds it from them!*

So, the CoC system must answer the question... just how in the world did Paul begat believers in Corinth through the gospel if he didn't baptize them? Because Paul clearly stated: *"for in Christ Jesus I have begotten you through the gospel" (1 Cor. 4:15).* Ironically, its characteristic ploy of trying to defend a lie with another lie has once again caught up with it, and has proved that the gospel Paul preached....was *Not* its watered-down "water gospel!"

The CoC system empties the gospel of its content, while preserving its vocabulary. For instance, it gives lip service to verses that define the gospel, which is the fulfillment of all righteousness through the sinless life, death, burial and resurrection of Christ (e.g. 1 Cor. 15:1-4). But then it puts a twist on them by teaching that all of this is to be found in water baptism! The CoC *replaces* the necessity of faith in the sufficiency of Jesus' obedience, with the act of baptism, which is only a *figure* or "likeness" of His death, burial and resurrection, whereby we identify with Christ and demonstrate what the Holy Spirit has *already* done *literally* (Rom. 6:3-5, 1 Cor. 12:13).

We become children of God by grace through faith (Gal. 3:26). *Then* we can be *figuratively* buried with Him in baptism through this *faith...which is the operation of God (Col. 2:12).* Once we are born again from above by the Holy Spirit, through faith in Jesus' fulfillment of all righteousness on behalf of sinners, we can then *figuratively* "put on Christ" in baptism (Gal. 3:27). Just as we can put clothes on a baby AFTER it's born. While the CoC will deny a literal, *physical* putting on of Christ, it still teaches that one spiritually puts on Christ *savingly* in water baptism. Even though, Jesus *clearly* taught that a physical process cannot produce a spiritual operation (Jn. 3:6).

But the final, fatal blow to baptismal regeneration is where Paul says he didn't receive the gospel from man (Gal. 1:12). This ruins the CoC interpretation of Acts 22:16, which claims that Ananias gave Paul *the gospel* by telling him to be baptized to wash his sins away. Yet his zeal for Paul to be baptized was not to get him saved, but was to signify that he had *already received the gospel from Jesus in person* and had *already* surrendered to Him as Lord (Acts 26:15,16). Jesus had *already* promised to rescue him from the people He was sending him to (Acts 26:16-17), and had *already* changed his heart from that of a persecutor, to a praying man who was given his sight back and the Holy Spirit (Acts 9:6, 11, 17,18). For he had *already* been God's *"chosen vessel,"* to have Jesus revealed in him (Gal. 1:11-16)!

So, naturally, AFTER all of this, Paul would want to finally come clean before the people in the act of baptism, to testify to the fact that God had changed him and that his sins had *already* been *literally* washed away by Jesus' blood (Heb. 9:22, 26)!! Who wouldn't? Baptism is a beautiful, symbolic ordinance to be once enjoyed by all who believe in the sufficiency of Jesus' perfect sacrifice. Whereas those who say it's a requirement for salvation, mar its beauty by implying His grace and sacrifice wasn't enough.

Therefore, the person going through the ordinances must know and believe beyond all shadow of a doubt that their salvation is by grace alone, through faith alone, in Jesus' perfect righteousness alone as their only hope of God's acceptance, or else the ordinance becomes a witness against them.

So why put limits on God's power? He's still performing miracles today, every time someone is saved!! It's not what we do that saves us, but Who we have. *"He who has the Son has life" (1 Jn. 5:12).* And to truly know Him is to know and believe His message. One cannot claim to belong to Him if they are blindly trusting in a false gospel that renounces the true gospel that He came to proclaim (Jn. 18:37). By placing so much emphasis on baptism, the evil spirit behind the CoC system causes its captives to worship an ordinance, rather than the God behind the ordinance.

"What Campbellism teaches is that God literally remits sin through an ordinance. Hence there is a complete misunderstanding on the part of Campbellites of the place and purpose of ordinances. The animal sacrifice ordinances could **"never take away sin"** (Heb. 10:11). They were only types and shadows of the Christ who came and actually did **"put away sin by the sacrifice of Himself"** (Heb. 9:26). Ordinances furnish us with a representation of the real substance. In the Lord's Supper the bread and wine represent the body and blood of Christ; they are not the real substance. Romanism contends that the bread and wine are the real body and blood of Christ, just as Campbellism contends that baptism is the literal means of "contacting the blood." Both are wrong. They grasp the shadow and miss the substance" (Emphasis in original). [1]

"Indeed it is a true profanation of the truth of baptism to confuse it with the reality it represents. It is Christ's death, and our union with Him in the sovereign grace of God that effects redemption (Eph. 1:7), not the action of baptism." "The frequent perversion of its meaning leading to a false trust in the rite itself, rather than true and repentant faith in Christ, is one of the greatest "pulpit crimes" of the entire history of the church."

"Those who make human autonomy and freewill definitive of their theology have little consistent basis for avoiding such excesses, but those who rest upon the sovereignty of God and His divine ordination of both the ends and the means are in a position to do honor to all of the biblical revelation. A child drawn to baptism out of a desire to be baptized is being put in spiritual danger for the rest of his or her life. Those who have had "their tickets punched" and have been assured, mistakenly, of their eternal salvation solely due to something *they* did, a card they filled out, a prayer they recited, are some of the hardest people in the world to reach with a real message of repentance and faith. It is a pulpit crime indeed to encourage such shallow "conversionism" that is not born in the heart by a mighty work of the Spirit of God resulting in repentance and faith in Christ" (Emphasis his). [2]

Baptismal Regeneration is a False Gospel

Notes:

[1] Bob L. Ross, *Campbellism: Its History and Heresies*, (Pasadena, TX: Pilgrim Publications, 1981), p. 90. Also see his chapter on Acts 2:38 for further proof of how the CoC misinterprets this verse *severely*.

Also see: CAnswersTV YouTube channel playlist entitled, *"Dealing with Saved by Works & Baptism," "Church of Christ,"* with 93 (and counting) videos on Campbellism at: https://www.youtube.com/playlist?list=PLBD55090718DA6D3D

[2] James R. White, *Pulpit Crimes: The Criminal Mishandling of God's Word*, (Birmingham, AL: Solid Ground Christian Books, 2006), pp. 133, 137 and 139.

For more examples of the CoC's criminal mishandling of God's Word, see: Dallas R. Burdette, *From Legalism to Freedom*, (Xulon Press, 2008)--(who staunchly defended Alexander Campbell at every turn) and Cecil Hook, *Free in Christ*, free PDF available at: https://cecilhook.wordpress.com/pdf-books/

The CoC's *controlled opposition* now admits to its legalism and appears willing to ditch issues it was once so dogmatic about. Yet these superficial adjustments and fair speeches mean nothing as long as it still refuses to relinquish its false gospel and continues to re-package it. For example, CoC preacher, Mr. Hook, admits: *"Though denying it, we have accepted the concept of baptismal regeneration."* Then he turns around and says: *"When baptism is said to save us, a part of the conversion process is used to represent the whole with baptism being the finalizing act"* (p. 55).

Simply put, everything involved in their *"process"* of justification, culminates in water baptism. Most CoC authors refrain from calling it "baptismal regeneration," but still unashamedly list baptism as a pre-requisite for salvation, contacting the blood, being born again, etc. It is *truly* unbelievable! Rather than completely renouncing the CoC's false gospel, their literature is full of claims to be "reforming" the *exclusive* aspects of it, by no longer requiring one to *fully realize* that one's baptism...*is indeed literally "for remission of sins"*...as long as one just gets baptized.

This double-speak helps the CoC to eliminate all of the tedious re-baptisms it had been fearfully inducing for years, and enables it to now accommodate "ecumenical unity." So as long as people just get water baptized...they now have their CoC "ticket punched," according to its ever-evolving sacramental system. Likewise, Rome's *Vatican II* allows the same baptismal regeneration "reformation," in order to round up even more ecumenical alliances against the true gospel.

Also see: A.W. Pink, *The Doctrine of Election*, (Lindenhurst, NY: Great Christian Books, 2013), p. 176 -- He states as follows: *"History bears ample testimony that Rome detests the very name of Calvinism. "From all sects there may be some hope of obtaining converts to Rome except Calvinism," said the late 'Cardinal' Manning. Yet thousands of "Protestant" Arminians are annually rushing into her arms."*

Chapter 20

The Galatian Heresy

"Christ is become of no effect unto you, whosoever of you are justified by the law; ye are fallen from grace" (Gal. 5:4).

"Churches of Christ" are a modern counterpart to first century Judaism. The parallels are clearly seen in their faith plus works heresies, which they call "obedient faith," or "works of obedience." Like most other works-based religions of men, they too are inspired by the teachings of Jesus, but that does not make them Christian. A massive fall from grace occurs when one trusts their own "freewill" initiative to enter into God's promises by human works and/or by a physical process. False teachers in Galatia had done this very thing. They came in with this *different gospel* and taught that although faith is needed, more must be added in order to be truly saved (Gal. 5:4).

By doing so, they were implying that Jesus' work on behalf of His people was not sufficient. They implied that human works had to be added to the equation of salvation in order to make Jesus' finished work effectual, which caused many Galatians to fall from grace into works. Apostle Paul stood strongly against this heresy, just as we should, because false religions are still committing the Galatian heresy today, by adding works to faith in Christ. The CoC even takes this to a level that is stunning, for it teaches that a so-called "salvation by circumcision" has been replaced with "salvation by water baptism." For example, its literature states as follows:

"Christians still have an act that represents circumcision--a witness to the acceptance of God's covenant. Refusal to accept baptism is a refusal to accept the covenant of Christ, just as an uncircumcised descendant of Abraham was a covenant breaker. Imagine someone in the days of Moses preaching that circumcision was not necessary for salvation. The covenant of God is established through baptism and without this covenant there is no salvation."[1]

No wonder those who are still captives of the CoC system are unable to grasp the biblical fact that neither circumcision nor baptism has ever saved anyone. *"For in Jesus Christ neither circumcision availeth anything, nor uncircumcision; but faith which worketh by love" (Gal. 5:6)*. Without this true, saving faith, all works are dead and done by those who are dead in sins and trespasses, unless they have their spirits quickened from the dead, by the power and indwelling of the Holy Spirit applying the gifts and merits of Jesus' work to their hearts (Eph. 4:8). Because those He died for *will* finally obtain the gift of faith that produces true works of righteousness, *done in love and done in Christ* (Rom. 12:3, Acts 13:48, 2 Thess. 3:2).

Scripture *never* indicates that baptismal regeneration has replaced circumcision regeneration (Rom. 2:29, Col. 2). For one, there's no biblical proof of the existence of either. Furthermore, it would be erroneous to include females, who were not even candidates of circumcision, on the basis of baptism! Yet the CoC still tries to build a bridge between Old Covenant circumcision and New Covenant baptism that collapses in the middle.

Circumcision was given to both the spiritual and physical seed of Abraham. Baptism is reserved only for those who call upon the name of the Lord in saving faith. Circumcision was only for males. Baptism is for both male and female. Circumcision marked out a national identity with the nation Israel, under national promises, which were only a shadow of the Heavenly ones to come. But not all of Israel are true Israelites (Rom. 9:7-8).

Baptism is reserved only for those who are born again into the New Covenant. Therefore, circumcision has no reference to the New Covenant in Christ's blood. In the case of Abraham, circumcision was the seal of the faith that he had *before* circumcision and *before* the Mosaic Law was even introduced, just as we are saved thru faith today, *before* baptism! There was no necessity of faith for circumcision under the Old Covenant. Faith is the prerequisite for the waters of New Testament baptism. (Emphasis mine) [2]

Colossians 2:11-12 is clear, that the work of salvation is done without hands, by the Lord. God Himself works on the heart apart from our performance of religious formulas. This circumcision is that of the heart (Rom. 2:28-29), which only God can purify by faith (Acts 15:9).

Even in the Old Testament, God's people were justified by trusting in the coming Messiah, for *"there is none other name under heaven given among men, whereby we must be saved" (Acts 4:12)*. Abel died for his faith in the promised Seed (Gen. 3:15). Old Simeon, the woman at the well and all of God's people had been waiting for His arrival (Lk. 2:34, Jn. 4:25). Abraham seen His day and rejoiced (Jn. 8:56). All of the prophets from Moses spoke concerning Him (Lk. 24-25). Moses chose the reproach of Christ over the riches of Egypt (Heb. 11:26). They all drank from the same spiritual Rock, *"and that Rock was Christ" (1 Cor. 10:3-4).* All works of the law pointed *forward* to Christ, Whom they were to believe in. Even now, the law (which extends to all works) points *back* to Christ, Whom we are to have faith in.

But the CoC avoids these Old Testament truths like the plague, for they threaten its works-based system. So, instead, it falsely teaches that people were saved in the Old Testament under the Old Covenant of law, so that it can portray itself as a system that possesses the New Covenant of a "believing immersion" in Christ, to replace the Old Covenant of a "believing circumcision."[3] However, Romans 11:6 makes it clear that salvation is by God's grace alone, not works, not even "believing" works....or else it would no longer be grace, and Christ would have died in vain (Gal. 2:21).

So the CoC system must hide O. T. pointers to faith in Christ, or else its members would conclude that salvation has *ALWAYS* been through faith in Jesus' imputed righteousness as the only hope for sinners. *"For Christ is the end of the law for righteousness to all who believe" (Rom. 10:4).* He fulfilled all righteousness on behalf of His people (past, present and future), so they don't work to *be* saved, they work *because* they are saved. He gives them a holy hatred of sin and a holy faith and love in Him, for His power works mightily in them...*to do His will* (Phil. 2:13, Eph. 1:19). But the CoC commits Rome's fatal error, by creating false distinctions between—

....."works of the law" (which they admit are not a condition for salvation) and "works" (which they insist are a condition of salvation). But contrary to the Catholic claim, Paul's statements against 'works' cannot be limited to only 'works of the [Mosaic] law (such as circumcision) but extend equally to all kinds of meritorious works, for all such works will in one way or another be works in accordance with God's law. They would not be *good* works if they were not in accordance with God's standard of goodness, namely, his law. Since God is the standard of all righteousness, it follows that all true works of righteousness will be according to his law and nature. It is only *our* righteousness (=self-righteousness) that is abhorrent in God's eyes" (cf. Isa. 64:6; Rom. 10:3, emphasis and brackets his). [4]

The CoC is caught in a hopeless contradiction concerning Romans 4, by claiming Paul's condemnation against works was only against works of the Mosaic Law, which hadn't even been introduced during Abraham's day! All of the verses against works salvation concerning Abraham have to do with *all works period, not* just works of the O.T. law! Yet when confronted with this, the CoC tries to save face, by claiming that Abraham was under the Patriarchal Law! But either way, the CoC creates a false dichotomy between "good works done in faith" and "works of the law." The fact is that *all good works* are in accordance with God's law (His perfect standard of righteousness). *Or else they would be lawless works and not good at all!*

Moreover, the "trees" (God's people) have to first be *declared* righteous and good by God, through the imputed righteousness of Christ, *before* they can actually produce good fruits of righteousness. But false religion always puts the fruit before the tree, which convolutes the entire gospel. A bad, dead in sins "tree" cannot go through a physical process, such as baptism, and expect to be saved as a result (Mt. 7:15-20). One must *FIRST* be *born from above* in the washing and renewing of Holy Spirit regeneration, not *born from below* in baptismal regeneration... *which doesn't exist* (Titus 3:5).

No wonder Paul feared his people's minds would be corrupted by the subtlety of the devil, from the simplicity that is in Christ (2 Cor. 11:3-4). He feared they would fall for a different gospel and put up with those who try to complicate the true gospel of God's grace alone, through faith alone, in Jesus' righteousness alone. And that's what had happened to me.

But to the praise of God's glorious grace, I was able to humbly repent for ever trying to make use of an ordinance to get saved, for it had been such an abomination to the Lord, and an insult to His free and sovereign, saving grace. So I was re-baptized *biblically,* in order to follow Christ *in spirit and in truth.* By publically renouncing the heretical CoC baptism that had spiritually paralyzed and stunted me so many years ago, it indicated that God had set my conscience free! I also testified to the fact that it's hard to die to self... *but Jesus is worth it.* It's hard to die to the world... *but Jesus is worth it.* It's hard to die to people, especially the people you love... *but Jesus is worth it.* Jesus is everything we need. Without Him we would have nothing.

What a beautiful testimony to the fact that *Christ rescued me!* And my loved ones even got to witness the demonstration of it, and were blessed by it. Words cannot describe the glorious freedom that is found only in Christ!

"Stand fast therefore in the liberty wherewith Christ hath made us free, and be not entangled again with the yoke of bondage" (Gal. 5:1).

The Galatian Heresy

Notes:

[1] La Vista Church of Christ, *Questions and Answers Regarding Circumcision and Baptism.* Retrieved May 3, 2018 from:
http://lavistachurchofchrist.org/LVanswers/2005/07-16.htm

[2] Robert M. Zins, Th.M., *Romanism: the Relentless Roman Catholic Assault on the Gospel of Jesus Christ*, Fourth Edition, (Charlotte, NC: A Christian Witness to Roman Catholicism, 2010), p. 105, paraphrased. It must be noted that some reformed Protestants (such as Presbyterians) will often try to make a connection between O.T. circumcision and N.T. baptism. But most do not take it to the level that the CoC does, such as sinfully making circumcision and baptism out to be *sacramentally redemptive,* which is completely heretical. Even now, the CoC still cannot construct a solid, biblical stance for such an unwarranted assumption. By God's decree, Paul devoted the Galatian Judaizers to an eternity in Hell for such heresy (Gal. 1-2).

[3] See: Allen Webster, *When the Fullness of Time Was Come.* Retrieved May 3, 2018 from: https://www.housetohouse.com/when-the-fullness-of-time-was-come/

The CoC teaches that the types and shadows in the Old Testament refer to "patterns" for an obedience-based system, rather than pointers to faith in Jesus' imputed righteousness alone. It teaches that faith in the O.T. was simply "faith" in a "pattern of obedience," which Messiah "allegedly" came to perfect. The CoC claims that *it is* that *"better system,"* with the so-called "New Testament Pattern." And it falsely claims that it was revealed and instituted by Jesus!

[4] Geisler, Norman L. & MacKenzie, Ralph E., *Roman Catholics and Evangelicals: Agreements and Differences,* (Grand Rapids: Baker Books, 1995), p. 234. Sadly, even though these authors annihilated Romanism, they were not courageous enough to declare that Roman Catholicism is not true Christianity. *"The fear of man bringeth a snare: but whoso putteth his trust in the Lord shall be safe" (Prov. 29:25).*

Part 4

How God *Really* Saves

Chapter 21

God Saves by Giving

"For the gifts and the calling of God are irrevocable" (Rom. 11:29, NKJV).

God saves by first GIVING us a revelation of our total depravity and how we are utterly destitute of any claim upon His favor. He saves by GIVING us a revelation of how lost and undone we are. He saves by GIVING us the revelation that we are undeserving of anything but eternal damnation. He saves by GIVING us the revelation that we must throw ourselves upon His mercy. He saves by showing us how desperately we need the Savior. He saves by GIVING us a revelation of the true Christ, and by GIVING us a will to come to Him for righteousness, in order to reconcile us to Himself. He saves by GIVING us faith in Jesus' righteousness alone as our only acceptance before His holy presence. He saves by GIVING us a revelation of how filthy our own self-righteousness is in His sight, how we must abandon it, renounce our own will, and be ruled by His. God saves by GIVING and *accepting* the perfect righteousness of Christ on our behalf, for Jesus GAVE Himself as a ransom for many (e.g. Mt. 20:28, Gal. 1:4; 2:20, Eph. 5:25).

However, the CoC teaches that God saves by expecting us to perfectly fulfill His laws and commandments, or at least to the "best of our ability." It teaches that God saves by expecting us to follow the pattern Jesus set forth. But, according to His Word, He saves by His blood, and His blood is not laws, commandments or patterns, but a redeeming price. We can contribute nothing to it, or else we could boast. God saves by GIVING to us, not by expecting from us. And once God GIVES, *then* we are enabled to serve Him acceptably through Jesus, for it's His power that works in us (Phil. 2:13).

Yet if we were expected to fulfill all of God's commands perfectly before we could be saved, then we'd all be doomed. Can any honest person claim to be able to fulfill God's impossible command to be perfect (Mt. 5:48)? Absolutely Not! James 2:10 makes it clear that we blew that possibility the first time we ever sinned. But what's impossible for man is not impossible with God (Mk. 10:27). Though Scripture reveals our responsibility to fulfill all of God's commands, it also reveals our inability to do so unless God intervenes (e.g. Ezek. 18; 36:22, 26 and 27, Rom. 8:7, 1 Cor. 2:14). For only He can *"make you perfect in every good work to do His will, working in you that which is well pleasing in His sight, through Jesus Christ" (Heb. 13:20).*

"For God so loved the world, that He GAVE His only begotten Son, that whosoever believeth in Him should not perish, but have everlasting life" (Jn. 3:16). John uses the word "world" here to reveal that salvation is not just for the Jews, but for *"whosoever believeth."* For God's divine power has GIVEN a diverse multitude of people all that they need for life and godliness, which would have to include the special graces of saving faith and repentance (2 Pet. 1:3). He saves *"not according to our works, but according to His own purpose and grace, which was GIVEN us in Christ Jesus before the world began" (2 Tim. 1:9).* And *"it is GIVEN in behalf of Christ, not only to believe on Him, but also to suffer for His sake" (Phil. 1:29). (Emphasis mine)*

God saves by GIVING the Savior to His people, and by GIVING His people to the Savior, Who says, *"All that the Father GIVETH Me shall come to Me; and him that cometh to Me I will in no wise cast out" (Jn. 6:37, emphasis mine).* For they are *"justified freely by His grace through the redemption that is in Christ Jesus"*…*"in Whom we have redemption through His blood, the forgiveness of sins, according to the riches of His grace" (Eph. 1:7).* All the glory goes to God the Father Who purposed salvation, God the Son Who purchased it and God the Holy Spirit Who applies it!!

Praise be to God, Who has been so merciful, kind and loving to GIVE His grace so freely to those who don't deserve it, to those who have no spiritual strength of their own. *"For when we were yet without strength, in due time Christ died for the ungodly" (Rom. 5:6).* God saves bad people.

Dear reader, are you a bad person? Then you're qualified for the Savior. And you need Him, for you cannot even dare to come to such a holy and righteous God without the Savior. His blood covers all sin, so that sinners can be *"accepted in the Beloved." (Eph. 1:6).* I encourage you to pray for His mercy, for it is God Who GIVES repentance and faith, which is why He never rejects those who repent and believe by the irresistible power of His might.

If you are at the end of your rope because you realize that you can never, in your own power, do enough to be acceptable to such a holy God, then I have Good News for you! His grace is enough. Jesus has already done the redeeming work and He said "it is finished." And He's saying to you now, *"Come unto Me, all ye that labour and are heavy laden, and I will GIVE you* rest" (Mt. 11:28, emphasis mine). Jesus is able to save to the uttermost (Heb. 7:25). And "uttermost" means to the most extreme, imaginable degree, because of the unchanging, never-ending nature of Jesus' perpetual priesthood. Jesus *"ever lives"* to intercede for His people, by pleading the merits of His blood in the presence of God the Father on *their* behalf.

So, as long as Jesus' blood has merit, and as long as He *"ever liveth"* (which is forever), His people have salvation! His precious blood can never lose its merit based on any inability within Himself or due to any weakness in His people, for He *"is able to do exceeding abundantly above all that we ask or think, according to the power that worketh in us"* (Eph. 3:20).

Jesus said, *"I GIVE unto them eternal life; and they shall never perish, neither shall any pluck them out of My hand. My Father, which GAVE them Me, is greater than all; and no man is able to pluck them out of My Father's hand"* (Jn. 10:28-29). So how could anyone ever believe salvation can be lost when it's based on Jesus' merit, not ours... *unless* one's "faith" is really in themselves and what they do, instead of in Jesus and what He's done.

"Are you so foolish? Having begun in the Spirit, are ye now made perfect by the flesh" (Gal. 3:3)? If we could ever possibly reach sinless perfection here, then we wouldn't need to be saved by an act still being performed by the Living Savior---His intercession! Apostle Paul knew this and made it clear that it's only because of Jesus continually pleading His blood, that believers are able to overcome and be brought safely home (Rom. 7:18-19, 8:26-39).

However, God's people can never boast that He loves them "just the way they are," for in deep humility and repentance they must admit that God loves them *despite* who they are. They are sinners who have had the price of their redemption paid for *in full* by Jesus' blood. And it was an actual payment, not a hypothetical one that's only applied if we "name it and claim it." We can't push Jesus aside and seat ourselves on God's throne and legalistically "plead the blood" as a formula for protection or deliverance. In fact, Scripture contains no record of phrases like those ever being used by the apostles, prophets or any other believer. For Jesus is the only One Who can truly plead His blood for the sheep (Jn. 10:15).

And He said, *"I pray not for the world, but for them which Thou hast GIVEN Me; for they are Thine"* (Jn. 17:9). Here He makes a distinction between the *whole* world and those who belong to God. Jesus' prayers for His people cannot fail, so He keeps their faith from failing (Lk. 22:32). His blood covers ALL the sins of those He died for (past, present and future), including the sin of unbelief. So those whom God has ordained to eternal life are enabled to *believe through grace* (Acts 13:48; 18:27). He doesn't begin the work of salvation and expect us to finish it, for only He *"is able to keep you from falling,"* because God saves to the uttermost (Jude 24, 25)!

Only by Jesus' merits does God GRANT His people the gift of faith to savingly trust in Jesus, and to them only *"it is GIVEN to know the mystery of the kingdom of God"* (Mk. 4:11, emphasis mine). Only by Jesus' merits does God GRANT reconciliation (2 Cor. 5:19, 21). Only by Jesus' merits does God GRANT repentance (2 Tim. 2:25). Only by Jesus' merits does God GRANT the ability to follow Him in obedience. All spiritual blessings are GIVEN only in Jesus Christ, *"Who of God is made unto us wisdom, and righteousness, and sanctification and redemption"* (1 Cor. 1:30). *"Without Me you can do nothing"* (Jn. 15:5). *"Their righteousness is of Me saith the Lord"* (Isa. 54:17).

Our duty to God is made clear.... *"If ye will fear the Lord, and serve Him, then shall ye continue following the Lord your God"* (1 Sam. 12:14)....along with the fact that only God can enable us to fulfill our duty.... *"I will put My fear in their hearts, that they shall not depart from Me"* (Jer.32:40). So His people can declare that their salvation is all God's work *(Isa. 26:12)*.

Jesus *"bore our sins in His own body on the tree, so that we, being dead to sins, should live unto righteousness"* (1 Pet. 2:24). He GAVE His life for the sheep (Jn. 10:11). He loves His Church and He GAVE Himself for it (Eph. 5:2, 25). And to whom much is GIVEN...*then* much is expected in return, for His people have a glorious stewardship to uphold (Lk. 12:48, 1 Cor. 4:2).

When God GRANTS true, saving faith, it is *then* in our possession to exercise that free gift as a good steward of His blessing. For it is *then* "our faith" and "our act," but only in the sense that it has been BESTOWED upon us (Eph. 2:8). And we are commanded to use the means that God has provided to increase our faith, but it is He Who GIVES the increase (1 Cor. 3:6). We are to *Never* take personal credit for it ourselves. For if it was a natural endowment we were born with, everyone would have it, and it wouldn't be referred to as a gift in God's Word (2 Thess. 3:2). *"What do you have that you did not receive? Now if you did indeed receive it, why do you glory as if you had not received it"* (1 Cor. 4:7, NKJV)? Everything that makes a Christian differ from others is GIVEN by God. Therefore, God gets all of the glory. So *"he that glorieth, let him glory in the Lord"* (1 Cor. 1:31).

Chapter 22

God's Perfect Redeeming Love

"What man of you, having an hundred sheep, if he lose one of them, doth not leave the ninety and nine in the wilderness, and go after that which is lost, until he find it? And when he hath found it, he layeth it on his shoulders, rejoicing" (Lk. 15:3-5).

The theological thoughts of many these days seem to resemble the lyrics of an old 80's song that says, "shove me in the shallow water, before I get too deep." No wonder so many are attracted to sermons that portray God's love as broad and shallow, like a wide river that welcomes all without exclusion, but with no depth to keep anyone afloat. As a result, they are led to believe that God allows all to approach Him, and by their own way, but that He doesn't secure the salvation of any.

But thankfully, the Bible shows that God's love goes so much deeper than that. The special love that God has for His own is like a narrow river, but it welcomes *all kinds* of people without distinction (from all walks of life), and is deep enough to keep them afloat all the way to the throne of God. In other words, God chooses those who approach Him and the Way they are to approach Him (through Jesus' blood), but He secures the salvation of all He has chosen (Ps. 65:4, Mt. 22:14, Jn. 5:21, 10:28, 29 and 1 Cor. 1:27-31).

The great wonder of God's love is not that He loves all (Rom. 9:13), as many assume, but that He loves *any* at all, and that His choice is based only on His sovereign mercy and loving kindness. Because if God didn't make the ultimate choice, no one would be saved at all, for our choices are governed by the sin that dwells in our flesh, unless the Holy Spirit quickens us, dwells within us and enables us to walk in the light as He is in the light (1 Jn. 1:7,8).

Yet Jesus warns, *"If therefore the light that is in thee be darkness, how great is that darkness" (Mt. 6:23).* Because the devil also poses as an angel of light and convinces many that Jesus' blood atonement provided an all-inclusive, shallow river that goes only halfway to the throne of Heaven so that all must walk the rest of the way themselves. And this causes many to shipwreck and walk in the "light" of legalism, while assuming those who end up in Hell just weren't as good as them. How prideful and insulting to God! Jesus paid His peoples sin debt in full. So why would any of them end up paying for their own sins again in Hell for eternity (Mt. 5:26)? God is just and doesn't demand a payment twice; first from Jesus, then again from those who have already had their sin debt cancelled. Those who end up in Hell are actually those whom God has turned over to their own lusts, who often think that they can come to God on their own terms (Rom. 1:28).

A shallow theology that keeps people from being assured that Jesus secures the salvation of all those He died for, also keeps them from taking a decided stance against evil. For they can never consistently declare, *"We know that we are of God, and the whole world lieth in wickedness" (1 Jn. 5:19).* And so, they fall prey to the harassing distractions of the world, and become less cautious about who they associate with and how they spend their time. Their attention spans get shortened, and the cares of the world disables their ability to ponder and study the deep things of God. For a half-hearted faith cannot give undivided attention to the cause of Christ and the privilege of being in constant prayer and loving communion with Him.

By compromising and conforming to the world, many show that they have not been perfected in the love of God (1 Jn. 5). They are unable to obey the command to *"love not the world, neither the things that are in the world. If any man love the world, the love of the Father is not in him" (1 Jn. 2:15).*

Some might say that is contradictory, for God loves the world. However, God loves the world only in the same sense that we should love it…by proclaiming the gospel to those we know in the world, which is the ultimate act of love…*Not* by an evil participation in the world.

That invisible, spiritual system of evil that hates God is a world that God hates, and it's to be overcome by His people through Jesus. There is also the beautiful world of nature that God created to be cared for and enjoyed. We are also to love all the people God has created in this world. But those who believe lies that keep them from saving faith in the trustworthiness of Christ, cannot fully experience the perfect love and forgiveness of God (Lk. 7:47), which would enable them to truly love and forgive others. And without this, it is not a good sign that they've truly been forgiven (Mt. 6:14).

But those who are rooted and grounded in love, through saving faith in Christ, are able to reciprocate with love and forgiveness toward others. And by this they can *know* that they have passed from death to life (1 Jn. 3:14).

They can then *"comprehend with all saints what is the breadth, and length, and depth, and height; And to know the love of Christ, which passeth knowledge" (Eph. 3:17-19).* By knowing the truth about Christ, they can know His perfect, redeeming love that casts out all fear of Hell (1 Jn. 4:18).

And though God's people can do whatever they want... thanks to His Fatherly, disciplining love, their *wants* have been changed, for He chastens those He loves (Heb. 12:6). Their hope in Christ purifies their life (1 Jn. 3:3) so that they have a continually decreasing desire for anything that offends God or opposes His truth, because *"all that is in the world, the lust of the flesh, and the lust of the eyes, and the pride of life, is not of the Father, but is of the world (1 Jn. 2:16).* Those who can freely sin and not be convicted and chastened by God... have no part in Him (Heb. 12:8).

Those perfected in God's love have a tendency to maintain a more watchful guard over their own hearts and minds. They are so effected by a sense of the love of Christ that their whole lives are ruled, dominated and motivated to stand against anything that is contrary to His holy nature. Rather than remaining desensitized to evil and approving of it by being entertained by it, they would rather say: *"I will set no wicked thing before mine eyes. I hate the work of them that turn aside; it shall not cleave to me." (Ps. 101:3).* Although their spirit is in a constant battle against sin, the flesh, the devil and the world, their inward prayer is often along the lines of what is found in the book of Psalms, where David is constantly seeking after God, while pleading for the ability to live holy for Him (e.g. Ps. 119).

But sadly, many worldly people think that if they are seeking what only God can provide, they must surely be seeking God. But Jesus told a multitude that they were only seeking Him for His earthly benefits, not for the fact that His miracles proved His Deity and eternal benefits. So they were *Not* really seeking God, and Jesus explained why---*"No man can come to Me, except the Father which hath sent Me draw him" (Jn. 6:26, 44, 66).*

Jesus' words were so offensive, many walked away. Because, like today, many admit God is sovereign over nations and temporal life, but they can't handle the fact that God is sovereign over all things, including eternal life. The unregenerate would rather walk away from the Sovereign Lordship of the true God and Savior and make up a god they are more comfortable with, for *"it's not in man that walketh to direct his own steps" (Jer. 10:23).* But those *ordained* to eternal life are savingly drawn to Jesus (Acts 13:48).

So why does God command us to seek Him and proclaim the gospel? Since only God changes hearts and draws sinners to Jesus to be saved, why should we take action at all? *Obviously,* the answer is simple...*He commands us to!* Although He knows some won't obey in spirit and truth, He knows some will. When God commanded light to shine out of darkness (Gen. 1), everything didn't become light, but what God *ordained* to be light, obeyed His command. That's why there is a universal call of the gospel, but not a universal redemption, *"for many be called, but few chosen" (Mt. 20:16).*

Although fallen humanity has the "light of conscience" and the "light of creation" to prompt them to an outward performance of God's commands, they cannot seek Jesus from a pure heart unless God commands the "light of the gospel" to shine into their hearts. And a mere outward response isn't the deciding factor, God is. In fact, God's supreme sovereignty in salvation is so obvious that Jesus recaps this point in John 6:65 by saying, *"No man can come unto Me, except it were given unto him of the Father."*

The false doctrine of "decisional regeneration" exalts man's will as the deciding factor in salvation. But only Holy Spirit regeneration can bring spiritual life. True believers *"have this treasure in earthen vessels so that the excellency of the power may be of God and not of us" (2 Cor. 4:3-7),* for those who receive God's free gift, aren't those with more "willpower," but are those whom God has given the power to become His (Jn. 1:12, 13). *"For it is not of man who wills or runs, but of God who shows mercy" (Rom. 9:16).*

"For who maketh thee to differ from another" (1 Cor. 4:7)? Are Christians different because they are better than others? Are they able to receive, repent, believe and obey the gospel by virtue of having more *"common grace"* of character, conviction, morality or ability to choose the things of God? Absolutely not! Or else they would not need the Savior, and could do without God's perfect, redeeming love and sovereign, saving grace.

So dear reader, although many turn away from such a sovereign God, I plead with you to submit to Him. You don't have to try to be better than others. Just cry out to God for mercy, confessing your desperate need for the Savior. He never turns away those who are truly broken-hearted over sin (Ps. 51:17). Jesus came to seek and save an endless multitude of people who are poor in spirit. So be encouraged, no one is closer to God's free grace than when they finally realize the poverty of their own sinfulness and powerlessness, compared to God's sovereign, majestic holiness!

Chapter 23

God's Foreknowledge and Predestination

"For whom He did foreknow He also did predestinate to be conformed to the image of His Son…..Moreover whom He did predestinate, them He also called: and whom He called, them He also justified: and whom He justified, them He also glorified" (Rom. 8:29-30).

So now we come to *the golden chain of redemption*, where we get a glorious glimpse of God's golden scepter of grace being extended throughout the corridors of time. It beautifully reveals that His predestined election is by grace, not by works, and not even by God's foreknowledge of our works. Because God saw sin on the horizon from the beginning, which is why He ordained His eternal plan of redemption in the first place, before time even began (e.g. Eph. 1, 2 Thess. 2:13, 2 Tim. 1:9).

God will not and cannot make another God. He is self-existent, self-sustaining and He alone is God. For He says: *"Before Me there was no God formed, neither shall there be after Me (Isa. 43:10).* It's the law of creation. And since only God is unchangeable, the creatures He made are changeable.

In the beginning God made everything good and upright. But since the creatures that He made cannot be God and cannot be unchangeable, it was inevitable that they would change and fall from their original righteousness into sin. However, God decreed to permit it in order to manifest His justice, mercy, grace and the glory of Jesus Christ, by redeeming those He has chosen *in Him* before the foundation of the world (1 Pet. 1:2, 20).

But many Bible verses are used to try to support the false, freewill doctrine. Even the fall of man is often used to try to prove the absolute, autonomous freewill of man. But by rightly dividing the Word of truth, it all ends up confirming God's absolute sovereignty that much more. Matthew 23:37, *in context,* reveals that Jesus reprimanded the Pharisees for putting stumbling blocks (obstructions and discouragements) before God's children in Jerusalem, for they were jealous of their desire to come to Christ (similar to what the CoC does). However, God's sovereignty is beautifully revealed in the fact that even though the Pharisees were not willing to let them enter into God's kingdom, those who were meant to come to Christ did anyway, because *nothing* can hinder them from doing so for very long (Mt. 23:13)!

Yet natural religions of the flesh still twist 1Timothy 2:1-4 to imply that God *tries* to save *all* people (without exclusion), which would imply that His efforts could be futile. But the *context* reveals that He purposes to save *all kinds* of people (without distinction), *even those in authority (v. 2),* which means that even king's hearts are at His disposal (Prov. 21:1). His will to save is *Not* determined by earthly factors, but solely upon His own sovereign purposes, which are *always* fulfilled (Isa. 46:11, Rom. 8:28).

2 Peter 3:9 says, *"The Lord is not slack concerning His promise, as some men count slackness; but is longsuffering to* **us-ward***, not willing that any should perish, but that all should come to repentance"* (Emphasis mine). But Arminianism puts a spin on this verse, to try to make it seem as if there are many in Hell that God planned to save, but couldn't, due to their almighty "freewill." Yet in context, it becomes clear who the "us-ward" are that Peter was writing to...*the elect!!*... "the children of *promise*"..."*that have obtained like precious faith*" (Gal. 4:28, 1 Pet. 1:2, 2 Pet. 1:1). Because the elect will *never* perish in Hell, for Jesus said, *"I give them eternal life; and they shall never perish, neither shall any man pluck them out of My hand (Jn. 10:28).*[1]

The key to understanding many of these verses is to know the difference between *God's preceptive will of command* and *God's decretive will of purpose*. We can resist His precepts and commands by not obeying Him. Yet even with this resistance, God must allow it. We cannot resist sovereignly and autonomously, for our will is limited. God's decretive will of purpose is what actually happens, because it's what God has divinely ordained and decreed, so that it cannot be resisted or changed. *"O the depth of the riches both of the wisdom and knowledge of God! How unsearchable are His judgments, and His ways past finding out"* (Rom. 11:33).

According to *God's preceptive will of command*, He commands the reasonable duty of all His creatures to obey His precepts, for they are good and holy, because they reflect His character and reveal His worthiness to be worshipped. So anytime we go against His perfect precepts and commands, we are sinning against Him. As God, He commands and deserves all of our worship and praise, for it is obviously all of creations *duty* to worship the Creator. This is why it's right for God to command all to repent, believe and obey the gospel of Jesus Christ, even though He knows all will not do this.

According to *God's decretive will of purpose*, He foreknew what would happen when people would be left to themselves. He foreknew that without His saving mercy, they would refuse to keep His commands and would reject Christ and His offer of salvation (Jn. 12:39-40). Thus, He could *infallibly declare* that they would not inherit salvation. He didn't make them wicked, and He didn't cause them to sin by leaving them to themselves. He just gives them over to their own desires. Neither does He predestine people to Hell in the same electing way He predestines people to Heaven, for the type of double predestination called "equal ultimacy" is heretical.

God simply foreknows that those He leaves to themselves will end up in Hell due to the natural consequences of sin. He takes *"no pleasure in the death of the wicked" (Ezek. 18:23, 32; 33:11),* and does no harm by leaving them in the condition He originally made them in---*upright image bearers of God* (Eccl. 7:29). So they are *without excuse*. This is one way He makes His power known and is one way He reveals how bad sin is. But He does all of this sinlessly and is justified in all that He does (Rom. 1:20, 24, 28; 9:22).

God foreknows all things because He foreordains all things (Rom. 11:36, Rev. 4:11). For example, God *prophesied* to Moses that He would harden Pharaoh's heart for *His purpose* of being glorified in the deliverance of Israel (Ex. 4:21). This is why God could *infallibly declare* to Moses that Pharaoh would refuse to listen, because He was going to leave Pharaoh to his own sinful, fallen will (Ex. 7:13, 22; 8:15; 9:12). And note, God could not have *infallibly declared* Pharaoh's destiny if Pharaoh could have repented and changed his own heart and mind apart from God's saving grace (Rom. 9:17).

God knows His own in a *special* way because He decreed that they would be holy and blameless before time began, for the purpose of glorifying His grace (Eph. 1:4-6). He also knows those who aren't His elect, but only in a *general* way, for He created them. *"The Lord hath made all things for Himself: yea, even the wicked for the day of evil" (Prov. 16:4).* Hell, the wicked and even the cross all reveal the glory of God's holy wrath and justice. Moreover, they all exist to reveal the incredible worth of the Savior!

Yet Arminianism makes Jesus and His finished work seem worthless, by teaching the lie that our "freewill" determines whether we are saved or not. It declares that we must "allow" God to save us by believing. But Scripture says just the opposite. *"As many as were ordained to eternal life believed" (Acts 13:48).* God intimately foreknew His people because He foreordained them to eternal life, the same way He foreordained Jesus to be a sacrifice for their sins (Acts 2:23). The same Greek word used for "foreknow" is also translated as "foreordain" in other verses as well (e.g. 1 Pet. 1:1, 20).

God foreknew those He has chosen to eternal life, for they've been *"called according to His purpose,"* not according to His mere observation of their future "freewill" choices. Jesus laid His life down *for the sheep*, knowing exactly who He was dying for on the cross (Jn. 13:1, Rom. 8:28). He died for *people,* not a nameless, faceless plan. And He says to those who are not His, *"ye believe not, because ye are not of My sheep"* (Mt. 25:32-34). But still, no one is excused from their reasonable duty to repent and believe the gospel, for God's sovereignty and man's responsibility are compatible.

Although God takes divine initiative in salvation, we are not excused from our reasonable duty to use the means that He provides. When Jesus taught that regeneration is a divine act (e.g. Jn. 3:5, 6:29, 37, 44, 63 and 65), someone raised an objection to His doctrine by asking *"are there few that be saved?"* And His reply was, *"strive to enter in at the strait gate; for many, I say unto you, will seek to enter in, and shall not be able"* (Lk. 13:23-24).

Our duty is to put all of our trust in Jesus and His power to save...*no matter what...* even before we know for sure that He died specifically for us or not. Only then can we know that He is faithful to all of His promises, and that He is sovereign over salvation, and that its main purpose is to glorify Him, which should bring us the most inexpressible joy imaginable! And it should be our greatest comfort ever to know that nothing takes God by surprise, for He's in complete control of all things. *"Before I formed thee in the belly I knew thee; and before thou camest forth out of the womb I sanctified thee, and I ordained thee a prophet unto the nations"* (Jer. 1:5).

"The foundation of God standeth sure, having this seal, The Lord knoweth them that are His" (2 Tim. 2:19).

Notes:

[1] For a fuller discussion and deeper, biblical exegesis on these particular verses, see: Dr. James White, *The Potters Freedom*, New Revised Ed., (Calvary Press Publishing, 2009). See his chapter 6 on the main "Big Three" verses that Arminianism twists.

Chapter 24

The True Nature of the Atonement of Christ

"...we also joy in God through our Lord Jesus Christ, by Whom we have now received the atonement" (Rom. 5:11).

It has been demonstrated throughout this book, how the freewill doctrine is at the root of every false religion, how it teaches that our will determines God's will, and shipwrecks faith in His Word. So now, let's more deeply observe how it perverts the atonement of Christ by promoting a universal atonement that makes salvation "possible" for *all*.... but certain for *none*.

An Arminian atonement has all believers being justified, but not glorified, which turns Scripture on its head, where it's made clear that those who are justified will *inevitably* be glorified. None who are justified by Christ can *ever* be condemned in Hell. They will all be glorified in Heaven, for the Father declares them righteous, based solely upon Jesus' perfect righteousness.

According to Scripture, those Jesus died for, are those God foreknew, predestined, called, justified *And* glorified---past tense and certain (Rom. 8:29-39). Yet Arminianism substitutes the effect for the cause and "puts the cart before the horse," by implying that we must *cause* Jesus to die and accomplish all of this for us... by believing, receiving, etc. How ridiculous!

How can we cause something that God *"determined before to be done" (Acts 4:28)*? *"Man can receive nothing, except it be given him from heaven" (Jn. 3:27).* Believing and receiving are fruits of Christ's effectual atonement, *Not* the cause, for we can only *"believe, according to the working of His mighty power, which He wrought in Christ" (Eph. 1:19-20; 3:7).*

Those whom Christ died for are *"elect according to the foreknowledge of God" (1 Pet. 1:2).* Not because of His foreknowledge concerning the exercise of their "freewill," but He elected them *"according to the good pleasure of His will"* (Eph. 1:4-5). God's election of grace is the *cause*, whereas faith, repentance and godliness are the *fruits*, given on account of the merits of Jesus' blood (Acts 18:27, Rom. 11:5-6). *"For the children being not yet born, neither having done any good or evil, that the purpose of God according to election might stand, not of works, but of Him that calleth" (Rom. 9:11).*

Jesus' death atoned for *all* the sins of *all* the elect throughout the entire world, including the sin of unbelief (Heb. 10:12), which is why none of the elect that Jesus died for can end up in Hell for unbelief. *"For who shall lay anything to the charge of God's elect? It is God that justifieth. Who is he that condemneth? It is Christ that died, yea that is risen again, Who is even at the right hand of God, Who also maketh intercession for us" (Rom. 8:34).* His intercession for them can never fail, so their faith can never finally fail (Lk. 22:32, Jn. 17:9, Heb. 7:25)... for it's *"the faith of God's elect" (Titus 1:1).*

Thank God in Heaven, the atonement of Christ did all that He intended; an actual payment, for actual sins, of actual people that He has ordained to eternal life....those He draws out of the well of darkness and sin *through the gift of faith (Eph. 2:8-10).* He didn't just provide an abstract "possibility" of salvation; He secured the actual purchase and sure salvation of actual people. God had their names in the Lambs book of life before the foundation of the world and promises to never blot them out (Rev. 3:5; 13:8; 17:8), which is why Jesus said that they *Shall* come to Him (Jn. 6:37).

And His Word says to them, *"God hath from the beginning chosen you to salvation, through sanctification of the Spirit and belief of the truth" (2 Thess. 2:13).* For when one is born of the Holy Spirit, they will be enabled to love, obey and believe the truth. This, in turn, will enable them to *make their calling and election sure (2 Pet. 1:10).* Because what God accomplished in times past, is worked out through human actions in the course of time.

Although it's not always easy for God's people to distinguish the working out of *God's* will in *their* coming to Christ, God is the *first cause* of their coming, for *"the preparations of the heart, and the answer of the tongue, is from the Lord" (Prov. 16:1).* In eternity past, God set them apart for Himself and effectually calls them by His grace, in His perfect timing (Gal. 1:15).

Regeneration and quickening by the Holy Spirit, occurs *before* anyone even has the *desire* to respond to the gospel call (1 Cor. 2:14, 4:7). Regeneration, faith and repentance are so inseparable that it's hard to tell where one begins and the other ends.

Jesus is the author, purchaser and finisher of His people's faith. Even their repentance is a *provision* of the gospel that Christ *procured,* in order to enable His people to follow His commands. *"There is therefore now no condemnation to them which are in Christ Jesus, who walk not after the flesh, but after the Spirit. For the law of the Spirit of life in Christ Jesus hath made me free from the law of sin and death"* (Rom. 8:1-2).

God has provided what He commands, or else no one would be saved. Yet false teachers convolute the whole gospel by teaching that we must *first* conjure up our *own* faith and repentance (in a degenerate, fallen state), and *then* Jesus' atonement would atone. How ridiculous! How could anyone wholeheartedly put their trust in Christ if His atonement didn't *actually* atone, unless our works are added to it...to *make* Jesus die for us? How ludicrous! How can anyone be called to trust in an inefficient atonement that allows some that He died for to slip thru the cracks? How can one trust in an atonement that can't even save people from themselves, let alone from Hell!? Yet this is the kind of blasphemy that's being preached today!

The true nature of the atonement is that it *actually* atoned and was *actually* purposed by God the Father to fulfill what it was intended to accomplish. God the Son *actually* purchased those it was intended for, with His own blood, and God the Holy Spirit *actually* applies the merits of it to the *"purchased possessions"* at God's divinely appointed time (Eph. 1:14).

The Father glorifies the Son (Jn. 17:1, 5), Christ came to glorify the Father (Jn. 12:28), and the Holy Spirit came to glorify Christ (Jn. 16:14). But Arminianism has all three Persons of the Trinity failing to be glorified! It has the Father failing to glorify Christ, by not giving Him people to *actually* save. It has Jesus failing to glorify His Father, by not *actually* accomplishing redemption for those the Father has given Him, and it has the Holy Spirit failing to glorify Jesus by not *actually* applying the merits of His blood to their account, which would have us conditionally earning or losing salvation based on our own merits. This, in turn, would keep *us* from glorifying God!

Arminianisms divergence from the true nature of the atonement and the beautifully harmonious splendor of how the Godhead operates in salvation, ultimately leads to absolute chaos, utter confusion and complete disaster.

But thank God for the truth! So that those who are truly concerned for the salvation of their souls can have the blessed assurance that Jesus' blood atonement *actually* secures, because it is an *unconditional* atonement, based solely on God's *"election of grace,"* not their works (Rom. 11:5-8). And those who end up in Hell can't blame it on an insufficient atonement and they can't blame it on God's election of grace. God is not unfair or unjust for justly sending people to Hell for their total corruption and rejection of Jesus Christ as their only hope.

God's judgment is righteous and He divides the darkness as He sees fit and He does it sinlessly and righteously. No one will be in Hell due to any unfairness on God's part, because we all deserve to be there. But He has graciously chosen to have mercy on some. Since He is God, He has the right to *"have mercy on whom He wills and to harden whom He wills" (Rom. 9:18).* And He has obviously set things up this way so that no one will have an excuse for their sin (which deserves Hell), and so that the elect cannot boast that they are any "better than others" like Arminianism does.

Although Arminianism denies Universalism, its heretical doctrine of *universal atonement* inevitably leads to that. Because if Jesus died for *all* the sins of *all* mankind then why wouldn't Universalism be correct in saying *all* will eventually be saved and end up in Heaven? Because if Jesus died for *all* the sins of *all* mankind, then their salvation would have been secure even before the beginning of time and no one would be in Hell. If Jesus died for *all* the sins of *all* people, then there has to be an explanation for *all* the people who were in Hell before the cross and all who have gone there since.

So did Jesus' atonement cover the sins of Cain, Pharaoh, *all* the Egyptians covered by the Red Sea, Absalom, *all* the wicked kings, Judas Iscariot, etc.? If so, then why does the Bible make it so clear that they are lost? Why does Scripture make a distinction between spiritual sheep and goats? The only answer is that Jesus' atonement covered the sins of all those it was ordained for, and it is *effectually* applied by the Spirit to all the elect throughout time.

But if Jesus died for *all* the sins of *all* mankind, as Arminianism teaches, then why would any be sent to Hell for the *sin* of unbelief? Did Jesus only die for *some* of the sins of *all* people? For if that were the case, then *no one would make it to Heaven*...because no sin can enter Heaven! So did Jesus die to atone for *all* the sins of *some* people (God's chosen) or *some* of the sins of *all* people? Let Scripture be the judge.

Recently I obtained another photo of a local CoC church sign that said: *"It takes courage to believe we are forgiven."* But according to Scripture, it doesn't take the innate power of "courage" to believe we are forgiven; it takes the supernatural power of the Holy Spirit *through faith in Christ.*

Yet in an earthly sense...it *would* take "courage" to believe the CoC's false gospel, for it cannot save anyone. It would take the most fleshly, blind courage a person could ever possibly muster up. For who could trust in a *false christ* who can't *actually* save anyone, unless they save themselves first, through some kind of *inherent* "inner power" such as courage, rather than the supernatural power of God through the *true* gospel!?

Who could trust in a universal atonement that allows many that Jesus supposedly died for to go to Hell? If the sins of all people were forgiven and paid for at the cross, then why would any have to spend an eternity in Hell paying for them again?? Exactly! The CoC doesn't have a leg to stand on. The only way it can be consistent is to plead a universal salvation, which actually seemed to be what this church sign was portraying to the world.

Either way is blasphemy! The CoC's false gospel is hopeless and not good news at all. It attempts to rob God of His glory and divide it between us and Him. And the logical conclusion of its universal atonement *always* leads to an ecumenical, universal salvation of all who are into false religion, including atheists, which is no wonder it is headed in that direction.

The true gospel is *"the power of God"* (Rom. 1:16), not *our own inborn "inner power."* The *true* Savior *actually saves* His people, for He paid their sin debt *in full*. The *true* Savior *actually rescues* His lost sheep from the penalty, power and practice of sin. The *true* Savior *actually saves* and leaves none of the saving up to those He died for. He took *their* place, suffered God's wrath against sin on *their* behalf, and reconciled *them* back to the Father, through the blood of His cross. He did *not* die for those who end up in Hell, for they never belonged to God (Jn. 17:9). They are those who never desire Jesus or believe His gospel, which proves that they were never His.

Those who Jesus died for on the cross belonged to God the Father Who gave them to Christ, for Him to redeem, purchase, pray for and die for (Jn. 17:9, Heb. 7:25). So for Arminianism to imply that anyone who has been redeemed and purchased by Jesus' precious blood could be tossed into Hell as worthless... is blasphemy to the nth degree (Heb. 10:29)! This is why it is so important to acknowledge that those who end up in Hell are those whom Christ *never* purchased, *never* redeemed, *never* prayed for and *never* knew as His own (Mt. 7:23, Jn. 17). They are those whom God has left to their own sinful desires, which is why they think they can be their own "freewill" god.

The truth is that those who realize God's right to be God and their desperate need of the *true* Savior, are those He has enabled to repent, by revealing the depths of their sin guilt before a holy God. They are those who *believe from the heart.* For the same power that rose Jesus from the dead is the same power that has raised their spirit to life in Christ, which had been *inherently dead in sin* (*not* inherently empowered). Their *literal* "washing and renewing" is *directly* by the Holy Spirit, not *indirectly* through water baptism as the CoC teaches (Titus 3:5). Their salvation is not half God and half them. He requires no human assistance. All the glory of salvation goes to God alone and He will not give it to another (Isa. 42:8).

Jesus is not only *able* to save; He is *willing* to save---all who come to Him rightly---*not* by their own righteousness, but *for* righteousness. They are those who lovingly choose Christ, for they were first lovingly chosen by God. He is the *primary cause,* and *their* choosing, loving, believing and obeying Him are the effects (1 Jn. 4:19). And the cause of God choosing, is due only to His good pleasure, not our works (e.g. Lk. 10:21; 12:32, 2 Thess. 1:11).

To further prove this would be to try to light a candle in the sun!! So we must surrender all to God's sovereign supremacy and throw ourselves upon the mercy of our Maker. He is our only hope of ever being able to believe the *true* gospel from the heart. He's our only hope of ever being granted repentance unto salvation. He's our only hope of being brought to life spiritually by the working of His mighty power, which He worked in Christ (Eph. 1:19). All glory goes to God's Truth that sets the captives free!

God secures His sheep and gives them His kingdom, prepared *for them* "*from the foundation of the world,*" with *everlasting* salvation and reserves the goats for *everlasting* torment (Mt. 25:31-46, Jn. 10), for they never desire God. But dear reader, if you *do* desire God, then be encouraged and use the means that He has so graciously provided for you.

Seek Him. Seek out His people. Hear and read what they teach from Scripture. Pray for discernment and protection from false teaching. Read God's Word and study it for yourself. Throw yourself upon God's mercy. Pray for the ability to believe the truth from the heart and for the ability to trust in Jesus' power to save. Coming to Jesus means entrusting all to Him alone. And when you do, He will never cast you out, for He has promised not to, and His Word is eternally trustworthy. Follow Him with all of your heart, knowing that He will never leave you or forsake you. Those who truly come to Him in complete surrender, with a desire to love Him and to be made holy by Him, could only mean that they've been truly regenerated! And their life will surely begin to show the results of such a radical change.

Part 5

Compelling Conclusions

Chapter 25

Whosoever Will

"Whosoever will, let him take the water of life freely" (Rev. 22:17).

There are two words that are obsessively repeated in Arminian circles, to the exclusion of what they really mean. So who is *"whosoever will?"* Is it those who have the strongest, natural "willpower?" No. Because according to Scripture, it's not even the will that determines our choices, it's the heart, and it moves our will to act. Therefore, the condition of our heart determines whether we will truly come to Christ or not (e.g. Prov. 4:23, Rom.10:9-10). The problem is that since the Fall, *"the heart is deceitful above all things and desperately wicked" (Jer. 17:9).*

Due to the extreme corruption that sin causes, just one sin in a lifetime is destructive enough to earn an eternity in Hell. Sin is what hardens hearts and causes people to refuse to come to Christ. So our will is free only in the sense that it is still free to choose according to our heart's desire. But a true, godly choice for Christ cannot possibly come from an unregenerate heart that loves sin more than God (Lk. 6:45-46). Therefore, whether or not we do what Jesus says to do, and come to Him *in truth,* depends upon whether God has cleansed our hearts from the love of sin, and filled it with love for Him, so that we *can* be willing to *"take the water of life freely."*

Every person will be held responsible for how they respond to the gospel call, for its everyone's duty to their Maker to repent, believe and receive Christ, whether they have Heavens help or not. God doesn't lower His standard just because sin has caused us to fall short of His glory. That would be like a criminal going before a judge and making the excuse that he can't help but break the law, and the judge corrupting justice by letting the criminal go due to the criminal's inability to abide by the law!

We all deserve Hell, so God could have chosen not to save any and would still be righteous in His judgment. There will be no one in Hell that doesn't deserve to be there, for God has never, and never will, force anyone to sin. Even God's act of reprobation causes no one to sin (Rom. 1:28). Because He does no harm by leaving people in the original condition that He made them in. *"God hath made man upright, but they have sought out many inventions" (Eccl. 7:29).* Sin is what has separated people from God (Isa. 59:2).

Yet God is merciful, and He has revealed this to us at the cross, where His justice and mercy meet. God can pardon the vilest of sinners and still be righteous, because His only begotten Son has given Himself as a ransom in order to purchase them and redeem them. The gospel of Christ *"is the power of God unto salvation to everyone that believeth" (Rom. 1:16).*

The power to believe comes from God. We can't come on our own terms or bribe God with our own works, for the only way to take the Water of Life is... *freely*. Even if one was stranded in a bone-dry desert without a CoC "baptismal mediator" or physical water to be baptized with, they could still be saved simply by trusting in Christ alone as their only hope of Heaven. The Living Water of the Spirit is *accessed only by faith in Jesus (Jn. 7:38-39).*

On the other hand, the CoC's freewill fable is not a Scriptural reality. *"For the time will come when they will not endure sound doctrine; but after their own lusts shall they heap to themselves teachers, having itching ears; and they shall turn their ears away from the truth, and shall be turned unto fables" (2 Tim. 4:3-4).* The CoC's freewill fable declares that, "God gives us a will that can reject Him, for He wants us to love Him willingly and freely." But it minimizes the seriousness of sin and how it has brought our will into bondage so that we cannot love Him willingly and freely. As a result, it diminishes our desperate need for the power of Christ to save us; for only through Him can we truly love God...*Not* by an unregenerate heart and mind that loves sin. Only God can produce holy inclinations in His people by virtue of Jesus' vicarious sacrifice, for only in Him can we be truly free.

But the CoC even uses the Garden of Eden scenario to try to prove that God allowed sin to be offered so we'd have freewill and not be robots. But that's like saying we'll be robots in Heaven, for God doesn't allow sin there! First of all, fear of being a "robot" for God is nothing but complete rebellion, and in effect, it reveals that the fallen will would rather choose to be a slave to sin. But "freewill" to choose sin is *Not* true freedom at all, or else God wouldn't be free, for He is holy and cannot choose sin (Job 34:10-12).

Ironically, the Garden scenario actually proves the freewill doctrine is a complete sham. For in the sequence of events leading up to the Fall, three faculties of Adam and Eve's soul were involved when they chose to eat forbidden fruit; their mind, heart and will....*in that order* (Gen. 3:1-6). The act of their will was preceded by the thoughts of their mind and the desires of their heart, proving that our will doesn't determine our choices. The act of our will is preceded and determined by other factors, which are now effected by the Fall. Our will no longer has the ability to choose God, unless the cleansing regeneration of the Holy Spirit brings our mind, heart and will into harmony with God's will by virtue of the merits of Christ (Titus 3:5). So those who do truly choose Christ are those *""Who were born, not of blood, nor of the will of the flesh, nor of the will of man, but of God" (Jn. 1:13).* We can't faithfully choose and love God until He intervenes in our lives with an irresistible love that breaks every barrier, even the barrier of a fallen will that's a slave to sin. And once we are saved we cannot brag that He saved us because we loved Him, for its *"not that we loved God, but that He loved us."* We can only *"love Him, because He first loved us" (1 Jn. 4:10, 19).*

John 3:16 doesn't say *"whosoever"* without exclusion has the *ability* to believe. Instead, the context shows that *"whosoever"* are those who will never perish because of unbelief, for God gave them His Son, Who procured their faith. Those who never believe have *already* been condemned (v. 18).

The verse also uses the word *"world"* to refer to *a certain group of people in the world* (e.g. Lk. 2:1, Jn. 12:19). The world *contains* those whom Jesus came to save from their sins (Mt. 1:22, Jn. 11:52). He didn't come to save everyone, but only God's elect that the world contains. Jesus came as *"God manifest in the flesh"* to be a *"ransom for many"* (not all)....from every tongue, tribe and nation *throughout the world* (Mt. 20:28, Mk. 10:45, 2 Cor. 5:19, 1 Tim. 3:16, Rev. 5:9). So all glory goes to Him alone.

Yet another verse the CoC distorts in a futile attempt to prove faith can be self-generated, is John 6:37, where Jesus says, *"and him that cometh to Me I will in no wise cast out."* But as many Greek scholars have observed:

"Even a cursory glance at the text reveals that this partial citation is the second half of a full sentence; that there is no indefinite relative pronoun here ("whoever"), but instead it literally reads, *"and the one coming."* The sentence defines who this "coming one" is: "All that the Father gives Me will come to Me." The one coming to Christ in John 6:37b is the one of the entire body of the elect given by the Father to the Son in 6:37a" (Emphasis his). [1]

No doubt, all who *truly* desire to come to Christ can, for God gave them that desire. But the CoC teaches that all are born with the *natural* ability to desire Christ, and that He died for the *whole* world, *even those in Hell*, which implies His death didn't procure the gift of faith or particular redemption for anyone. Case in point....it suggests that His death accomplished *nothing!*

And this is the sinister trade-off that enables the CoC to teach that we're no longer responsible to God if we lose our natural abilities, or that God can't hold us accountable if we don't have freewill. It implies that a loss of cognitive function is a direct ticket to Heaven. It's like telling criminals they're no longer held responsible for their crimes if they can't help but commit them! And, ironically, it's not even consistent with the CoC's obedience-based system of salvation. But it just goes to further illustrate its inconsistency, and how it picks and chooses which commands to keep and which ones to reject, based on subjective morality.

While the CoC occasionally uses grace terminology, such as: "Only God can change the heart," the very basis of its belief system dictates that "we must choose to *allow* God to change our heart." For its foundational freewill fallacy contradicts any references it may make about God's sovereignty. In effect, the only sovereignty it allows God to have is the "sovereignty" to grant *humans* sovereignty over their own fallen will! Not only is that a ridiculously self-defeating argument, it reveals a lack of reverence toward God, for He "quickeneth whom *He will*" (Jn. 5:21, emphasis mine). Jesus fulfills the will of the Father, so that none of His people will perish in Hell.

However, today one often hears people referring to their salvation in first person—"I went to the altar, I said this prayer, I made a decision for Christ, I invited Jesus into my heart, I got baptized, I did this or that ...THEN God saved me"-- rather than second person—"God first loved me; God's Word convinced me I was a sinner in need of the Savior; God changed my heart and granted me the grace to repent, believe and obey the gospel; God secured my salvation in Jesus...*before* I could've had anything to do with it."

The former makes God's grace sound cheap, as if it's only effective if we do something first, or that it only enables us to attain our own salvation. Yet the latter *"praises the glory of His grace" (Eph. 1:6)*, by emphasizing the miracle of what Jesus already attained by His death, burial and resurrection, to secure the eternal plan of redemption, by which God has determined to save, through Christ, sinners whom He has chosen, and how He freely bestows the grace necessary for them to respond in faith and repentance.

Creaturely freewill can only act in harmony with its nature (Rom. 8:7-9). For example, in the natural scheme of things, those who have no legs cannot choose to run. And though many of us can choose to either walk or run, we can't choose to flap our wings and fly. Our limited nature prevents us from doing so. Likewise, freewill is limited by our fallen nature. Before the Fall, mankind had freewill to either obey or disobey God. But now, the will is only "free" in the sense that it still has the natural ability to disobey God and the audacity to try to attain salvation through works (Rom. 10:3).

Man's fallen will has no desire to seek salvation in the righteousness of another. It is deluded into believing it can appease God's wrath, when only the righteousness of Christ can. Man's "freedom of choice" can still choose what is *morally* good, despite the remaining "freedom" to choose evil, but because of indwelling sin he cannot choose what is *spiritually* good *unto salvation*, unless God grants him faith in Jesus as his only hope of salvation.

If we *did* have absolute freewill that could tie up God's hands and thwart His every move, then He would be a small "g" god with frustrated plans and purposes, and that's exactly the kind of powerless god Arminianism portrays. He's an unhappy god who has to sit back and watch people make a mess of everything, while trying to clean it all up the best he can.

In Eden, he was wringing his hands, hoping Adam and Eve would make the right choice, but to his dismay and disappointment he had to come up with "Plan B," and send his son to die on a cross to make salvation "possible" for everyone...*if only* they would "freely" choose him. But even if they did, he couldn't guarantee that he would keep them from Hell. He *tried* to save everyone, but couldn't...because man's almighty "freewill" hindered him. But thank God in Heaven...that's *Not* the God of the Bible!!

God Is absolutely sovereign and grants the free grace necessary for His people to truly repent, believe and obey the gospel. For our natural inability to repent enough, believe enough or be good enough is no barrier to His ability to change all of that and save us from Hell. His grace is enough. Although God resists the proud, He gives grace to the humble and poor in spirit (1 Pet. 5:5). And He often refines them in the furnace of affliction to remind them that they can never earn it (Isa. 48:9-11). God in His mercy has already provided the means of salvation in Jesus' blood atonement and He sends the Holy Spirit Who applies the merits of that sacrifice, while regenerating the dead spirit that was once held captive by sin.

God's grace also helps believers overcome the external compulsion to sin, which still makes our position one of major accountability. At the same time, believers have an advocate with the Father, Who intercedes for us in our weaknesses. Jesus Christ is the author and finisher of our faith; not by violating our will, but by changing our heart so that our will is free to obey Him in spirit and in truth, rather than legalistic bondage.

Because being seated in heavenly places by God's free grace, with a full, rapturous view of the splendor and beauty of Christ.... *is far better any day than being seated on the high horse of human freewill by our own works.*

Notes:

[1] Dr. James R. White, *The Potters Freedom*, New Revised Edition, (Calvary Press Publishing, 2009), p. 28.

Chapter 26

Subjective Morality: The Iniquity of Holy Things

*"**For you were hypocrites in your hearts** when you sent me to the Lord your God, saying, 'Pray for us to the Lord our God, and according to all that the Lord your God says, so declare to us and **we will do it**" (Jer. 42:20, emphasis mine).*

God's perfect standard of righteousness is downplayed in "Churches of Christ" by what's called "subjective morality." In a nutshell, they set the standard for righteousness on a subjective, *individual* level, dependent upon whether an *individual* has "done the best *they* can." If so, they say that God will "make up the difference." This is one way exhausted members are kept from dropping out and giving up, for they are told that God doesn't expect perfection as long as they just "do their best." So they end up thinking they can actually pull off a *degree* of righteousness that God will accept.

This is because CoC's entertain the idea that Jesus made a way for God to lower His perfect standard of righteousness so that our imperfect works can now be accepted as a means to appease God and enter Heaven. Their underlying assumption is that Jesus made a way for our imperfect works to have saving merit (worth)....as if God now accepts *imperfect* obedience, which would make Christ's *perfect* obedience pointless! They too *"have put no difference between the holy and profane"* (Ezek. 22:26).

As a fatal consequence, CoC's create a very low view of how hideously evil sin is and how unattainably holy God is. In turn, they create a very low view of Jesus and the cross. Although Jesus enables His people to produce good fruits, their works still have no saving merit. All the credit and glory goes to their Savior, but Arminian operatives want at least *part* of the credit.

According to CoC doctrines, there is no such thing as being justified by faith alone in the finished work of Christ alone. This is why CoC's emphasize *faith plus works* as the grounds of justification. And *that* faith is not even a saving faith, for it is mere mental assent to basic facts about Jesus' existence and ministry that even non-Christians could affirm. Ultimately, it is a blind and misguided trust in a system that Christ never instituted, and *that kind of faith cannot save (Jas. 2:14).* The CoC overturns and destroys true faith, nullifies the cross of Jesus Christ and hides the way of salvation, for the substance of true faith is Jesus Christ Himself...*Not* a performance-based system that is set up by man to *replace* direct access to Jesus.

God's standard of righteousness is not a sliding scale of requirements that adapts itself to the ability of its subjects. God's standard involves *objective* morality, which is not based on an individual person's *subjective* ability, but is based upon *absolute* Truth. One of Jesus' most shocking statements in Scripture came during His Sermon on the Mount when He said, *"Be ye therefore perfect, even as your Father which is in heaven is perfect" (Mt. 5:48).* Yet false religion comes up with its own perversion of this truth, due to a refusal to accept God's perfect standard, which is Christ.

For instance, the CoC teaches that the word *perfect* here merely means "spiritual maturity" or "perfect love." Yet the paralleled perfection of the Father presented here as our standard, is obviously not just "spiritual maturity." Plus, no one can love perfectly unless they themselves are perfect. Jesus' point is that we must come to Him for what we lack, because *"all have sinned and come short of the glory of God" (Rom. 3:23).*

Jesus made it clear that it's impossible for man to save himself (Mt. 19:25-27). This is why we must *seek God's mercy and pray for Him to credit Jesus' perfection to our account* (Heb. 13:20). But, to the contrary, the CoC encourages sinners on their way to Hell to "keep trying," "don't give up" or "you can do it!" Its unspoken motto is: "Never mind Jesus' words about perfection; just make up your own standard of righteousness by doing the best *you* can." One can almost hear the hiss of the serpent behind such lies.

God's standard of righteousness is unattainable by fallen, sinful man. The only way one can reach it is by having Jesus' righteousness credited to their account by a sovereign act of God, Who alone can purify the heart by faith (Acts 15:8-9). But false religion doesn't encourage people to pray and seek the Lord for this perfect righteousness and holiness, which is the only way one can ever hope to see the Lord (Heb. 12:14). The inevitable outcome of the CoC's soul-destroying error ultimately leads to a type of Antinomianism, which is a turn from true liberty in Christ, to an "anything goes" theology.

Apostle Paul taught against the *dietary law* and *ceremonial law,* but he upheld the moral law. *"Do we, then, nullify the law by this faith? Not at all! Rather, we uphold the law" (Rom. 3:31).* He taught that true, saving faith in Jesus is a faith that obeys, for Christ enables His people to obey and follow the moral principles of the law in every aspect of life. *"According as His divine power hath given unto us all things that pertain unto life and godliness" (2 Pet. 1:3)*. However, the CoC denies that the human race fell hopelessly into sin *in Adam*. Instead, it puts sin on a *subjective* level that can be overcome with *subjective* morality. But God *Never* lowered His standard of righteousness. He still demands that it be met. God's law remains the same because it's a reflection of His holy character, which never changes. His Word shows that lost sinners are spiritually dead and cursed by the law of sin and death, whereas those who are saved are risen to new life by *"the law of the Spirit of life in Christ Jesus" (Rom. 8:2)*, where the true purpose of the Law is found. *"Wherefore the Law was our schoolmaster to bring us unto Christ, that we might be justified by faith" (Gal. 3:24)*.

Still, the CoC views God's law as a minimal set of performance markers, where a "do more, try harder" moralism produces devilish pride when one thinks they are pulling it off, and a paralyzing, legalistic fear when one fails. And when things don't pan out, it produces a deep down resentment for being restricted, which eventually breaks out in complete rebellion.

Yet those who are in Christ are no longer under the condemnation of the law, but rather delight in it (Rom. 7:22), for they see it as instructive rather than restrictive. They believe *"doers of the law shall be justified" (Rom. 2:13)*, and that none are perfect doers, except Jesus Christ, *"Who was delivered for our offences, and was raised again for our justification" (Rom. 4:25)*. His resurrection from the dead proved that God had discharged all the sins He bore for His people. In virtue of His victory, Jesus fulfilled the demands of *God's holiness and justice,* so that His people can receive *God's mercy and grace,* which then enables them to be doers and not just hearers.

This is why true believers are "to declare *His* righteousness---*"for the remission of sins"* (Rom. 3:25), instead of their own works of righteousness, such as baptism. In the parable of the Pharisee and the publican, Jesus said the publican was justified, because he pleaded to God for mercy when he realized that he had no saving righteousness of his own. But the Pharisee declared *his own* "works of obedience" for approval, because he didn't want to fully rely upon the righteousness of another to save him. He boasted in himself and what he had done in his own power to "activate" salvation.

Likewise, the CoC implies one can "activate" salvation by *"coming into contact with Jesus' blood in baptism,"* for it misinterprets all of the Bible verses that have to do with baptism "for the remission of sins." By doing so, it makes use of an ordinance to soothe people's conscience, which is an abomination to God. But true believers are baptized from a different motive....gratefulness and love to God for granting them faith in the righteousness of Christ alone---*for the remission of sins*. Only those, whom God has renewed in heart and spirit, are divinely enabled to perceive the true beauty and purpose of God's ordinances.

Yet the Pharisee mindset is displayed when many boast about how they think they are accepted by God based on their works, with no emphasis on Jesus and His *perfect* atoning sacrifice. But the humble mindset fully relies upon the mercy of God through Christ. And those with this heart condition have truly had their sins remitted by the work Jesus did on the cross.

"He made Him Who knew no sin to be sin on our behalf, that we might become the righteousness of God in Him" (2 Cor. 5:21). "Not having a righteousness of my own derived from the law, but that which is through faith in Christ, the righteousness which comes from God on the basis of faith" (Phil. 3:9). When God *makes us righteous*, it means He *declares us righteous* on the basis of Jesus' righteousness alone. It does not mean that we have any actual righteousness of our own that merits salvation.

We cannot be justified by our own righteousness. *"For we do not present our pleas before You because of our righteousness, but because of Your great mercy" (Dan. 9:18, ESV). "They which receive abundance of grace and of the **gift of righteousness** shall reign in life by One, Jesus Christ....by the obedience of One shall many be made righteous" (Rom. 5:17, 19, emphasis mine).* This doesn't mean that one can become sinless this side of Heaven, or savingly righteous in and of themselves. What it does mean is that God can justify a sinner without tainting His own righteousness, because Jesus made a propitiation for His people, in order to fully satisfy divine justice, so that His righteousness can be imputed to their account. That *"He might be just and the justifier of the one who has faith in Jesus" (Rom. 3:26, NKJV).*

But Pharisees *"trusted in themselves that they were righteous" (Lk. 18:9).* Though the CoC places great emphasis on getting people into its church, it does not have the true gospel of Jesus Christ, for it perverts the doctrine of the cross, while proudly sporting one on a church steeple. And though it sings "Amazing Grace," it despises the true, biblical doctrine of grace, which is God's merciful disposition toward His people and replaces it with something that's "imparted" or *infused*.... in exchange for good works.

Subjective Morality: The Iniquity of Holy Things

The CoC makes a gigantic, outward show of religion, but ignores righteousness, peace and joy in the Holy Spirit, for it doesn't even teach the imputed righteousness of Christ, the peace and joy of eternal security, or the true, biblical doctrine of believers being *eternally* indwelled and *sealed* by the Holy Spirit (Rom. 4; 14:17). Instead, it offers a form of godliness, but denies the power of God, by teaching that the power of salvation is in man's freewill and the unregenerate works of the flesh (Rom. 1:16, 2 Tim. 3:5).

Pharisaical religions in every generation are like white-washed tombs full of dead men's bones that have never been regenerated by the Holy Spirit. They encourage people to *make themselves* righteous in will worship (Col. 2:23). And by doing so, they actually deny Christ by their works (Titus 1:16).

The CoC is a formal, ritualistic, ceremonial, outward religion void of the true gospel of Jesus Christ. *"This people honor me with their lips, but their heart is far from me" (Mt. 15:8).* But in all honesty, the CoC doesn't even honor God verbally, for it refers to salvation in first person and gives all the glory of salvation to people's "freewill" in getting baptized....in doing this or doing that... rather than acknowledging the fact that true salvation is all to the glory of God. This is why the CoC creates false converts who are unable to submit to the sovereign Lordship of Jesus Christ in order to be saved, because it doesn't even teach that God is sovereign in salvation!

This is why another preferred perversion of the CoC is an unbiblical eisegesis of Romans 9:13, where it tries to claim that God hated Esau because he was evil, and that He chose Jacob because he was good. But Scripture in no way bears that assertion out, for Jacob was inherently a con-man. God even calls him a worm, and yet He chose him, according to His mercy and grace, *not according to works* (Isa. 41:14).

"Not everyone that saith unto Me, Lord, Lord, shall enter into the kingdom of heaven; but he that **doeth** *the will of My Father which is in heaven. Many will say to Me in that day, Lord, Lord, have we not prophesied in Thy name? and in Thy name have cast out devils? and in Thy name* **done many wonderful works**? *And then will I profess unto them, I never knew you: depart from Me, ye that* **work iniquity**.*" (Mt. 7:21-23, emphasis mine)*

In this passage, the CoC puts extreme focus on the "doing" and inserts its preconceived notion of works salvation without giving a biblical exegesis of the entire context, because that would expose its heresies. For this passage actually reveals that Jesus warns about those who come to Him expecting to be accepted by their own works, and how He considers this as *iniquity*, due to their wicked attempts to supplement His righteousness with their own.

And note, *not once* did these *"workers of iniquity"* ever mention that their *only* hope was in Jesus' righteousness alone, which is the *only* righteousness God will accept for salvation! Here Jesus even warns that He will tell them to depart from Him...w*hich puts those in the CoC system on dangerous ground...* for they too are taught to bribe God with their works.

This is why the CoC never expounds upon these verses in context, for it would expose its system as sinfully and fatally flawed. So, instead, it grossly misrepresents Jesus here and deceptively teaches that He was only reprimanding *the wrong kind of works for salvation!*

When Jesus was asked, **"What shall we do,** *that we might work the works of God? Jesus answered and said unto them, 'This is the work of God, that ye* **believe on Him** *whom He hath sent'"* (Jn. 6:28-29, emphasis mine). But if a biblical exposition of this passage was ever given in the CoC, which would glorify God and *the work He does* in the hearts of those Jesus came to save, one would be called on the carpet for being a heretic and for not stressing the "issues" enough....such as the *necessity* of good works, the *necessity* of having no instrumental music, of having the Lord's Supper *every* Sunday, water baptism, etc.,....*all for the purpose of attaining salvation.*

But one may ask, "How can anything moral or holy be sinful?" It seems contradictory doesn't it? But it's not, for in Exodus 28:38 we're shown that the High Priest Aaron (Moses' brother and an Old Testament type, who prefigured Christ) had to offer blood atonement for God's people even when they offered *"holy things."* Because even their moral, holy things (service to God) had to be purified before they could be acceptable to God, for everything we do is tainted with sin. God is completely pure and holy, so that NOTHING less than perfect holiness can enter His holy presence.

This O.T. scenario was only a shadow of what Jesus, as High Priest, does for His people today. He's always in the presence of God the Father, interceding for His people and pleading His finished work on the cross, where He took upon Himself the guilt, not only of sins actually committed but the guilt of a corrupted, sinful nature, which had alienated us from God.

"All we like sheep have gone astray; we have turned every one to his own way and the Lord hath laid on Him the iniquity of us all" (Isa. 53:6). Jesus came to earth to live the perfect life we could never live because of our

fallen condition, which is why Jesus came to fulfill all righteousness on our behalf. Because even when we've done all that He's commanded (including baptism), we've still fallen short of His glory.

Yet the CoC teaches that we've not fallen so far from God that we can't still please Him. The CoC motto is: "We're not that bad, so God's not that mad." This, in turn, nurtured the deep-down belief that we were not bad enough to go to Hell, but not good enough to go to Heaven. Similar to the lie of "Purgatory," we too were stuck in a type of spiritual middle ground.

And so, we began to think that surely God wouldn't expect perfection and hold us to that standard, which rendered Christ's work completely void in our minds. We were not taught that nothing less than perfect holiness can enter His holy presence. Jesus said that even if we did all that's commanded and required of us, we must say to ourselves, *"I am an unprofitable servant" (Lk. 17:10)*. For nothing that we "do" could ever possibly save us. Even our good works (holy things) must be repented of, for they fall short of perfection, which is what God's perfect holiness requires. God hasn't lowered His standard just because of our fallenness, which is why we need the Savior. *"The wages of sin is death, but the gift of God is eternal life through Jesus Christ" (Rom. 6:23)*.

Jesus bore the *"iniquity of holy things,"* by taking upon Himself the guilt of any error, mistake or wrong motive His people would ever have while offering service to God. Our holy things can only be accepted by God through the perfect holiness and righteousness of Jesus Christ. And, even then, they are not meritorious works on our part that have any saving power. The only power of salvation is in the gospel of God's grace. So any futile attempt to appease God by works is repulsive to Him. *"We are all as an unclean thing, and all our righteousnesses are as filthy rags" (Isa. 64:6)*.

So instead, we must put all of our hope and trust in Jesus Christ, Who alone can present us holy and unblameable before God (Col. 1:22). Just as the High Priest in the O.T. *figuratively* bore and took away the *"iniquity of holy things"* by sacrifice and intercession, Jesus, as High Priest, *literally* does this today, as He presents His own holiness to God the Father on behalf of His people, so that they can *"offer up spiritual sacrifices acceptable to God by Jesus Christ" (1 Pet. 2:5)*. And they are acceptable only for rewards, *Not* for salvation itself, because only Jesus' work is acceptable for salvation.

Chapter 27

Deism Leads to Me-ism

*"For by Him were all things created, that are in heaven, and that are in earth, visible and invisible, whether they be thrones, or dominions, or principalities, or powers: all things were created by Him, and **for Him**: And He is before all things, and by Him all things consist" (Col. 1:16-17, emphasis mine).*

Recently I came across a CoC publication that many are finding in their mailboxes and inboxes today. The main subject of this one was why there's suffering in the world.[1] I had also just recently heard a speech on the same subject, by a well-known Christian, Joni Eareckson Tada, who's been quadriplegic most of her life. She explained how many today push the heretical idea that God is just a distant observer Who is not really personally involved in His creation, and that evil and suffering just randomly happens.

And this was exactly what the CoC literature was pushing, and it is called deism; a system of thought based upon human morality and natural reason, rather than divine revelation. And every *consistent* Arminian is a deist. It's a fallible and feeble attempt to explain suffering in the world, by portraying the sovereign God of the Universe as a passive onlooker who has forfeited His sovereignty, in order to push the idea that the full government of God's creation is now in the hands of mere humans. Yet Scripture is clear:

"For unto us a child is born, unto us a Son is given: and the government shall be upon His shoulder: and His name shall be called Wonderful, Counsellor, The Mighty God, The Everlasting Father, The Prince of Peace. Of the increase of His government and peace there shall be no end, upon the throne of David, and upon His kingdom, to order it, and to establish it with judgment and with justice from henceforth even for ever. The zeal of the Lord of hosts will perform this" (Isa. 9:6-7).

However, deisms systematic subversions are an attempt to undermine and overthrow the sovereign government of God Almighty. But Joni Eareckson Tada honored God's sovereignty by explaining what she called the "theology of suffering," where *God allows what He hates in order to accomplish what He loves.* And she said God's sovereignty in our suffering can be better understood if we look to the suffering of Jesus. For example, in Acts 2:23 and 4:28, we see that God determined beforehand what would happen to Jesus. We also see here how God ordained for Jesus' crucifixion to be brought about by *"wicked hands."* God restrained and directed the evil that was already in their heart, in order to fulfill His redemptive purposes, even though they didn't even realize it (Prov. 20:24, Jer. 10:23). And though the wicked do it from evil motives, God does it sinlessly, for He cannot sin.

Even as far back as Genesis 45:5-8, we see God restraining and directing the evil actions of the wicked in order to bring about His purposes. Joseph's brothers meant evil against him, but Genesis 50:20 says God meant it for good, because He is good and all that He does is good. *"And we know that all things work together for good to them that love God, to them who are the called according to His purpose" (Rom. 8:28).* So we can be comforted in knowing that there is no random, purposeless evil or suffering in this world.

But one may ask, "Does this excuse the wicked?" And the answer is absolutely not! For God did not cause them to be wicked or infuse evil into their heart. We are all responsible to God no matter what (Rom. 9:20). And even when God works good from our evil, we cannot take any credit for it. Yet if God had not set things up this way, we would think that we could be justified in trying to control all things or in trying to take credit for our own salvation. But God has set things up so perfectly that we have no excuse but to acknowledge and submit to His complete sovereignty in all things.

Deism, on the other hand, leads to me, me, me-ism; for it is a natural consequence of Arminian theology, which attempts to put man or "mother nature" in charge and portrays God as a helpless bystander. And there can be no assurance of salvation in that kind of false god, which is an idol.

Thankfully, Scripture reveals that God's hands are not tied by His laws of nature or by the so-called "freewill" of man (e.g. Dan. 4:35, Eph. 1:21). For example, Jonah was *Not* willing to do what God called him to do....*far from it!* Jonah tried to run from God and found out that he couldn't! Why? Because God always catches up with His own! He never leaves them to themselves, but He seeks and rescues them, which is why God prepared the fish to swallow Jonah and spew him out on land again. God knows how to incline His people to be willing to obey (Ps. 110:3). *His hands are Not tied!!*

Much of our suffering, even as Christians, is due to the sin that dwells in the flesh. Many times, even depression begins with sin (worry, impatience, doubting God, believing the devils lies, etc.), not "low self-esteem." Yet therapeutic deism turns people to idolatry, rather than to God for mercy.

The Savior can never be treasured as long as one thinks they are basically "good." Deism is a self-help religion that downplays how terrible sin is and labors to boost pride. But Scripture shows us that's the last thing we need. We already love ourselves too much! We are naturally selfish and every other bad thing. Our greatest need is to have Jesus, Who alone can cover our sins, reconcile us to God, and give us love for Him, Who is able to love us more than we could ever love ourselves. And only His trustworthiness can secure ones salvation from the eternal damnation that sinners deserve.

However, deism idolizes the carnal mind by falsely claiming the gospel can be obeyed by natural abilities, rather than supernatural enablement by God. But *"the carnal mind is enmity against God; for it is not subject to the law of God, neither indeed can be"* (Rom. 8:7). *"The natural man receiveth not the things of the Spirit of God; for they are foolishness unto him; neither can he know them, because they are spiritually discerned"* (1 Cor. 2:14).

Although the gospel is completely reasonable, those who are in rebellion against God cannot bring themselves to wholeheartedly obey it. But God never leaves His people to their own fallen will, for in His time He opens their spiritual understanding and *grants* them repentance so that they *can* recover themselves from evil and obey the true gospel (2 Tim. 2:25-26).

After writing about the sovereignty of God for years now, I still can't completely wrap my feeble, finite mind around it. And it seems that along with all that I've written, God in His mercy has often disciplined me through some very painful depths of suffering to bring me to the end of myself. Perhaps to save me from the prideful pitfalls that often happen when one tries to proclaim the beauty of God's supreme sovereignty in salvation. All I know is that it's been only in my weaknesses that I've truly been able to realize the strength of God's grace. So when it comes to God's sovereignty... in puddles of tears and pleas for mercy, I have to confess, *"Such knowledge is too wonderful for me; it is high, I cannot attain unto it"* (Ps. 139:6).

Notes:

[1] Allen Webster, *Why Do Bad Things Happen?* Volume 18, Issue #4, pp. 1-3. Retrieved May 30, 2018 from: https://housetohouse.com/wp-content/uploads/2016/02/v18n4.pdf

Chapter 28

Open-Theism Opens the Door to Doubt

*"And it repented the L*ORD *that He had made man on the earth, and it grieved Him at His heart" (Gen.6:6).*

God grieves when His preceptive will is not obeyed, for His divine precepts are reflective of how holy and good He is. However, nothing takes God by surprise. When the world had become so filled with evil in Noah's day, it grieved God so much that He sent a destructive flood that covered the entire earth. But He already foreknew all that was going to happen and had already divinely decreed that He would use the situation as an object lesson that would spiritually impact every generation from then on.

Once again, perilous times have come. We are so troubled on every side that if we are not on guard against the devils schemes, we will end up compromising the truth just so we can try to make sense of why evil exists. Scripture makes it clear that *"God divided the light from the darkness"* as He has seen fit, and *"in Him is no darkness at all"* (Gen. 1:4, 1 Jn. 1:5). Yet anytime we go beyond God's Word to try to explain why He's ordained for evil to exist, then we've crossed over into what the Bible calls heresy.

The CoC highly promotes one such heresy, and its called open-theism, for the only *consistent* Arminian is an open-theist. Even though God says, *"I am the Lord, I change not" (Mal. 3:16)*, it claims that God doesn't know the future and is therefore subject to change, based on the misinterpretation of certain verses, such as Exodus 32:14, where it says, *"the* LORD *repented of the evil which He thought to do unto His people."*

Here the CoC's false interpretation has God being controlled by the whims of man. However, a biblical exposition of this passage reveals just another instance of God using threats of judgment to move His people to repent. And the fact that He accepted Moses' appeal for mercy proves that He had not "set in stone" or divinely decreed that they would be judged, or else they would have been, for God's divine decree cannot be broken.

Yet the heretical implication of open-theism is that God is learning as time goes by. It implies that evil randomly happens with no divine purpose or meaning at all. It also implies that God cannot be fully depended upon, for it portrays Him as neither sovereign, all-powerful or all-knowing. This, in turn, easily descends into rank atheism when taken to its logical conclusion.

"Open theism is specifically designed to undercut and deny the sovereignty of God and the idea that He is accomplishing a specific, freely chosen purpose in this world. Open theism is fundamentally incompatible with Christian theism, and is hence opposed to Christian truth."[1]

Yet, if the CoC is cornered on the truth of God's foreknowledge, it will only admit that He foreknows people's *actions.* This way it can teach that God bases His choice of their salvation or damnation upon their *actions.* It teaches a general, "corporate election" of a nameless, faceless class of people, *who supposedly put themselves in Christ by their own "freewill."* But Scripture reveals that God foreknows *people*, not just their actions. He foreknows those who are His, because He chose them in Christ, based on His *own* good will, *not* on their actions (Rom. 9:11, Eph. 1:11).

But despite our churches false teaching and an unwillingness to submit to God and His uncomfortable doctrines, He removed my obstinate heart, moved my will and enabled me to find comfort in the God Who is anything but comfortable! But it did not happen overnight, for it is not natural or easy to accept that we are totally dependent upon an absolutely sovereign God, Who turns some over to their own reprobate mind (Rom. 1:28).

At one point in my Christian walk, I sunk into another depression, due to a painful realization that there was nothing I could do to convince people to believe the gospel, unless God opened their heart to it (Acts 16:14). It felt as though I was dying, for I desperately wanted all of my loved ones to be saved. Severe mental and spiritual anguish at the thoughts of any of them going to Hell tormented me and tempted me to question God's goodness, wondering how He could ever allow anyone that I loved to go to Hell.

But by God's grace, I finally repented for entertaining such thoughts and began pleading for God to help me still believe that He was good no matter what happens. And I prayed that He would forgive me if my curiosity had caused me to seek forbidden knowledge beyond the bounds of His Word. I even prayed that He would remove from my memory the depths of the knowledge of His sovereignty, unless He gave me the ability to handle it.

Many dark months went by before I received an answer to that prayer. I went to get some fresh farm eggs and milk from a large homeschooling family we knew, and they happened to be doing some spring cleaning that day. They had found an old book by John Bunyan, and wondered if I wanted it, for they knew that I loved his writings. And as soon as I seen the title, "Reprobation Asserted".... I just knew it was an answer to my prayer.

It was humbling to realize that I had never had a problem with the fact that God didn't choose to save *any* of the fallen angels who are much higher beings than we are. Yet I had the audacity to think God was unfair for not saving all fallen humans, for it's a miracle of His mercy that He has chosen to save *any*! It was humbling to learn that whenever "God must be fair" is our stance in life, and we get to determine the definition of "fair," then we're not submitting to God's will, but exalting our own (Job 35:2; 36: 21).

That was the very sin Elihu confronted Job with in chapters 32-37. Surprisingly, Elihu wasn't one of Job's three friends who had to repent in the end. On the contrary, Elihu was a godly bystander who finally got to the root of Jobs suffering. From there, God confirmed to Job that we are to NEVER question His ways or doubt His goodness, for we are in no position to do so. Only God can see the big picture, so we must trust that only He can know what's best. Like Job, we must submit to His inescapable sovereignty, be humbled into the ground by His truth, and repent in dust and ashes.

We also need to remember Jesus' words: *"Think ye that they were sinners above all men?...I tell you, Nay: but except ye repent, ye shall all likewise perish"* (Lk. 13:2-5). Though all sins are not equal in degree (Jn. 19:11), all sin is still terrible in God's eyes. And sin has so corrupted every faculty of our nature that we must be pulled out of the fire by the force of God's love. But the CoC teaches that we should reject a God Who would "force"...or as Scripture puts it..."*make you*" free *and willing* by His power (Ps. 110:3, Jn. 8:36). But by rejecting God's sovereignty in salvation, the CoC suggests that it would be better for us all to be left to our own fallen will.

By claiming that God's sovereignty in salvation would make Him a puppet master and we His mere puppets, the CoC implies that it would be better to be in bondage to sin as one of the devils puppets! It cannot be stressed enough... that fear of being a "robot" for God is nothing but rebellion and reveals a complete misunderstanding of how God's people *willingly* serve

Him because they *want* to. Yet the CoC exalts man's *creaturely* "free" will to sin, which is not free at all, for it's a slave to the devils will (2 Tim. 2:25).

The truth is that we all need to run as fast as we can to Jesus' embrace. For *"If the Son therefore shall make you free, ye shall be free indeed."* Because there has never been one single, truly saved person who has ever resented God's divine intervention in their lives and there never will be!

God's people are chosen according to His great mercy and distinguishing love. He *causes* them to be *born again* (1 Pet. 1:3, NASB). They don't birth themselves by going thru water baptism or any other ordinance! When a person is *"born of God,"* they have become a *"new creation"* in Christ (2 Cor. 5:17). The Creator does not expect His creatures to re-create themselves. *"Can the Ethiopian change his skin, or the leopard his spots" (Jer. 13:23)?*

God Himself accomplishes the *"work of faith with power" (2 Thess. 1:11),* which is why true believers in Christ can say, *"His divine power has granted to us everything pertaining to life and godliness" (2 Pet. 1:3).* Because they realize that it's only by God's grace that they have been given the gift of faith in Christ, repentance from sin and the ability to follow Him in spirit and in truth (Eph. 2:8-10), for they are *"His workmanship!"*

This is why all the glory goes to God, not mankind, *"that every mouth may be stopped, and all the world become guilty before God" (Rom.3:19).* *"So that no flesh shall glory in His presence" (1 Cor. 1:29).* We are hedged about and surrounded by the all-encompassing truth of God's sovereign purposes that are not based on our own works (Rom. 9, 2 Tim. 1:9).

The God of the Bible is *Not* the false god of open-theism, who has to wait on pins and needles to see how things turn out. He's also not the *"whatever will be, will be"...* fatalistic...*"it is what it is"* god of Arminianism; casually sitting back while humans call all the shots. On the contrary, God is...

"Declaring the end from the beginning, and from ancient times the things that are not yet done, saying, My counsel shall stand, and I will do all My pleasure" (Isa. 46:10).

Notes:

[1] Dr. James R. White, *The Potters Freedom*, New Revised Edition, (Calvary Press Publishing, 2009), p. 61. Also revisit # 6 in my *Introduction notes* on fatalism.

Chapter 29

The Authority and Sufficiency of Scripture

"All Scripture is given by inspiration of God" (2 Tim. 3:16).
...inspired of God—(theopneustos) ...means "God-breathed" (NASB Greek Lexicon)
"For ever, O Lord, Thy Word is settled in heaven" (Ps. 119:89).

As it has been clearly and repeatedly shown, one of the most common pitfalls of the fallen masses is the false, freewill doctrine of man. And when it's taken to its logical conclusion, it completely shipwrecks faith in God's Word which is the foundation of all truth and knowledge. And all true worshippers of God must worship Him *"in spirit and in truth" (Jn. 4:23).* But *"if the foundations be destroyed, what can the righteous do?" (Ps. 11:3).* If Arminianism is right, and man's will is absolutely free to resist God, and if God chose to have autonomous men, with an *absolute* free will, to write down His Word, then the Bible message would have been altered.

But *"who hath resisted His will?" "The prophecy came not in old time by the will of man; but holy men of God spake as they were moved by the Holy Ghost" (Rom. 9:19, 2 Pet. 1:21).* Although the CoC will confess that God's Word is inspired, it steers clear of the implications of anyone being *moved* by God to do anything, for that would threaten its man-centered control.

Yet the truth remains; God is in control, not man. He *"worketh all things after the counsel of His own will"* (Eph. 1:11). *"Of His own will,* begat He us with the Word of truth" (Jas. 1:18, emphasis mine). His Word reveals the truth about creation, Christ's Deity, His virgin birth, perfect life, death, burial, resurrection, ascension and intercession to save us from sin. And *"Scripture cannot be broken" (Jn. 10:35),* which means that none of the prophecies and promises of God through Jesus Christ can ever fail.

However, the CoC teaches that we must have complete freedom of will to choose either good or evil, or else we deserve no reward if we are moved out of mere necessity. This, in turn, leads to doubting Jesus Christ, Who came in the flesh-- *out of necessity* (Jn. 12:48). It was *necessary* that He do the will of His Father, Whose Word and will cannot be broken. So in order for the CoC to be consistent with its freewill doctrine, it would have to conclude that all Jesus did on earth was unworthy of reward or praise, for His will was not "free" to choose anything against His Fathers will!

But rather than repent of the heretically horrid implications of its false doctrines, the CoC still stops at nothing to exalt the praise of man. This is why it goes to great lengths to try to deceptively integrate humanistic psychology into God's Word to further its man-centered agenda. However--

"The Bible claims to be the authoritative treatise on the doctrine of man, including the fallen nature, salvation, sanctification, faith and obedience. Therefore, if one is to study the human condition one must begin with Scripture rather than psychology. The commitment must be, first of all, that the Bible is in and of itself completely sufficient for matters of life and conduct. That does not mean that it is merely a sufficient framework on which to suspend unproven psychological theories."[1]

"Because many in the church believe that theories and techniques of counseling psychology are based upon empirical evidence, they put them on the same level of authority as the Bible. In so doing, the subjective observations and biased opinions of mere mortals are placed on the same authoritative level as the inspired Word of God. Furthermore, trying to syncretize psychology with Christianity denies the sufficiency of the Word of God and the sufficiency of the Spirit of God in all matters of life and conduct. It suggests that the Bible needs substantiation, confirmation, expansion, and assistance in matters of life and godliness."[2]

It's true that those who exalt self will be "in sync" with all that CoC syncretism has to offer: *self*-esteem, *self*-seeking, *self*-worth, *self*-love, *self*-fulfillment, *self*-improvement, *self*-help and *self*-pity. But Christians are to take Jesus' words to heart---that we must *deny self*. Because God is not an idle spectator with limited sovereignty that can be hindered or controlled by man's self-will. Also, according to Scripture, Jesus is God in the flesh and His Word is infallible, which happens to reveal that He does indeed override man's will. Just to name a few: Abimelech, Jonah and Saul of Tarsus all prove that no one can thwart God's power to supersede man's will.

But sadly, since the CoC teaches that God won't overcome man's will, it cannot *consistently* teach that God's Word is infallible (reliable). This is why the CoC keeps inching ever closer to its logical conclusion of complete apostasy. For a classic example, CoC author, Leroy Garrett, stated:

The Authority and Sufficiency of Scripture

"I revealed that I didn't believe in biblical inerrancy. I pointed out that the Bible makes no such claim for itself. Fundamentalists among us seem unaware that Alexander Campbell, who also didn't believe in the inerrancy of Scripture, was among the first modern translators to "mess with the Bible."[3]

When Alexander Campbell found errors in the KJV *translation,* he ignorantly concluded that the Bible wasn't inerrant (without error). His belief in the heretical doctrine of autonomous, human freewill caused him to conclude that mere men hindered God from preserving His message. He didn't realize that although *translators* are fallible, it does *NOT* mean God's Word is.

Only what the *original writers* wrote was divinely inspired. And it wasn't by being put into a mindless trance to perform the pagan practice of "automatic writing." For God supernaturally worked through them without deleting their individual personalities, writing styles, backgrounds, etc., which is evident throughout Scripture. And He has supernaturally preserved His message. All of Holy Scripture is inspired, infallible and inerrant, *NOT* its *translators* over the centuries who cannot make such a claim, which is why-

..."it is vital to emphasize that demonstrating errors in the KJV version in no way demonstrates errors in the Bible. The first involves recognizing the fallibility of human translators, while the second questions the very inspiration of Scripture itself."[4]

So the CoC needs to *seriously* rethink its Campbellistic freewill-ism, which inevitably shipwrecks faith in God's Word, and take heed to the fact that--

"God has preserved His text; He simply has chosen to do so in a far more miraculous way than you would allow Him to. It is a far more real miracle for God to take the work of multiple authors, written in multiple locations, in multiple contexts, writing to multiple audiences, during a time of Imperial persecution, working through the very mechanisms of history (just like He did with His people in the Old Covenant), and in that process create the single most attested text of all antiquity where less than one percent of the text requires us to engage in serious examination of the sources to determine the original reading. Fifty-seven-hundred-plus manuscripts, fifteen hundred years of trans-missional history, multiple authors, and the combined wrath of Rome and the Gnostics, yet we have the New Testament we possess today. *That* is miraculous indeed! Textual variation is merely an artifact of the mechanism of preservation" (Emphasis his).[5]

Notes:

[1] Martin and Deidre Bobgan, *Prophets of Psychoheresy I*, (Santa Barbara, CA: EastGate Publishers, 1989), pp. 215-216.
[2] *Ibid.*, pp. 332-333.
[3] Leroy Garrett, *A Lover's Quarrel, An Autobiography: My Pilgrimage of Freedom in Churches of Christ,* (Abilene, TX: A.C.U Press, 2003), pp. 226-227.
[4] James R. White, *The King James Only Controversy: Can You Trust the Modern Translations?* (Minneapolis, MN: Bethany House, 2009), p. 277.
[5] *Ibid.*, p. 307.

Chapter 30

Sad and Natural Outcomes of CoC Theology

"Jesus answered and said, I thank Thee, O Father, Lord of heaven and earth, because Thou hast hid these things from the wise and prudent, and hast revealed them unto babes...for so it seemed good in Thy sight" (Mt. 11:25, 26).

As I was growing up, my grandmother had always been my hero of "the faith," for she seemed to be the epitome of all the perfectionism our church stood for. As a child, I remember hugging her and looking up to say..."I want to be just like you when I grow up grandma, because you're perfect." And instead of correcting me and telling me that only Jesus is perfect and our only hope of being saved, she would just smile and beam with pride.

A few years ago, I painted a portrait of her sitting with her stack of Bibles, depicting how religious I had always viewed her. But from childhood to old age, she had always expressed doubts about the Bible and God's existence. Since the CoC taught that God wouldn't overrule man's fallen will, it nurtured the idea that the Bible could not be infallible, for God used human instruments to write His Word, who could have supposedly resisted Him by their almighty "freewill." So as long as we were under CoC influence we could never *consistently* believe that the Bible was infallibly true.

Yet grandma still kept a strict adherence and devotion to the CoC system and a compulsory reading of Scripture, which had earned her the title of "Bible Lady." After all, the CoC was *Big* on the Bible, the do's and don'ts of it anyway, for the overarching assumption was that all of its passages concerning works were a "prescription" for salvation, rather than a "description" of how a truly saved person will live to obey God by the sanctifying power of the Spirit, in virtue of their eternal union with Christ.

So our approach to Scripture was -- "What do I do?" Rather than seeking a perfect righteousness outside of ourselves that could only be imputed to us by God, through faith in Christ (Mt. 6:33, Rom. 1:17). Like the Jews in John 5:39-44, we searched the Scriptures diligently for eternal life but missed the only source and main theme of the entire Bible….namely, Jesus.

No wonder my grandmother spent the last few years of her life repeating the mantra, "I don't know what to do." Although she would sometimes say that she wanted to *do* what God wanted her to *do*, her "want to" wanted nothing to do with Jesus as her only hope. Instead, she ended up in a never ending maze of compulsory Bible reading marathons for hours on end, even through all hours of the night, looking for a loophole that she never could find. While doing so, she'd violently clap her hands, slap her legs, stomp her feet, spit, yell, squirm and rock violently in her rocking chair. It was truly heart-breaking. As many Christian theologians have conclusively noted:

"There may be a temporary willingness and mental consent in the unregenerate which makes them for a time ready to profess Christ while the natural enmity of their heart toward God is still unremoved (Mt. 13:20). Where the truth is preached there will be a general kind of conviction wrought by the Spirit which disturbs men's consciences and makes them willing to look for some relief. Yet until they have been quickened into newness of life by the special call and operation of the Spirit they will certainly not receive relief in the divinely appointed way, by coming to Christ. They will proceed to act on that principle which lies at the root of all natural religion, the belief that *man can do something to put himself right with God.* Thus Herod, with his conscience disturbed by the preaching of John the Baptist, was willing to do 'many things' (Mk.6:20). This willingness in Herod existed side by side with a basic attitude of hostility towards a holy God" (Emphasis his). [1]

My family would take grandma's "want to" to mean that she really was a Christian, whereas when she would blaspheme God, they took it to just be dementia, which revealed the inconsistency of such a view. Either she was able to respond spiritually or she wasn't. The answer couldn't be yes only when she said what was desired, and no when she didn't. Although grandma would restrain herself and act pious and religious around her own kind, she would slam her walker into walls and get hostile with her humble, assisted living neighbors who loved sharing their testimony of salvation.

Her hostility finally got so bad that she was no longer allowed to eat with other residents because she would spit food at them and mock them if they mentioned Jesus. When one told her that they were looking forward to being with Him, grandma got so furious that she turned blood red and exclaimed over and over again, "When we die, we just die and that's the end of us!" This too became a daily mantra for grandma up until her death.

Naturally, there were times when she *would* admit there was a God, but then she would say that no one knew for sure what *"it"* was, which mirrored Romans 1:21, about how all know there is a God, but not all want to acknowledge their accountability to Him. When I would patiently show her Hebrews 9:27 and all of Jesus' warnings about Hell and how He was the only escape, she would start hitting the Bible while saying it was just a book written by a bunch of men who didn't know what they were talking about.

So one day, I finally asked grandma why she ever even went to church all those years if she never even really believed in the God and Savior of the Bible. She said, "Well, because that's just what was expected of us." I said, "But grandma, that's what the Bible calls being a hypocrite." She laughed out loud and proudly said, "Well then, I guess I'm a hypocrite." It was so devastating to hear her talk like that, and it hurt me so bad to find out that my hero in "the faith" had only acted religious all those years... *because she just did what she thought "religious" people expected of her.*

When anyone would mention God, she would often ask them angrily, "How do you know there's a God, have you ever seen Him?" Most would be so shocked and offended that they would usually just walk away in an embarrassed silence. But when she would ask me, I would always say, "I don't walk by sight, but by faith.... I know Him by faith grandma." She would then get so abusive that she would hiss, huff and spit at me, while tempting me to sit in judgment upon God and His Word. She would sneeringly ask, "If you think God is so good then why did He create Hell?!"

So I would try to explain to her that without the existence of Hell, we would never know how bad sin is; an offense against the eternal God, with eternal consequences. I would try to explain that without the reality of Hell, we would never know how holy God is, how much He hates sin or how just He is against evil. I would then always try to direct her to God's grace.

Although my grandmother was the one who taught me to sing *Amazing Grace*, when I would try to sing it with her in her later years, she would abruptly interrupt when I'd get to the part about God saving a wretch like me. With an air of offended pride, she would argue that sin wasn't that bad. When I'd try to explain that we have all sinned and deserve Hell, she would angrily argue that she had never sinned bad enough to go to Hell.

But one day, just out of the blue, she yelled out, "I've sinned!--So what?!"--to which I gently replied, "Then repent and turn to Christ as your only hope grandma." She derided me and told me that she didn't need a Savior, and that Jesus was just created like us. So I asked, "Grandma if you don't want the Savior, Who is eternal, not "created"….then how are you going to escape Hell?" She indignantly shouted: "By doing right!"

During such moments I would cringe in fear for her soul and would always gently respond by trying to explain what the CoC never taught us. I would lovingly tell her that we can never do enough good to make up for a single sin that we've committed. I would then joyfully proclaim that Jesus completely satisfied God's divine justice, for He was sinless. Then I'd try to plead with her to accept that her only hope was in Him, Who sacrificed His own life to save sinners like us. But she would always mock me and say things like… "So we're all saved and don't have to worry about it then."

But I'd try to explain that not everyone is saved, because Jesus didn't just die to lower God's perfect standard of righteousness so that anyone could just slip in. He fulfilled God's standard perfectly, which means only those who put their complete trust in His righteousness alone are saved. But she'd get so mad that she'd scream ---"*I don't have to do no such thing!*"

One day she began reading one of the gospels out loud and exclaimed that Jesus was so bad that they had to kill Him!! As shocked and sickened as I was, I prayed for God's protection and resisted the devil by patiently showing her from Scripture that Jesus was good and in complete control of all that happened to Him. He *gave Himself* to save sinners (Gal. 1:4). He laid His life down *of His own accord.* He *fulfilled* the Fathers will (Who decreed that He die by *"wicked hands")…* and *raised Himself* from the dead (Jn. 2:19-22). He was *NOT* a criminal or failed victim, as the Pope sinfully proclaims. Jesus, the eternal High Priest, *offered Himself* as the sinless sacrifice (Jn. 10:18, Acts 2:23, Heb. 7:27)… and *prevailed to justify many* (Isa. 53:11).

But grandma dismissed it all and kept shaking her head no. For the CoC's deism, open-theism and Arminian sacramentalism that had been so deeply engrained into her, could never give her any reason to believe that God was truly in control of anything, or that Jesus' death accomplished anything more than a mere system, whereby one must try to save themselves.

So when I'd hear her say such horrible things, I would uncontrollably start trembling all over and feel deathly sick, for a twinge of horror would come over me. And during those times, there would be such a choking sense of darkness in her room that I'd barely even be able to breathe. Then, to compound the problem, other CoC'ers would *strangely* show up at the *exact* same time, treating me with contempt. Finally, after pondering Scripture, I realized that she could not have been speaking by the Spirit of God and that I was up against powers of darkness, not flesh and blood (1 Cor. 12:3).

But most would just chalk her blasphemy up to psyche meds, dementia or old age. Some even tried to take Ecclesiastes 12:1 out of context to prove that we are only expected to remember our Creator in youth, and that old age or dementia excuses one from that....as if aging and physical brain deterioration are excuses for blaspheming and outright rejecting the Jesus of the Bible! So I beautifully framed Ecclesiastes 12:1, *in context,* by including verses 6 and 7, and I set it up in grandma's room as a testimony to the fact that we are also to remember our Creator in old age *and* before we die. Even in old age, John Newton retained what he had held most dear:

"Although my memory's fading, I remember two things very clearly: I am a great sinner and Christ is a great Savior."[2]

Even despite memory loss, God's people *"shall still bring forth fruit in old age" (Ps. 92:14),* which is why so many of them can even have *severe* brain damage, diseases and disorders, and yet be some of the most godly, Jesus-loving saints in the world. For in many cases, brain deterioration is one way that God draws them closer to Him. Yet the world will often make excuses for the elderly, demented or drugged to outright reject Christ.

Some are even deceived into thinking that old age is always proof that one must have honored their parents and received the first commandment with promise..."long life on this earth"...and that it proves them to be a Christian, whether they acknowledge Jesus as their Savior or not!

But God's Word reveals that true Christians desire to win souls to Christ, rather than planting seeds of doubt against Him and His message! God also reveals that following commands is not what makes a Christian. For example, Job lived hundreds of years and had witnessed for himself that old age is not always proof of right standing with God. In fact, God sometimes allows the wicked to grow old and hardened in their sins, in order for them to store up even more of His wrath (Job 21, Ps. 73). Scripture is clear... *our age is nothing before Him (Ps. 39:5).*

"The mind cannot *really* become diseased any more than the intellect can become abscessed. Furthermore, the idea that mental "diseases" are actually brain diseases creates a strange category of "diseases" which are, by definition, without known cause. Body and behavior become intertwined in this confusion until they are no longer distinguishable. It is necessary to return to first principles: a disease is something you *have*, behavior is something you *do*" (Emphasis his). [3]

"Since the mind is not a physical organ, it cannot have a disease. While one can have a diseased brain, one cannot have a diseased mind, although he may have a sinful or unredeemed mind."[4]

As hard as it is for our sinful flesh to accept, the Bible makes it clear that there is such a thing as a *reprobate mind* (Rom. 1:28), which proves that it is a spiritual matter whenever sin is involved, *intentional or not*. Yet we live in a time where the spiritual needs of the feeble-minded are so neglected because of the psychologically sophisticated deception of confusing the physical brain with the non-physical mind.

"One can understand what a diseased body is, but what is a diseased mind? And if one cannot have a diseased mind it is obvious that one cannot have a diseased emotion, a diseased behavior, or a diseased relationship. Nevertheless, therapists and authors continually refer to mental, emotional, behavioral and now relational problems as illnesses."[5]

In our post-Christian era, the social, pseudo-science perspective, psycho-therapy and psyche drugs have all been strategically used to try to *replace* the gospel of Christ, and to blind minds from the truth, in a futile attempt to explain away sin and the biblical reality of demonic oppression.

"Although the brain is a physical entity and may require physical/chemical treatment, the mind and the soul are nonphysical entities. Whereas the former can be studied through scientific investigation and become physically ill; matters of the psyche and the soul are studied through philosophy and theology. And, indeed, those aspects of psychology which attempt to investigate and understand the mind and the soul resemble religion more than science."[6]

If it's true that mind-altering drugs can cause one to blaspheme God, then shouldn't they be avoided at all costs? Besides, the word *sorcery* in the book of Revelation is derived from the Greek word *pharmakia;* the same Greek word *Pharmacy* is derived from. Could it be that those who get hooked on such dangerous drugs are under God's judgment because they had rebelled against Him and His Word? One way to discern whether a situation is the result of God's judgment or a result of God's chastening love is that God's judgment hardens people in their sins, whereas afflictions that are sanctified by God's love irresistibly draw His people closer to Jesus as their only hope, with a repentant heart.

"The Bible refers to the soul of man. The words *psychological* and *psychology* are derived from the Greek word *psyche*, which means soul. It is the invisible aspect of man which cannot be observed. The study of the soul is thus a metaphysical endeavor. Thus psychology has intruded upon the very same matters of the soul which the Bible addresses and for which the Bible should be the sole guide."[7]

By simply trusting God and His Word, I made it a point to honor grandma by doing for her what I hoped someone would do for me in such a sad case. I kept re-directing her to the true Jesus of the Bible as her all in all, and comforting her in the truth that all she had to "do" was trust her all to Him, so that she could have *"the peace of God, which passeth all understanding" (Phil. 4:7),* and so that her *heart and mind* could be kept through Him.

Knowing the difference between the brain and the mind also helped me to stay focused on reaching out to grandma's soul with the gospel, despite all of the devils efforts to discourage me. Demented or not, *she still had a spirit that needed Jesus, Who alone can grant* **the spirit of a sound mind** *(2 Tim. 1:7)*. For God's people can have **the mind of Christ** (1 Cor. 2:16).

There are many testimonies of those with dementia being healed and delivered by Jesus. Even the medical field has often been forced to testify to the fact that many Christians, who have an *extremely* limited mental and physical capacity to communicate, still have the *spiritual* capacity to pour forth praise to Jesus for saving their soul, which can't be explained scientifically. For, like Mary, who sat at the feet of Jesus, they have *"the one thing needful"* that cannot be taken away, even after losing everything else.

While it may be true that some can be so brain damaged that they cannot express themselves, grandma was without that excuse, for she was able to express herself *very clearly!* And she was always *very consistent* with her beliefs and made it abundantly clear that she *meant what she said!*

After all, Jesus said, *"Those things which proceed out of the mouth come forth from the heart" (Mt. 15:18),* and that *"Ye shall know them by their fruits" (Mt. 7:16).* God secures His sheep in perseverance of the faith, but they are not passive in the process. He keeps them *through faith (1 Pet. 1:5)* and their hearts pour forth the fruits of that faith. God promises to keep His people, for He says *"I will put My fear in their hearts so that they will not depart from Me" (Jer. 32-40).* So those who do fall away from Christ, reveal that they were never true believers to begin with (1 Jn. 2:19).

As difficult as it was, I had to refuse to utilize all of my past Arminian escape hatches to try to explain away God's sovereign purposes for allowing some to be hardened in their sins. God's Word was my only guide. For I could not allow my love for grandma to destroy my faith in Jesus and the fact that He never allows the faith of His sheep to finally fail, because He forever intercedes for them, and His intercession never fails (Lk. 22:32, Heb. 7:25). His true followers *"are not of them who draw back unto perdition; but of them that believe to the saving of the soul" (Heb. 10:39).* They live in the hope of His righteousness on their behalf, *Not* in the hope of non-existence after death, Universalism, atheism or "having done their best."

Jesus delivers His people from spiritual torment and puts them back into **a *right mind*...** not due to their own ability to choose Him with their natural mind, but because He sets them free *spiritually* (Mk. 5:15, Eph. 4:23). For only then can they "do right" and *come to Him rightly.*

Although I had vigilantly tried to utilize every opportunity to reach my grandmother with the gospel, even by being her personal caregiver for years at the expense of my own health and finances, I began to pray that God would release me from that burden. For 2 Timothy 2:24-26 helped me to come to terms with the fact that although I had always been gentle and patient with grandma, refusing to argue with her...only God could grant her repentance to acknowledge the truth and escape the devils snare.

Two weeks later I received an answer to my prayer when another caregiver called to tell me that she had lost her client and was available to help with grandma. I took the offer and began to slowly distance myself from grandma, for I could no longer in good conscience continue to listen to her blaspheme God forty hours a week.... *It was literally killing me*.

The final straw was the day that she thought she had finally found the "loophole." She was reading Hebrews 9:22 out loud and exclaimed that she had come to the conclusion that we needed to shed our own blood to cover our sins!! Out of all the surrounding verses that mention Christ, she singled out one that she thought *she could do* to cover her own sins! Because, just like Romanism, the CoC had taught her all those years that Jesus' blood was *necessary,* but not *sufficient* unless we *did* all that we could *do* first, which meant that she could never know for sure if she had ever *done* enough.

CoC theology always gave false assurance that one might finally reach a degree of righteousness that God would accept. And since the CoC was very selective about the sins it would attack, false humility and self-righteousness was never at the top of the list. Though false religion can put a very shiny appearance on the surface, once the gloss begins to wear off, the things that led one to embrace error in the first place starts to come to the surface.

No wonder I discovered that out of all the diaries grandma had kept since she was thirteen, not once could I find that she had ever acknowledged God's direct hand in any of life's providences. Even so, I found it to be so fascinating and quite ironic that it had always been right in front of her. For instance, she wrote about her and my aunt visiting me right after I was born, and how it seemed as if I was really trying to tell them something!

I was reminded that Jesus said...*out of the mouth of babes God would perfect praise (Mt. 21:16).* Amazingly, grandma's first impression of me seemed to sum up God's call upon my life to "really try to tell them something"...*that they still couldn't seem to comprehend!* Sadly, many seem more consumed with storing up treasures on earth instead of in Heaven (Mt. 6:19-21). Grandma's only recorded testimony was that of works, with no mention of Jesus ever saving her. But before she died she told us to burn her diaries, for she said they were worthless...yet they became a shrine.

When I went to see grandma one last time before she died, I talked with her about many things and she would readily respond, but when I would begin to mention anything about Jesus or ask whether she knew Him as her Savior, she would refuse to answer and would make mean faces. Strangely, her whole room even seemed engulfed in a darkness that could be felt.

Although she would positively respond to me and tell me that she loved me too, when I'd come back around to the gospel and Jesus, she would stiffen up and cringe at the very mention of His name. Then she would start violently thrashing her arms. To the utter breaking of my heart, she never could answer the question...."Grandma, do you know Jesus as your Savior?"

Consequently, I was rushed to the emergency room, due to collapsing to my knees with severe chest pain and an inability to move the left side of my body. At that point, my husband told me that I needed to let go of my grandma and pray from a distance before grief over her soul killed me.

I was reminded of Bible passages that reveal how the gospel torments those who become hardened in their rejection of the truth (e.g. Acts 7:54, Rev. 11:10). To the self-righteous, the gospel doesn't sound like good news at all, but becomes like an aroma of death to them (2 Cor. 2:16). And, as God often purposes, the gospel actually becomes a testimony against them. So even if the gospel falls on deaf ears, it is still triumphant.

Although I had tried to reach grandma for years with the gospel through my *Theological Thoughts* articles and other books and gospel tracts, they would either be confiscated by family members, or I would find them in the garbage. At one particular point, her walker bag was even removed by family members so that I could no longer keep Charles Spurgeon books, articles and gospel tracts in it, which she had initially seemed to enjoy reading years before... *until they really seemed to hit home.*

Revealingly, no one else in the family ever even bothered to confiscate or throw away New Age "Guideposts," Mormon, Jehovah Witness or evolution materials from grandma's room, due to their common ground with the CoC.

It was also heartbreaking to me, that instead of directing grandma to Christ as her only hope of facing such a holy God, CoC members kept laying the impossible burdens of "try harder" legalism on her. She was even told that God would guide her "if" she really *wanted to do* what God wanted her *to do.* They could not understand that her "want to" was in bondage unless Jesus set her free. They did not realize that a dying soul needs more assurance of acceptance with God than its own obedience.

So when grandma lost consciousness after all of their "do more," "try harder" prodding's, they took that to mean that she had finally "found peace." And, of course, grandma may *have* found peace where there was no peace. False assurance in such neutral, work-righteous God-talk could have directed her to *any* conceptualized deity....*except* the true Deity of Christ.

By glorifying their efforts, they unintentionally revealed that they *did* realize deep down that she *was* spiritually distressed. Yet they still didn't seem to realize the full-orbed truth that *"there is no other name under heaven given among men, whereby we must be saved" (Acts 4:12).*

Sadly, grandma had fearfully and obsessively mumbled the mantra, "What do I do?" until she lost consciousness, and only then did my mother get brave enough to even so much as mention the name of Jesus to her right before she died....*and only after my aunts had left the room.*

As painful as it was, God had removed yet another idol from my life. But at the funeral home, one would have thought that she had been the Pope of the "Church of Christ," and that the golden chariot of its system of works had carried her straight to the throne of Heaven. Yet if she was truly saved on her death bed (*and I hope against hope that she was*), it was despite its sacramental system of salvation that had kept her in such spiritual darkness, bondage, torment and hostility toward the gospel her entire life.

As Christians, we are to use all the means that God provides in order to reach others with the gospel, while patiently and lovingly walking them thru it. But we must remember that they will only respond in true repentance and faith if God is pleased to exert His power to make those means effectual in their life. If not, we must humbly submit to the fact that He gives some over to believe lies and uses the situation as an object lesson to reveal how spiritually fatal false religion really is, in contrast to the glory of His truth.

It's been a little over a year and a half now since grandma passed away on my birthday. And though I was desperately hoping for a different ending to this book, I've had to accept that the whole scenario seems to have been set forth as a warning from God, as an example for all others in the CoC to beware, lest they end up *consistently* taking its toxic theology to its sad and natural outcome, and end up bringing reproach upon the doctrine of Christ.

It is truly tragic to think of how many have gone to eternity cherishing the false hope of Campbellism. For anyone who has the regrettable persistence to follow CoC doctrine all the way through to its logical conclusion will be hopelessly lost in the end. Beliefs have consequences, and the false belief that Christ is an *incomplete* Savior, will eventually reap the natural consequence of *complete* apostasy.

"Although the fig tree shall not blossom, neither shall fruit be in the vines; the labour of the olive shall fail, and the fields shall yield no meat; the flock shall be cut off from the fold, and there shall be no herd in the stalls: Yet I will rejoice in the Lord, I will joy in the God of my salvation" (Hab. 3:17-18).

Notes:

[1] Iain Murray, *The Invitation System*, (Carlisle, PN: Banner of Truth, 2002), pp. 20-21.
[2] John Newton. (n.d.). Retrieved December 20, 2017 from: http://www.azquotes.com/quote/351005
[3] E. Fuller Torrey, *The Death of Psychiatry*, (Radnor: Chilton Book Company, 1974), p. 40.
[4] Martin and Deidre Bobgan, *The Twelve Steps to Destruction; Codependency Recovery Heresies,* (Santa Barbara, CA: EastGate Publishers, 1991), p. 29. See also: Citizens Commission on Human Rights. (n.d.). *Real disease vs. mental "disorder."* Retrieved May 7, 2018 from: http://ww.cchr.org/quick-facts/real-disease-vs-mental-disorder.
[5] Martin and Deidre Bobgan, *The Twelve Steps to Destruction; Codependency Recovery Heresies,* (Santa Barbara, CA: EastGate Publishers, 1991), p. 30.
[6] Martin and Deidre Bobgan, *Prophets of Psychoheresy I,* (Santa Barbara, CA: EastGate Publishers, 1989), pp. 34-36.

Appendix 1

Acts 2:38

Exegesis/The Greek Rule

"Then Peter said unto them, ye repent and be baptized every one of you in the name of Jesus Christ for the remission of sins and ye shall receive the Holy Spirit."

Clause--- Any kind of phrase within or as a sentence

Two types ---Independent clause and Dependent clause

Independent--- Can stand alone as its own sentence.

Dependent--- Can't make sense on its own and depends on the sentence as a whole.

Acts 2:38 has three clauses:

1. "Ye repent"
2. "Every one of you be baptized"
3. "Ye shall receive the Holy Spirit"

Verb--- A word that shows action or state of being

Subject---Part of a sentence or clause that indicates what it is about or who or what performs the action.

In a sentence every verb must have a subject. The basic rule states that a singular subject takes a singular verb, while a plural subject takes a plural verb.

Grammatical person--- First, second and third

First person--- The person speaking or writing

Second person--- The person being spoken to or written to

Third person---The person, people, thing or things being spoken to or written about. Each clause has a subject and a verb that possess person and number.

First Clause Subject--- "ye"...second person and plural in number

First Clause Verb--- "repent"....second person and plural in number

Second Clause Subject--- "each one"......third person and singular in number

Second Clause Verb--- "be baptized"....third person and singular in number

Third Clause Subject--- "ye"....second person and plural in number

Third Clause Verb--- "shall receive"....Second person and plural in number

The Greek Rule---Subject and verb must agree in both person and number

The subject and verb of the first clause agree in person and in number so they go together.

The subject and verb of the second clause agree in person and in number so they go together.

The subject and verb of the first clause, and the subject and verb of the second clause, do *not* agree in person and in number, so they *cannot* be conjoined together; they *cannot* read: "repent, each one and be baptized."

The first and third clause, agreeing in subject and verb, in person and in number, *can* be conjoined together; they *can* read: "ye repent and ye shall receive the gift of the Holy Spirit."

The subject and verb of the second clause, and the subject and verb of the third clause, do *not* agree in person and in number, so they *cannot* be conjoined together; they *cannot* read: "each one be baptized and ye shall receive the Holy Spirit." The change in number of person from the first clause to the second clause marks a break in thought here. The English

Appendix 1: Acts 2:38 Exegesis/The Greek Rule

translation does not preserve this break in thought, so application of the Greek Rule is required.

Peter is saying first to repent. We are to act as we are acted upon by God (Who grants repentance by giving a new heart and a new spirit). *Then* we are to be baptized *after* this change has occurred.

A Modifying Phrase--- is one that describes something----"for the remission of sins" is a modifying phrase that can only go with either the first or second clause but *not* with both.

First Clause Modified--- "ye repent for the remission of sins"

This rules out baptism having a part in receiving the remission of sins; meaning remission of sins is received prior to baptism. That someone can receive remission of their sins and the gift of the Holy Spirit without baptism is proven in Acts 10:44.

Second Clause Modified---"each one of you be baptized for the remission of sins."

This would rule out repentance having a part in receiving the remission of sins; meaning a person would only need to be baptized without repentance for remission of their sins. This is clearly *not* the case, since a non-believer can be baptized without being saved, and still remain under condemnation of the law of God.

Therefore, the conclusion of Acts 2:38 and Acts 10: 44-48 is that water baptism does not *cause* salvation, but it *is* a public confession of what has *already* occurred.

Notes:

--- adapted from *Baptism is Not Salvation/ The Greek Rule (Acts 2:38)*. Retrieved June 4, 2018 from *The Message of the Cross* YouTube channel at: https://www.youtube.com/watch?v=TWYSCVZzWWw

For an even more in-depth overview of this subject, see: Bob L. Ross, *Campbellism: Its History and Heresies*, (Pasadena, TX: Pilgrim Publications, 1981), pp. 84-94.

Appendix 2

Breaking Through the CoC's Heretical Language Barrier

"The breaker is come up before them: they have broken up, and have passed through the gate, and are gone out by it: and their king shall pass before them, and the Lord on the head of them" (Micah 2:13).

There have been those who have tried to remedy the legalistic problems in the "Church of Christ." And yet, they have completely missed the mark by looking past Christ and focusing on peripheral issues. As a result, the heart of the matter is never addressed. So the main focus of this section will be on addressing some of the CoC's failed attempts to forge a superficial reconstruction that can never constitute a supernatural renovation, which can only come from God. Consequently, it will be demonstrated that there is nothing hidden that shall not be revealed (Mt. 10:26), despite the CoC's attempt to hide its heresies by redefining biblical terminology.

Though it claims to "speak only where the Bible speaks"... it "speaks" by redefining biblical terms when it suits its agenda. It preserves biblical vocabulary, while emptying it of its true meaning when it's convenient to do so. When confronted, it tones down its heretical rhetoric with superficial adjustments, causing its language to come off in such a way that it seems to convey a surface-level agreement with Scripture and true Christianity.

Its heretical language is so couched in spiritual terms that it's hard to distinguish the truth from fiction, unless God grants the discernment to do so. When someone *does* start to catch on, or objects by saying, "But the Bible says"...they are quickly silenced with a "yes, but" response. This is how the CoC elusively smuggles in "answers" to objections, without ever actually having to *exegetically* deal with those objections.

For instance, the CoC will admit that no one can ever be good enough to earn salvation. Yet then, it will turn right around and throw in a "but" that completely contradicts its first statement. This is how it always creates confusion to throw off the one objecting to its heresies. Therefore, the CoC must always have a readily accessible "yes, but" escape hatch, in order to evade being pinned down as the false religion that it is. For a classic illustration, the CoC's top of the chain author, Flavil Yeakley Jr., wrote this:

"Churches of Christ do not believe that people are born good. We have to learn to be good. **But** we are born with the **power of free will**" (Emphasis added). [1]

The problem is that the CoC cannot explain exactly to *what degree* one must muster up the willpower to "be good." When is it ever *enough?* And who sets the standard if it's not God's *perfect* standard…. Jesus Christ?

The CoC denies the biblical doctrine of original sin by teaching the idea that we are born "neutral," which creates a messed up mindset that nourishes the belief that we can actually pull off work-righteousness. So in order to be consistent, we had to follow where our heresy led. Yet we were anything but consistent when it came to *explanations* for our beliefs.

This is why one will hear a lot of double-talk in the CoC about how people aren't *really* born good; they supposedly have to learn to be good. And yet, it teaches that they have the *inherent ability* to do the kind of spiritual good that's worthy of salvation, which undermines God's gospel of grace.

Like semi-Pelagianism, the CoC denies our desperate need of the Savior as soon as we're conceived (Ps. 51:5; 58:3). Never mind that infants often have to pay *the wages of sin*, which is death. Although they are innocent of *volitional* sin (Jer. 2:34), they have *inherent* sin, or else no babies would ever die. *"For the wages of sin is death; but the gift of God is eternal life through Jesus Christ our Lord (Rom. 6:23).*

But as an end run to avoid the clear teaching of Scripture (which stands forcefully against the CoC's misleading doctrines), it goes so far as to teach that Jesus was born just as we are, and therefore, concludes that we must not be born into sin either. And so, the CoC falsely accuses those who oppose its false doctrine, of being monsters who imply Jesus was born into sin! Because…*the CoC specializes in the art of deflection.* But its ridiculous rhetoric is only a rabbit trail that leads to *such dangerous ground.* For by trying to falsely frame others, the CoC implies that either Jesus' birth was *not* divinely miraculous or that our birth *was!* Either way, the CoC is trapped in a hopeless contradiction by trying to defend the indefensible. [2]

The irony is that although the CoC admits that Rome's doctrine of

Appendix 2: Breaking Through....

"Mary's Immaculate Conception" is heresy; it substantially teaches the same thing by applying a pre-emptive salvation to *every* human, not just Mary!

The CoC teaches that babies are saved because they are without sin. So we must ask... *then what exactly are they saved from?* According to the heretical implications of CoC doctrine, *they are saved from having to be saved!* This is yet another way that the CoC redefines the biblical doctrine of salvation in the context of eternal life. In the CoC, the doctrine of salvation for infants is a salvation from having to be saved...a theoretical construct that can never square with Scripture!

The Bible makes it clear that *Jesus was Not born into sin like us.* Adams sin was not imputed to Him. He is fully man *and* fully God. But we, on the other hand, are born guilty of Adam's sin, not just our own sinning. This is why Jesus "shall save His people *from their sins*" (Mt. 1:21, emphasis mine). He only saves *sinners*, the *ungodly....those without any spiritual strength or power of their own* (Rom. 5:6).

We are all born with a fallen, *creaturely will* that's in bondage to sin, because Adams sin was imputed to us, for he was humanity's federal head (Rom. 5:12, 19). So we are *Not* born sinless or "neutral." Yet if the CoC is right, and babies are born without sin, then that would mean Heaven is full of those whom Jesus never died for....*because He only died for sinners!*

The CoC initially gives the false impression that it's being noble for protecting the innocence of infants from "monsters" who believe in inherited sin; "monsters" who supposedly assign babies to Hell. But nothing could be further from the truth! What the CoC is actually "protecting" is its sacramental system of salvation, even at the expense of disqualifying infants from entering Heaven. For the only humans in Heaven are those who Christ has redeemed from sin; those who've had their sin covered by the blood of the Lamb; those who have been sanctified by the Holy Spirit!

Sadly, it just goes to show the extremes that the CoC will go to in order to try to keep its whole Arminian system from collapsing, even at the expense of disqualifying little babies from salvation in Jesus, under the false pretense of protecting God's attribute of love, to the exclusion of His holiness!

As a result, the CoC actually undermines God's message of love that was displayed on the cross for His people, and disqualifies itself from being compatible with genuine Christianity. For the implications of CoC theology is that Heaven is full of humans who have never been saved from sin, redeemed by Christ or sanctified by the Holy Spirit! *(Also see: Mt. 21:16).*

Once again, the CoC is trapped in a hopeless contradiction. This is how ridiculous the CoC system gets when it fights tooth and nail for the "neutral," *not so fallen,* "freewill" of man. As a natural consequence, it ends up implying that Jesus was born with the same so-called "neutral" nature as us.... with the ability to sin!

Yet, to try to cover its tracks, the spirit behind the CoC causes its captives to falsely accuse those who believe in the biblical doctrine of original sin, of also believing Jesus had a sin nature, which is a gross distortion. For the true Christian position is that *Jesus was not born like us*. But CoC pulpiteers often claim that He was, and often even go to the extent of saying Jesus' temptation in the wilderness was proof that He could've chosen to sin, which also implies that He could've chosen not to do the Fathers will!$_2$

But the genuine Christian view is that Jesus was and is the God man, *with no inclination toward sin whatsoever!* The Bible makes it clear that He was born into this world by a miraculous work of the Holy Spirit, *unlike us* (Mt. 1:18, Lk. 1:35). Though He was exposed to the same temptations as we are, it was *impossible* for Him to sin, which made Him the perfect Lamb sacrifice.

Yet the spirit behind the CoC suggests that He was born like us and was therefore "neutral," which blasphemously implies that He would've been capable of damnable sin once He reached the so-called *"age of accountability"* (another Arminian doctrine found nowhere in Scripture and a culprit as to why some murder their children before they reach that "socially designated age," thinking that will assure them salvation).

At the opposite end of the spectrum, the Christian position is that Jesus did not come just to give us a plan whereby we must attain our own personal righteousness by an act of "freewill." Jesus' righteousness is the only one God will accept. Scripture warns us not to think more highly of ourselves and our abilities than we ought to (Rom. 12:3).

No one, including infants, can get to Heaven apart from Jesus' blood. He died to save His people from sin, which would surely include babies. Thank God they qualify for the Savior! Thank God they qualify for Heaven! Despite the CoC's heretical doctrines that imply babies are disqualified.

But what more can one expect from the CoC's typical, pulpit puppetry. As mentioned before, CoC advocate, Flavil Yeakley, Jr., in *Why they Left,* even boastfully based his analogies upon the psychological theories of atheists, such as Carl Jung, to try to explain away the CoC's contradictions and why people are leaving the "Churches of Christ" because of them.

No wonder he tried to advise CoC's not to appear so "cult-like." And no wonder he wrote... *at the very end of his book*... that we should be Christ-centered! ₃ For this is how the CoC system operates. It tacks on the name of Christ as an afterthought, in order to soft-peddle perversions of the gospel. Not only are CoC advocates theologically conditioned to speak out both sides of their mouth with a forked tongue if called into question, but they are also adept at tying themselves into theological knots when they attempt to defend the blasphemy of fallen man's *absolute autonomy....an attribute that only God possesses!* For a perfect illustration, Yeakley stated:

..."we do not become autonomous persons in response to propositions but rather in response to persons." (p. 202)

Yeakley wrote this in a section where he undermined the doctrines of Christ (or what he called "propositions"), and tried to replace them with "personal relationship." Furthermore, on page 202, he also stated:

.."We do not become ourselves by ourselves. If there were no others and no dealing with others, there would be no you. That is how we become fully-functioning autonomous persons. That is also the process by which Christ is formed in us."

Then, as an afterthought, Yeakley *finally* mentioned the power of Christ, but then turned around and denied His power by putting down His doctrines, which is a classic example of how the CoC creates a false dichotomy between Christ and His teachings.₄ It also reveals how ridiculous and confusing its muddled maze of mixed up terminology gets when its system is called into question concerning its "autonomous" freewill fables.

One of the devils favorite ploys is to separate Christ from the doctrines He taught, because it inevitably leads to thinking one doesn't need the Bible in order to know Christ. But the truth is that the very gospel itself is a "proposition" based upon the knowledge of what God has done in Christ, which is revealed *only* in His Word. And one cannot be saved by simply hearing the Word, for it must be attended by the regenerating power of the Holy Spirit, Who works conviction, repentance and faith in the Lord Jesus

(Heb. 4:7). Scripture even warns that *whoever does not have the doctrine of Christ…. does not have Christ* (2 Jn. 9)!

"Evil men and seducers will wax worse and worse, deceiving, and being deceived. But continue thou in the things which thou hast learned and hast been assured of, knowing of whom thou hast learned them; And that from a child thou hast known the Holy Scriptures, which are able to make thee wise unto salvation through faith which is in Christ Jesus. All Scripture is given by inspiration of God, and is profitable **for doctrine**, *for reproof, for correction, for instruction in righteousness; That the man of God may be perfect, thoroughly furnished unto all good works"* (2 Tim. 3:13-17, emphasis mine).

Although the CoC system claims allegiance to the authority of Scripture, it waters down Scripture and leads people down repulsive roads to Rome through baptismal bridges and freewill funnels that direct a downward flow. *"They profess to know God; but in works they deny Him, being abominable, and disobedient, and unto every good work reprobate"* (Titus 1:16).

This is why one must *think critically* and pray for discernment when listening to CoC sermons or reading its literature, in order to see past the whitewash. One must ask, how can Christ be formed in us, without us even knowing His "propositions" of the gospel? *That would be equivalent to saying we can be saved without believing the gospel!* If the gospel wasn't doctrinally relevant then the gospel would be useless! How can we have a personal relationship with Christ if we don't even know the doctrines He taught? Could it be that the CoC doesn't want people to know that *the way one is saved is central to the gospel itself*… because the CoC has the wrong way? That would explain why it suppresses the content of the gospel to accommodate the requirements of its sacramental system of works.

"It seems obvious that faith is empty if God can be stripped of His content. His content is expressed through doctrinal propositions which He Himself has revealed. The first ingredient toward apostasy is the assertion, "It is not the truth *about* Jesus that is the basis of conversion, but rather the truth *of* Jesus that really counts." This terribly unnatural separation of the doctrinal truths of Christianity from Christianity itself has led to the ruination of the Gospel. Indeed, it has taken root in Evangelicalism already. We are being told that one is saved by coming to a person— not by believing something said about the person. This is typical ecumenical nonsense, and leads easily into the Roman error of coming to Jesus *in the Eucharist*.

Appendix 2: Breaking Through....

We are converted only when we come to the right person, believing the correct message about Him. One cannot hope to separate Jesus from the message He preached. One cannot hope to have a relationship with God except on God's terms" (Emphasis his). [5]

The CoC, on the other hand, contains just enough Bible to be dangerous. In fact, it will be demonstrated that the Bible in the hands of the CoC system is like a sword in the hands of a deranged orangutan. Anyone who gets in its way will be mentally massacred with a mish-mash of juiced up jargon that has nothing to do with Jesus and leads to utter confusion.

So, back to page 202 of Yeakley's book. *What in the world* could CoC authors like him mean by implying that "we become ourselves"... *by dealing with others?* Do we create ourselves by choosing who we hang out with? Or do others create us through their influence upon us? And how in the world does this "process" of becoming a "fully-functioning, autonomous person" *cause* "Christ to be formed in us?" Is it by hanging out with "Church of Christ" people? It sounds that way doesn't it? How convenient.

Does the Bible proclaim that Christ exerts His power to make us "autonomous" persons? Or does it proclaim that He calls us to *deny ourselves, take up our cross and follow Him*? Should we trust God and His Word or the godless imaginations of those who promote the opinions of man? The CoC system has a form of godliness, but denies the gospel of God's power by attempting to *replace* it with man's "will power" to convert himself and others (Rom. 1:16, 2 Tim. 3:5).

Therefore, the CoC and its blind leaders of the blind come under the same condemnation as the Pharisees in Matthew 23:12-13, where Jesus says, *"And whosoever shall exalt himself shall be abased; and he that shall humble himself shall be exalted. But woe unto you, scribes and Pharisees, hypocrites! For ye shut up the kingdom of heaven against men; for ye neither go in yourselves, neither suffer ye them that are entering to go in."*

Even though Jesus says that *He Himself* is the door of entry to salvation (Jn. 10:9), the CoC blasphemously claims that *baptism* is the entry point of salvation! By doing so, it obscures the narrow way to Heaven and opens a broad way to everlasting destruction. For a classic example of how it utilizes a sleight-of-hand theology that's designed to shut up the only entry way to God's kingdom by offering another way, Flavil Yeakley, Jr., stated as follows:

"Baptism is not *why* we are saved. Grace is why we are saved. Baptism is not *how* we are saved. It is only our faith that God counts for righteousness. **But** baptism is *when* we are saved" (Emphasis added). [6]

Did you catch that? Another CoC "yes, but" escape clause to keep its baptismal regeneration doctrine from being so easily detected! This is how it redefines the biblical phrase "saved by grace through faith" to mean "saved on account of grace given to make a sacramental system available, which will save if worked in faith by us," just as Romanism does.

In the CoC, "faith" is to ultimately be in a system of works that are thought to be counted as righteousness by God. Although it claims that no one can take credit for the system of merit that God has supposedly provided, it teaches that one *can* take credit for "appropriating" God's grace by a "freewill" response to come to Christ "in faith".... *by being baptized*. In the same way, the Roman Catholic church claims that one can take credit for "appropriating" God's grace by a "freewill" response to come to Christ "in faith".... *by eating Him in the Eucharist!*

The Christian position is that the *ground* of our justification is in nothing that grace produces. For instance, faith itself is not even the *ground* of our justification, but only the sole instrument. Justification is *through* faith not *because* of faith. The only ground of justification is the righteousness of Christ *imputed* to the sinner by God's grace; a topic avoided by the CoC like the plague. Although it vaguely teaches that Jesus died for our sins, it never mentions that He lived (and still does) for our righteousness. *"For if, when we were enemies, we were reconciled to God by the death of His Son, much more, being reconciled, we shall be saved by His life" (Rom. 5:10).*

"For He hath made Him to be sin for us, who knew no sin; that we might be made the righteousness of God in Him" (2 Cor. 5:21). In the CoC we were never taught that there was a double imputation; our sins to Him and His righteousness to us. We were never taught that *this righteousness is a gift, just as saving faith is a gift* (Rom. 5:17, Eph. 2:8). Instead, we were taught that it was something we could attain by God's grace *plus* our own efforts, which was a denial of the necessity of Jesus' imputed righteousness.

Dangerously parallel to Romanism, the CoC system denies that faith in Jesus' righteousness is sufficient to save, so it teaches that the merits of Jesus must be initially applied in baptism. Then it also adds other "works of obedience" that must be performed to supplement Jesus' merits with our own. And, like Rome, the CoC makes this out to be "faith working by love." They've both institutionalized the merits of Christ into a system of works, where God is supposedly obligated to save those who "work the system."

The CoC eloquently calls this….*appropriating God's promises through "obedient faith."* Yet in Christianity, *faith itself is obedience to the gospel* as evidenced in John. 3:36, where the Greek word used for the first occurrence of "believes" is *pisteuo*, which means "to trust;" and the Greek word used for the second occurrence of "believes" in that verse is *apeitheo*, which means "disobedient." So one who *"believes not"* is *disobedient* to the gospel, for it calls for *faith* in the righteousness of Christ as our only hope. Thus, the CoC is completely at odds with genuine Christianity.

"We ask, "Can one be saved while denying imputed righteousness?" Salvation is not for those who later deny the very essence of salvation. Yes, one can be saved without a full grasp of imputed righteousness, but one cannot maintain that he is saved while denying this essential element of the Gospel. He will have only believed in a caricature of the gospel and a Jesus of His own imagination. This is idolatry, not salvation."[7]

To say one believes the gospel while holding to beliefs that deny the gospel is simply silly. True faith is confidence in God's divine mercy, which remits sins for Christ's sake. True salvation is in the object of our faith (Jesus), not in faith itself. Though the CoC teaches the *necessity* of faith, anything less than the *exclusivity* of faith in Christ alone, *Not* in our works…is a false faith.

"The failure to proclaim justification by faith alone is not simply a sin. It is out and out displacement of the Gospel of Christ with another gospel. Anyone who does this is anti-Christian and is not to be considered a brother or sister in Christ. Anyone who does this boldly and as a matter of doctrinal formulation is guilty, not of sin only, but in worshipping a false god and promulgating a pagan religion."[8]

Apostle Paul stressed so strongly that our justification *begins* with faith and *ends* with faith, that he used the double force of double prepositions…*"from faith to faith" (Rom. 1:17, 3:22).* For a faith generated by God is maintained by God. But the content of the CoC's version of faith constitutes works (things that are seen), whereas the substance that makes up a Christians faith is Christ Himself…. the evidence of what is not seen (Rom. 8:24-25,

Heb. 11:1). A Christian's instant, *declarative* justification, based on faith in Jesus alone, is not to be confused with sanctification; the process of God making us in reality what we already are positionally *in Christ (Heb. 10:14).*

Yet the CoC promotes *self*-justification that must be progressively pursued as we "work out our salvation with fear and trembling," which is why it *always* isolates this passage from the verse that follows, *"For it is God which worketh in you to will and to do of His good pleasure" (Phil. 2:12-13).*

Christians will inevitably work out (sanctification) what God has worked within (regeneration). But *justification* is a finished work of God, found only outside of our selves...*in Jesus' perfect obedience on behalf of guilty sinners.* Those, whom God has graciously provided with this perfect righteousness, are *"justified by His blood."* It is a judicial act of God (Rom. 5:9, 17-21).

Those, whom God has purposed to pronounce as "not guilty," are *"justified freely by His grace through the redemption that is in Christ Jesus" (Rom. 3:24).* This saving grace is not a mere aid to gain justification through works, but is God's divine power that actually accomplishes His purposes. True, He accepts a Christian's work done in Christ, but not as a means to *get* them to Heaven, but *"their works do follow them"* to Heaven (Rev. 14:13).

Yet again, like Romanism, the CoC has a contractual model of salvation, where one's works *are* accepted as a means of salvation and as a means of getting one to Heaven... once one is first initiated into a "grace relationship" with God *through baptism*. Once one is baptized, one allegedly enters into a right relationship with God, where He then accepts "the best one can do," which means that one can never know for sure if they've ever done enough. What a sad state of affairs...*where one can never have peace with God.*

But Scripture is clear; *"Being justified by faith, we have peace with God through our Lord Jesus Christ" (Rom. 5:1).* God's grace is an *undeserved gift* of reconciliation that is not granted upon a condition of our obedience. It's granted upon Jesus' perfect obedience and purchased by His precious blood. God's mercy is Him *not* giving what Christians *really deserve,* for Jesus paid the penalty of their sins in full. Yet substitutionary atonement was unheard of in the CoC.

Strikingly similar to Romanism, the CoC implies that God's grace merely gives us a foundational system that we must work in order to get ourselves to Heaven. It teaches that *grace is something that is operative when we do something*, which blurs the lines of distinction between grace and works.

And, like Romanism, the CoC teaches that a "grace relationship," initiated through *baptism,* makes our works worthy and acceptable *as a means of salvation*. It teaches that grace is the *foundation* of salvation, but invalidates grace as an irrevocable gift from God (Rom. 11:29). Its version of grace starts out as being offered as a gift, but ends up being something we obtain and keep by our response, cooperation or "works of obedience." So, just like Rome, the CoC is guilty of institutionalizing grace into a system of works.

But, once again, if CoC proponents are called out on this, they are conditioned to give a "yes, but," surface-agreement response, in order to slip in a *redefined* version of the CoC's false, baptismal regeneration doctrine, as a "passive" work. For a classic example, in his book, *What Must the Church of Christ Do to Be Saved?*—Leroy Garrett stated as follows:

"Campbell wanted to show that God's grace is *unconditionally* bestowed to all mankind, apart from any worth, merit, or works on man's part. But the appropriation and enjoyment of the grace is *conditional*" (p. 168). "*That is where baptism comes in.* It is God's way of having us accept the gift. And even baptism is not something we do as much as it is something done to us" (p. 169, emphasis his).

One thing is for sure when dealing with the CoC, baptismal regeneration will somehow *always* be slipped in, without it ever even being called that, which makes it all the more sneaky. In the same book, Leroy Garrett wrote:

"Baptism is not our "work of righteousness" but the work of God's grace upon us." "It is a passive act. God is doing something to us, it is God's "washing of regeneration" upon us, an act of His grace. In baptism we have the assurance of pardon and the remission of sins. I can know I am a Christian and saved because "I have been to the river and I have been baptized" (p. 126, emphasis his). (SCMe-Prints@stone-campbell.org., ©2010).

Ironically, fasting (not eating) could be considered a *passive* work. Yet, like baptism, it's still a work and should never be used as an attempt to gain salvation! Moreover, the CoC makes the deadly mistake of taking the baptism of the Holy Spirit, which is how God *literally* puts His people into the Body of Christ (e.g. Mk. 1:8, 1 Cor. 12:13), and confuses it with *water* baptism. There is only *ONE spiritual* baptism into the Body of Christ, which is indeed passive on our part, for it is God's work (Eph. 4:5). But *the physical aspect*, which is the outer and *figurative expression* of what has already occurred *inwardly*...is something done by us and can in no way, shape or form be truly "passive," unless it's used as a medium to the spiritual realm.

However, the CoC falsely accuses Christians, who hold the biblical view of baptism, of taking a Gnostic approach that separates the physical from the spiritual, so that it can falsely claim to take a more "balanced approach."[9]

But the CoC is actually the one guilty of a Gnostic view (revisit p. 19), and for taking a *completely unbalanced* approach to baptism, which has parallel implications with Romanism and occult practices that require *passivity* in order to seek Jesus experientially....*through human mediators who facilitate spiritual encounters*. Pagans have *always* used a "water portal" to facilitate *passive* spiritual experiences and strong delusions to give false confirmation.

This is why those who *passively participate in baptism as a way to be saved* are subtly induced and inoculated with an unbiblical view of Jesus and the gospel, so that they become totally resistant to truth. This is due to the subtle form of divination that takes place while participating in a *passive* perversion of the truth that involves human mediators and the spiritual realm, which is an abomination to God (Deut. 18:9-14, 1 Tim. 2:5).

Falsely assuming God will cooperate with *another gospel* is an unbiblical attempt to manipulate Him, and an attempt to save oneself outside of God's sanction and protection, which puts participants in direct contact with *another Jesus; a demonic imposter* who works to confirm the lies that have been implanted through the CoC's false, baptismal regeneration doctrine.

This is where discernment is crucial for recognizing the difference between man-initiated encounters with God and the biblical pattern that confirms the fact that...*true encounters with God are always initiated and facilitated by Him alone*. In fact, the only scriptural references for man-initiated encounters are instances of divination, which is a severe offense and abomination to the Lord (e.g. Lev. 20:6, Jer. 14:14, Acts 16:16).

Ezekiel 13:6-8 perfectly describes baptismal regeneration "encounters," where God condemns conjuring up vain visions of lying divinations while claiming they are from Him and causing people to hope in false confirmation. Colossians 2:18 also speaks against intruding into things not seen and being vainly puffed up by the fleshly mind. Though our God-given imagination can be used to express love for God or to convey the gospel, *it's never to be used as a way to hear and receive from God,* which leads to rank

Appendix 2: Breaking Through....

superstition and creates an idol in the mind. Jesus and His cleansing blood is near all who call upon Him *in truth*....*Not* in error (Ps. 145:18, Eph. 2:13).

Jesus is the only mediator between God and man (1 Tim. 2:5). He has not left us with a sacramental system that restricts access to His blood, for it is readily accessible outside of any system (Rom. 5:9). He Himself pleads His blood before the Father, on behalf of His people. They already have access to *pure rivers* of Living Water that flows unto salvation, so that they never have to drown in a *polluted river* of baptismal "rebirth," where undercurrents of spiritual bondage lead to mystical, man-mediated encounters that shipwreck faith in Christ-mediated reconciliation with God. Strikingly comparable to Jeremiah 2:13, the CoC has ironically forsaken the fountain of Living Waters for broken cisterns that can hold no water!

It must be noted that although the grace of God may enable a CoC member to live above their theology and see beyond the baptismal regeneration formula enough to grasp the gospel and be saved, still it cannot be said that the CoC teaches *the way* of salvation or that one should stay in a false religion once they've been saved. God convicts His people of such and separates them from those who promote it (2 Cor. 6:17). And Yeakley unwittingly quoted an ex-CoC member who hit the nail on the head:

"I left Churches of Christ because I got tired of the "Yes but" approach to the doctrine of salvation by grace."

But what was Yeakley's response you might ask? Well...none other than the "yes, but" approach of course!! On the very same page he slyly stated:

"God's grace is essential to receive the free gift of salvation, **but** that response involves works of obedience and not works of merit" (Emphasis mine).[10]

This is the CoC's typical "grasping for straws strategy" when caught in hopeless contradictions. It's tricky double-speak not only creates artificial categories, it creates a false dichotomy between "works of obedience" and "works of merit," *just like Romanism*. As one Christian theologian put it:

"The Roman Catholic phrase "Christ alone merits our salvation" means nothing when it comes to the articulation of the Gospel. It is an open door for all manner of cults and religions of man. It is so because it puts Christ in the position of only opening the door to Heaven. It is the old heresy that "Christ has done His share, and now you must do yours," or that "God is pleased with Christ, so now here is what man must do." This means that "Christ has merited the opportunity, and now man must merit the salvation itself." Romanists think that Christ has made salvation possible and hence has merited our salvation. What they are really saying is that we could never save ourselves unless Christ had first merited the chance for us to do so. Romanists sincerely believe that Christ enabled God to accept what sorry works we have to offer for our own salvation."[11]

Like Romanism, the CoC affirms grace as a saving principle, but then it turns around and couples grace with obedience (works). And it is forbidden fruit to mix mercy with merit, grace with works or truth with error. Yet the CoC system capitalizes on compartmentalizing conflicting concepts, which creates a *double-minded* approach that causes confusion and shuts down people's capacity to critically think through its theological mind games. *"A double minded man is unstable in all his ways" (Jas. 1:8).* And Scripture makes it clear that this kind of man, whose "faith" wavers between works and grace (because they doubt the sufficiency of both), *cannot expect to receive anything from the Lord (v. 7).*

On page 60, in the same book, Yeakley used the false analogy of "The Blind Men and the Elephant" to try to excuse the blindness of the CoC system when it comes to "dialoguing" with those who have left. The irony is that although a blind man may focus on an elephants ear and conclude that it is the whole elephant instead of just a *part* of the elephant, this does not excuse the CoC's blindness to the wholeness of Christ and His gospel!

Instead of taking the testimonies of those who have left seriously, he elusively smoothed over CoC heresies with a shallow psychoanalysis that made it look as if Christ can be a Savior *in part*. This leads to being *"carried about with every wind of doctrine" (Eph. 4:14),* devoid of any absolutes. Yet the *absolute truth* is that Jesus will either be *all* of one's salvation....or none.

The CoC confuses works and grace by isolating certain Bible verses to try to prove that we *inherently* have the power to *keep ourselves (1 Jn. 5:18, NASB).* But Scripture in no way bears this assertion out. For instance, the best Greek renderings of this verse reveal that Jesus is the One begotten of God, Who keeps those given to Him, so that the evil one touches them not.

Besides, God's Word completely clears up the "yes, but" confusion between works and grace by stating: *"Even so at this present time also there*

Appendix 2: Breaking Through....

is a remnant according to the election of grace. And if by grace, then is it no more of works; otherwise grace is no more grace. But if it be of works, then is it no more grace; otherwise work is no more work" (Rom. 11:5-6).

Human work is still human work no matter which way you slice it or dice it. Though the CoC appears to agree with Christian doctrine on the surface, by grudgingly admitting one can't earn salvation, it camouflages words with an eloquent veil of human wisdom, to try to keep from being so obvious.

Like Romanism, the CoC attaches double meaning to words and makes grace and works interchangeable. But mutually exclusive assertions cannot possibly both, in the same context, be true. Yet such thought twisting tactics are a powerful CoC weapon when combined with trick terminology that is deliberately vague. Then its final, fatal blow to biblical discernment is softened by sugar-coated language that suggests its heresies are not really poisonous and deadly after all. So when dealing with such shady religious systems, we must pray for spiritual discernment and learn to break through the heretical language barrier by using the means that God provides....the very means that the evil spirit behind the CoC system tries so hard to hide.

With the upsurge of reformed theology, the CoC system has had to develop even more sophisticated arguments in order to try to counteract the threat of being exposed. This is due to the fact that the CoC has the same basic soteriology as the Roman Catholic Church, *which the early reformers successfully stood against to the death.*

So the spirit behind the CoC must first attempt to turn people against reformed confessions of faith by suggesting that they are only "man-made creeds." Then, in order to discourage them from ever trying to find out the truths they contain and how they match up with Scripture, the CoC's domain of expertise is highly trained to misrepresent them. And sadly, Yeakley followed suite with the charade by telling people that reformed theology had no explanations for certain Bible verses (e.g. Heb. 6:4-6, 2 Pet. 2:20-22, Gal. 5:4). Furthermore, he propagated this lie again by stating:

"Calvinism has no emphasis or clear understanding concerning the role of the Christian evangelist or the role of the convert."[12]

This is a gross distortion and a severe confusion of categories, which displays ignorance concerning the difference between Calvinism and *Hyper-*

Calvinism. For one of the great hallmarks of reformed theology is that it has *entire books* written on these very verses and on every subject that the CoC says it has no explanation for! Yet, in order to keep its false gospel from being exposed, the CoC must misrepresent Christian theology by building a straw-man that's easier to attack, and falsely calling it Calvinism. Like other Arminian circles, the CoC inoculates people against the truth by giving them a caricature of Calvinism, rather than the genuine article.

On page 151 Yeakley charged reformed theologians of "ignoring the role and the responsibility of the convert." This is a patently false statement, for it flies in the face of hundreds of years' worth of evidence to the contrary.

"The error of Arminianism is not that it holds the biblical doctrine of responsibility but that it equates this doctrine with the unbiblical doctrine of "free-will" and preaches the two things as though they were synonymous. But man's will is always exercised in harmony with his nature and, as his nature is at enmity with God, so is his will. Man being fallen, his will cannot be neutral or 'free' to act contrary to his nature.....Man's spiritual inability is due solely to his sin and therefore it in no way lessens his responsibility. That man must be able to believe and repent in order to be responsible for unbelief and impenitency is a philosophical conception nowhere found in Scripture."[13]

"Reformed theologians, when speaking of man's free-agency, which is essential to moral responsibility, occasionally refer to man's will being 'free,' that is from any external compulsion to sin; in this sense man has a free-will, which is obviously different from the Arminian usage of the term, and it makes our position one of terrible personal accountability for our actions."[14]

Amazing! And this is only one of *thousands* of expositions on the subject of man's responsibility and free agency within the confines of God's decree, which has clearly *not* been neglected or ignored by reformed theologians!

Yet Yeakley sugar-coated the CoC's neglect of full, biblical expositions of Scripture on difficult doctrines that the flesh doesn't want to accept, by making the typical, lame excuse that *we just can't know everything* (p. 174). But Scripture is clear; there's *truth to be known, truth that saves, truth that's to be received with love.* Yet there will be those who don't love it or receive it... and will be sent a *strong delusion* (Mt. 13:10-15, 2 Th. 2:10-13).

No wonder the CoC gives shallow, *general* explanations for everything, especially for the doctrine of election (e.g. pp. 159-162). Then, it has the

Appendix 2: Breaking Through....

audacity to falsely portray itself as the only source with any explanations at all, and discourages anyone from going *"outside the camp"* to find true, biblical *exegesis* of Scripture, for that would expose its unbiblical *eisegesis*.

So the CoC's top of the chain author followed suit with the devils cover up agenda, by taking the typical minimalist approach that failed to acknowledge clear category distinctions. For a classic illustration, he stated:

"What is rejected is Calvin's doctrine that people are saved by a direct operation of the Holy Spirit totally separate and apart from the influence of God's Word."[15]

He has presented a "Calvinism" straw-man, for John Calvin even stated:

"...the Word is the instrument by which the illumination of the Spirit is dispensed. Since the human mind, through its weakness, was altogether unable to come to God if not aided and upheld by His sacred Word, it necessarily followed that all mankind, the Jews excepted, inasmuch as they sought God without the Word, were laboring under vanity and error."[16]

Reformed theology has *always* acknowledged the harmonious working of the Holy Spirit *and* the Word in salvation.[17] True believers are born again *directly* by the Holy Spirit (Jn. 3:5) *through faith* in God's Word (1 Pet. 1:23). The Word is a means of conversion and the Spirit is the effectual agent. The reformers realized that they needed their minds renewed by the Holy Spirit in order to understand God's Word, which led to doctrinal balance.

But the CoC's unbiblical belief in man's *inherent* spiritual ability through absolute, "freewill" autonomy, *apart* from a direct operation of the Spirit... is exactly what leads to a "Word only" stance, which Yeakley pretended to reject, and yet he ended up promoting it (which will soon be demonstrated).

The prevalence of such unbiblical principles inevitably leads to abandoning prayer, for prayer requires one to appeal to God for divine intervention, which the CoC refuses to acknowledge a need for, as long as it just has the Bible. It makes, *"calling upon the name of the Lord"* synonymous with being baptized, which makes Acts 22:16 contradict Acts 2:21; 10:2; 22:8, 10 and 26:15, where it's clearly shown that prayer comes *BEFORE* baptism.

False, CoC interpretations make prayer a vain, empty duty, void of any spiritual meaning whatsoever. This is the natural consequence of its false notions of the indwelling of the Spirit being synonymous with the Word being memorized. By convincing people that they already have all the divine intervention they need by possessing the written Word, they are not led to pray for the Spirit... *Who is promised only to those who ask* (Lk. 11:13).

"Campbellism openly proclaims that sinners are pardoned without one word of prayer. Such a doctrine is God dishonoring and soul destroying in its tendency. It is calculated to make "blind leaders of the blind," and to induce whoever receives it to cry, "peace, peace," while there is no peace, and to expect salvation in a way that God has never ordained" (Emphasis his). [18]

While the CoC says Scripture is *essential,* it leaves out the fact that it's made *effectual* for God's people *by the Holy Spirit.* This is why they *shall* come to Him *for* righteousness, not by their *own* righteousness, for they are the poor in spirit who *thirst for righteousness (Mt. 5:6, Jn. 6:37).* They *shall* come to Him thru the power of prayer and not by a power of their own (Rom. 8:26).

"But as many as received Him, to them gave He power to become the sons of God, even to them that believe on His name; Which were born, not of blood, nor of the will of the flesh, nor of the will of man, but of God" (Jn. 1:12-13). And those who receive Him are the same ones whom God has given the power to do so, because *"a man can receive nothing, except it be given him from heaven (Jn. 3:27).*

The CoC, on the other hand, teaches that "receiving Christ" or "accepting Christ" merely means intellectually receiving or accepting facts about Him, rather than acknowledging *the desperate need to be accepted by God on the basis of receiving Jesus' imputed righteousness (Eph. 1:6, Jas. 4:6).*

One could allegedly "accept Christ," and yet, reject His message, which is not really accepting Him at all. The CoC does just that, by rejecting Jesus' message on divine intervention (Jn. 6: 65), and replacing it with a general, *inborn power* to "receive Christ," which leads to a perverted, *generic* view of the indwelling of the Holy Spirit. Thus, Yeakley continually followed suit:

"Every blessing the Bible attributes to the indwelling of the Holy Spirit the Bible also attributes to the influence of the inspired Word as recorded in the Scriptures." [19]

The CoC equates the indwelling of the Spirit with the mere *influence* of Scripture. But when pressed to define terms and answer biblical objections, Yeakley tried to smooth over the CoC's heresies concerning the Holy Spirit,

Appendix 2: Breaking Through....

by covering futile ground with philosophical theories that cannot be integrated into a cohesive and consistent whole. The use of such mind-numbing maneuvers and pseudo-parables could easily distract the reader from what's really being said... *for just a few paragraphs later he also wrote*:

> "Some people think that members of the Church of Christ do not believe in the indwelling of the Holy Spirit. Some went so far that they adopted a "Word Only" doctrine that limited the Holy Spirit's indwelling to nothing more than the influence of the Bible in our lives."[20]

But that wasn't Yeakley of course. That wasn't any of the CoC's he was familiar with. That was just those *"bad CoC's"* that teach such a terrible thing. Unbelievable!! This is your typical CoC, "heretical hop-scotching" attempt to avoid answering a charge by misdirecting it. CoC operatives are notorious for trying to take the heat off, by dodging the obvious. When questioned... *it's always those other CoC's that believe such heresy*... NOT!

This is why it's so important to stay focused and backtrack when reading CoC literature, because it *always* contradicts itself, which shows a lack of respect for the reader by assuming they won't detect such contradiction. It also reveals a lack of respect for the issues at hand... *by blurring the issues*.

On page 72, Yeakley taught the CoC's typical *general* doctrine of the indwelling of the Holy Spirit, which is just the mere outward *influence* of the Word, *made effective by baptism and lost when one sins.* Yet he seemed to *wonder* why anyone would dare to think that the CoC doesn't really believe in the indwelling of the Spirit! *Ugh!* Playing dumb is not going to cut it.

This is exactly how the CoC system commits intellectual and theological suicide. Beyond a shadow of a doubt, it never ceases to amaze the thinking mind just how blasphemous, deceptive and contradictory the CoC's pulpit puppetry is trained to be. And it's literature from start to finish is *full* of this kind of stuff, as evidenced in my overflowing filing cabinet.

> "For such are false apostles, deceitful workers, transforming themselves into the apostles of Christ. And no marvel: for Satan himself is transformed into an angel of light. Therefore it is no great thing if his ministers also be transformed as the ministers of righteousness; whose end shall be according to their works" (2 Cor. 11:13-15).

Behind the whitewash and philosophical gymnastics, we find that it's actually the CoC that has no clear emphasis or understanding when it comes to the truths of Scripture, because it abuses the name of Christ and misleads people into believing lies about Him. After unraveling its theologically tangled mess, it has been thoroughly demonstrated that it hoodwinks people by engaging in a psychological operation of the worst caliber.

The main supports for CoC arguments are isolated texts of Scripture pulled out of context, to form shallow, loosely-knit analogies, allegories and psychological theories that cannot be harmonized with the full counsel of God. When confronted, its enthusiasts are highly trained to heretically hop-scotch around the obvious, to evade the clear teaching of Scripture.

Though the CoC initially gives the impression that it's the real deal, after close inspection it becomes painfully obvious that it is absolutely at odds with genuine Christianity and proves to be a very deceptive counterfeit.

Although its enslaved captives are always learning, they're never able to come to the knowledge of the truth....*unless Jesus rescues them.* For the CoC system is designed to short-circuit the capacity to *think theology through*. By framing words in a futile fashion that's fatal to logic, it tickles itching ears with smooth speeches and flesh-flattering, freewill fables that cause fragmented thinking, division and offenses that scatter the sheep.

"Mark them which cause divisions and offences contrary to the doctrine which ye have learned and avoid them. For they that are such serve not our Lord Jesus Christ, but their own belly and by good words and fair speeches deceive the hearts of the simple" (Rom. 16:17-18).

Notes:

[1] Flavil R. Yeakley Jr., *Why They Left*, (Nashville, TN: Gospel Advocate Company, 2012), p. 71.
[2] Alvin Jennings, General Editor, *Introducing the Church of Christ* (Fort Worth, TX: Star Bible Publications, Inc., 1981), pp. 115-119. For a typical illustration, also see: YouTube channel, *Biblical Truth*, with CoC preacher Wesley Simons, who unsuccessfully tried to refute what he called "The False Doctrines of Calvinism." Retrieved Friday February 9, 2018 from:
https://www.youtube.com/watch?v=Yhvo2sBlwIM
[3] Flavil Yeakley Jr., *Why They Left*, pp. 117, 118 and 203. Also see pp. 105-118 for his promotion of athiest Carl Jung and his psycho-heresies. Also see: Brian Staron, *Why Our Youth are Leaving the Church*. Retrieved February 1, 2018 from:

Appendix 2: Breaking Through....

http://www.gospeladvocate.com/gospel-advocate-magazine-november-2013-why-our-youth-are-leaving-the-church-by-brian-staron.

[4] *Ibid.*, p. 202.

[5] Robert M. Zins, Th.M., *On the Edge of Apostasy: The Evangelical Romance with Rome*, (Huntsville, AL: White Horse Publications, 1998), p. 116.

[6] Flavil R. Yeakley Jr., *Why They Left*, (Nashville, TN: Gospel Advocate Company, 2012), p. 70.

[7] Robert M. Zins, Th.M., *On the Edge of Apostasy: The Evangelical Romance with Rome*, (Huntsville, AL: White Horse Publications, 1998), p. 125.

[8] *Ibid.*, p. 234.

[9] For a classic example of this false accusation, see: Benjamin J. Williams, General Editor, *Why We Stayed*, (Los Angeles/London: Keledei Publishing, 2018), p. 69. Also see page 129 for the CoC's view of "sacramental encounters" with God and page 160 for its view on baptism being a spiritual "portal." Also see: *Council of Trent, Canon 8* for the CoC's heretical parallelism with Rome when it comes to viewing God's ordinances *"sacramentally and really."*

[10] Flavil R. Yeakley Jr., *Why They Left*, (Nashville, TN: Gospel Advocate Company, 2012), p. 69.

[11] Robert M. Zins, Th.M., *On the Edge of Apostasy: The Evangelical Romance with Rome*, (Huntsville, AL: White Horse Publications, 1998), pp. 222, 223.

[12] Flavil R. Yeakley Jr., *Why They Left*, (Nashville, TN: Gospel Advocate Company, 2012), pp. 158-160.

[13] Iain Murray, *The Forgotten Spurgeon*, (Carlisle, PA: The Banner of Truth Trust, 1994), pp. 61, 62.

[14] *Ibid.*, p. 62.

[15] Flavil R. Yeakley Jr., *Why They Left*, (Nashville, TN: Gospel Advocate Company, 2012), p. 71.

[16] John Calvin, *The Institutes of Christian Religion*, Edited by Henry Beveridge, (Pacific Publishing Studio, 2011), pp. 27, 41.

[17] For an in-depth study of reformed theology, see: R.C. Sproul, *What is Reformed Theology? Understanding the Basics*, (Grand Rapids, MI: Baker Books, 1997).

[18] William Phillips, *Campbellism Exposed*, (Cincinnati, OH: J.F. Wright & L. Swormstedt, 1837), p. 255. Also see page 254-- "Now it is not contended that every Campbellite has gone to this extreme, but it is confidently asserted that some have, and firmly believed that in so doing they have only carried out their system of doctrines to its legitimate results."

[19] Flavil R. Yeakley Jr., *Why They Left*, (Nashville, TN: Gospel Advocate Company, 2012), p. 71.

[20] *Ibid.*, p. 74.

"Therefore let us go forth to Him, outside the camp, bearing His reproach."
(Heb. 13:13, NKJV).

About the Author

Lee Anne (Ford) Ferguson is an honors graduate of Western Kentucky University, with a Bachelor of Science Degree in Social Work. And though the secular world was clueless about *the grace of God* that was behind it all, she was also the recipient of the Outstanding Student Award for endurance, perseverance and sacrificial service toward others, while under extreme circumstances. She and her husband Tony now enjoy a simple, quiet life in Kentucky, where they live, love, "eat, sleep and breathe" the gospel, while sharing it with others. Between the two of them, they have seven grown children and six grandchildren (and counting). Lee Anne also blogs at www.christrescuedme.com

Made in the USA
Las Vegas, NV
13 October 2022